Navajo Multi-Household Social Units

Navajo Multi-Household Social Units: Archaeology on Black Mesa, Arizona

Thomas R. Rocek

The University of Arizona Press / Tucson & London

The University of Arizona Press
Copyright © 1995
Arizona Board of Regents
All rights reserved

Manufactured in the United States of America

00 99 98 97 96 95   6 5 4 3 2 1

Library of Congress Cataloging-in-Publication Data

Rocek, Thomas R.
    Navajo multi-household social units : archaeology on Black Mesa,
Arizona / by Thomas R. Rocek.
        p.   cm.
    Includes bibliographical references and index.
    ISBN 0-8165-1472-0 (alk. paper)
    1. Navajo Indians—History—Sources. 2. Navajo Indians—Kinship.
3. Navajo Indians—Antiquities. 4. Social structure—Arizona—Black
Mesa (Navajo County and Apache County). 5. Social archaeology—
Arizona—Black Mesa (Navajo County and Apache County).
6. Ethnohistory—Arizona—Black Mesa (Navajo County and Apache
County). 7. Black Mesa (Navajo County and Apache County, Ariz.)—
Antiquities. I. Title.
E99.N3R58   1995   94-33277
979.1'35—dc20   CIP

British Library Cataloguing-in-Publication Data
A catalogue record for this book is available from the British Library.

For Anna Bondy Porges Trojan

Contents

Illustrations

Tables

Acknowledgments

I can only begin to acknowledge the long list of people to whom I owe debts of thanks. David Aberle, William Adams, Garrick Bailey, David Braun, David Brugge, Richard Ford, Karl Hutterer, Klara Kelley, Susan Kent, Keith Kintigh, Louise Lamphere, John Nystuen, Karen Rosenberg, Carla Sinopoli, John Speth, Gil Stein, Patty Wattenmaker, Paul Welch, Wirt Wills, Robert Whallon, and Henry Wright, as well as two anonymous reviewers all read portions of the work in various forms, and provided invaluable advice and comments. It is impossible to adequately express my appreciation for their help; this book would not have been possible without the time they gave me.

John Speth provided overall guidance, advice, and encouragement, as well as support and friendship. His willingness to give time and thought to my research has been a major factor in its completion, and this work is partially his, whether he likes it or not. Jeff Dean gave me access to, and invaluable advice about, the tree-ring data that are central to this work. Scott Russell, who collected much of the local ethnographic data included in this study, introduced me to the historic archaeological record of Black Mesa. Keith Kintigh wrote several of the pieces of software used in the analysis. William Erickson provided statistical counseling, and derived some of the formulas used in my work. John O'Shea provided access to a digitizer, and gave instruction in its use. Milford Wolpoff provided generous and invaluable computing help. Kay Clahassey helped with drafting advice and access to drafting and photographic facilities. Teryl Lynn drew several of the illustrations. Dorothy Hubbell allowed me to visit her home and discuss her unparalleled knowledge of the trading-post system and its recent history.

Several institutions provided crucial assistance during my research. The Black Mesa Archaeological Project made available the data used in this study. Staff members also provided computer tape, microfiche, and photocopies of field notes and other data. I am particularly indebted to George Gumerman, former director of the Center for Archaeological Investigations at Southern Illinois University, Deborah Nichols, who directed the investigation of Navajo sites, and Shirley Powell, who directed the project. Several other members of the project facilitated my access to the data, including Belinda Blomberg, Becky Bottlemy, Brian Butler, Lee Newsom, and Pam Reed. Bill Parry and Kim Smiley helped greatly in guiding me to Black Mesa Project information that I needed and in arranging access to it. The staff of the University of Arizona Library Special Collections Department, particularly Clint Colby and Louis Hieb, greatly facilitated access to Hubbell Collections trading-post data.

During part of the time I was preparing this work, I received funds from a Rackham Fellowship, Rackham Grant, and the Black Mesa Archaeological Project. My research was made possible by the Peabody Coal Corporation. My first season of fieldwork at Black Mesa and the first three years of my graduate career were funded by an NSF predoctoral fellowship. The School of American Research provided me with a wonderful opportunity to continue this work with a Weatherhead fellowship. I have also received generous support from the Department of Anthropology at the University of Michigan and at the University of Delaware. In addition to his friendship, Juan Villamarin has provided absolutely essential and enthusiastic support for my research and writing at the University of Delaware.

Although it is impossible to list them by name, the people of Black Mesa made fieldwork a true pleasure. Whatever its inaccuracies and its foreign perspective, this work is intended to document one small part of their history.

At the University of Arizona Press, Chris Szuter and Linda Gregonis gave me rapid and very valuable editorial guidance.

Finally, six special sources of inspiration and support have been crucial for me. Karen R. Rosenberg has given advice, help, and encouragement, which has given me the strength to do what needs to be done. Miriam and Laura have put up with a grouchy father who always has to rush off to the office. My parents, brother, and grandmother have given love and support far beyond what can be expressed here. They helped me throughout every phase of my education and shared in my enthusiasm for archaeology and the Southwest. I look forward to sharing the satisfaction in the completion of this work with my whole family.

Navajo Multi-Household Social Units

1

Introduction

In the classic autobiography *Son of Old Man Hat* and its sequel, *Left Handed* (Dyk 1967; Dyk and Dyk 1980), the Navajo narrator shares boyhood memories of his emerging awareness of natural and social surroundings in the western Navajo country of the late nineteenth century. Initially, he is conscious of a limited range of activities and places. Events and people simply appear without explanation: "In the spring, all at once, I discovered we were moving" (Dyk 1967:22). His knowledge of people and places is also limited, restricted to his family's homesite and its surroundings.

Gradually, however, he starts recognizing a broader web of people, places, and the pattern of their interaction. His family's residence remains a critical focus to his life, but he is also aware of a rhythm of contact with people outside of his family, and patterns of cooperation with them. By the time Left Handed reaches his early adulthood in the late 1880s, he sees his family not only interacting with others, but actively planning cooperation in a variety of activities, and relying on other families for material as well as emotional support. This is well expressed by one of Left Handed's clan uncles, Slim Man, who tells of a pair of children grieving the death of their mother:

> Now you both are alone and there isn't anybody living around here close to you. You'll be lonesome and you sure will miss your mother. . . . I live down here at the foot of the mountain and we both are living down there, I and my father . . . [he is referring to Left Handed]. I'm living right close to him because we help each other right along and we are getting along nicely. There are other people down there and they are the

same clan as your mother, so there are five families down there right close to each other, five with us two. So it's up to you both, if you want to move down there it will be fine. (Dyk and Dyk 1980:112)

Elsewhere, Left Handed describes a variety of activities shared among the cooperating families, including sheep shearing, horse and cattle round-ups, assistance with herding, farm work, construction, travel to distant trading posts, sponsorship of ceremonies, and so forth.

In Left Handed's autobiography, as well as in other accounts of Navajo life, we are presented with a contrast between individual autonomy and group cooperation. Critical property such as sheep, the economic mainstay, is owned individually. As Left Handed's clan uncle's statement illustrates, personal decisions, such as residence moves, are ultimately a matter for the individual. Residence is in isolated rural settlements, typically housing an extended family of a dozen or so people. Patterns of cooperation, however, may involve larger groups of twenty or more people. The small, seemingly isolated social units are actually part of these larger groups, which they depend upon. These alternative levels of social interaction are found not only among the Navajos, but in other societies as well, and they add complexity to the anthropological study of social groups.

Anthropologists study groups of people. These groups vary in size and function, and this variation suggests alternative, sometimes conflicting scales of analysis. As a result, anthropologists use multiple scales and types of analytical units.

Many researchers have explicitly studied criteria for defining boundaries of large-scale units such as ethnic groups or populations. They have examined the reality and stability of such social groups, and considered how they function. Other anthropologists have focused on a smaller scale of social units such as households and families.

This smaller scale of analysis is the basis of a substantial body of literature, as well as several sociological journals (e.g., Goody 1958, 1976; Laslett and Wall 1972; Netting et al. 1984; Segalen 1986; Wilk and Rathje 1982; *Journal of Family History*; *Journal of Marriage and the Family*). The focus on larger-scale units also has a long tradition in anthropology, expressed in diverse approaches. For instance, students of cultural ecology have had to consider the biological and economic significance of large-scale social boundaries as a starting point for ecological research (e.g., Rappaport 1984). Students of political systems have confronted the issues of boundedness and fluidity among large groups (e.g., Barth 1969; Fried 1967, 1975).

As anthropologists have examined the small domestic groups and the larger units that delimit societies, a medium scale or "middle-level" of social units has received only sporadic attention. The few studies of medium-sized groups have traditionally focused on kinship units, primarily those that are unilineally structured (Mitchell 1963). Some analyses have also dealt with more loosely defined units, which are often based around the concept of the "kindred"— ego-based categories of bilateral and (depending on who defines the term) affinal kin (e.g., Appell 1967; Freeman 1961; Keesing 1966; Mitchell 1963; Murdock 1964). Descriptions of medium-scale units have been limited, however, and the criteria for defining them remain inconsistent. Particularly variable is the degree to which middle-level social units are described as abstract categories of kin, or as actual groups possessing functional significance (e.g., Freeman 1961; Murdock 1964). In fact, it is likely that the importance of such units varies among societies and depends on particular circumstances within a society and on changes over time. Recent work, particularly (though not exclusively) by archaeologists, has begun to examine a broader range of middle-level social units (e.g., Hayden and Cannon 1982; Netting et al. 1989; Stone 1991, 1992). Clearly, however, a vast amount of work remains to be done to examine the variability among such groups and to investigate their dynamics over time.

In this book, I examine small- and medium-scale social units among the Navajos and compare them to similar units found in other cultures. The work has two goals, one descriptive and the other analytical. The first is to document (through a combination of archaeological, ethnohistorical, and historical data) the conditions experienced by a particular group of people—Navajo occupants of northern Black Mesa, Arizona (fig. 1.1)—during a particular period in their history in the early nineteenth through mid-twentieth century. These data regarding conditions of Navajo life on Northern Black Mesa are the basis of the second goal of this work.

The second goal is to investigate the ways in which the economic and demographic circumstances under which a people live shape the social units that make up their society. In focusing on this question, I restrict myself to examining those units with physical consequences recognizable in settlement patterns, and consider functional groups *without* restriction to the particular kinship or nonkinship criteria by which members are recruited. I suggest that

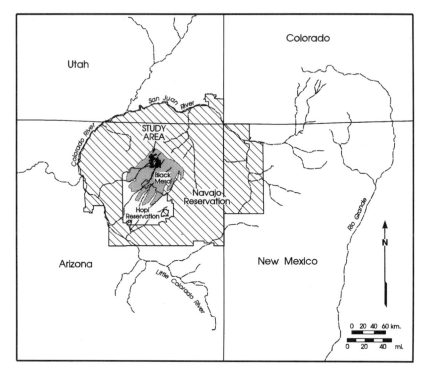

Figure 1.1. Location of the Black Mesa Study Area

functioning middle-level units emerge and fade in response to the changing circumstances of the society in which they operate, and I use the Navajo case, as well as comparative discussion of other societies, to examine this proposition. I argue that past anthropological analyses that focused on the household and family or on the community and "tribe" have neglected an important intermediate level of organization that has developed under certain circumstances in societies worldwide.

Although examining medium-scale units, I also consider concurrent changes in the finer-scale units (residence groups) that compose the medium-scale units. Ultimately, the analytical portion of this work suggests correlations of changes in both fine-scale and medium-scale units with what I believe are causal economic and demographic variables. Failure to recognize the impact of these variables limits our understanding of inter- and intracultural variability in social organization.

Navajo culture is commonly cited as an example of flexibility and potential for cultural change (e.g., Vogt 1961:325 and references therein). Discussion of such changes has tended to concentrate on the historical particulars of Navajo culture (e.g., Hester 1962; Vogt 1961; but cf. Kelley 1986). If, however, we accept the view that cultures serve as adaptive mechanisms (Binford 1965; White 1959), changes such as those seen among the Navajos may be analyzed in terms of responses to changes in their biological, social, economic, and political environment. So, the details of culture change in a particular region and time can show the operation of cultural adaptation in a much broader sense. At the same time, the detailed study of particular cases increases the reliability of generalizations about culture process.

Thus, the archaeological research I discuss in subsequent chapters combines the goals of processual analysis characteristic of anthropological archaeology with the control of idiosyncratic particulars permitted by ethnographic and ethnohistoric data (Spores 1980). It is a specific case study that is intended to shed light on the broader questions of the role of social units in cultural adaptation. I address these broader questions explicitly in the comparative discussion of ethnographic cases in the final chapter.

The Navajo case involves processes of transformation in a culture that, until recently, was largely preindustrial and based upon familial units of production and consumption. The Navajos are not, by any means, "pristinely" independent of a market economy and have not been so for a considerable period. During the period of Navajo history I examine, however, they can reasonably be viewed as organized in relatively independent "familial" or "domestic" production units typical of prestate societies (Sahlins 1968:74–75, 1972:141–48). Such a view is also appropriate for many of the examples of social units in chapter 8 that I compare to the Navajo case.

The particular focus of my investigation of northern Black Mesa Navajo history is on changes in the composition of, and interrelations among, social units through time. Navajo culture has traditionally been based on the individual and the family as the units of ownership and generalized sharing, and on the extended family camp or "residence group" as the major unit of day-to-day cooperation and production. The degree of local integration in Navajo society above the level of the residence group has been a subject of considerable disagreement and uncertainty. Much of the debate has centered on the term "outfit" (Kluckhohn and Leighton 1946:62), used to describe the members of several residence groups who provide mutual assistance under particular circumstances. However, a variety of alternative terms and descriptions have been proposed for these middle-range supraresidence units (see chapter 3).

Left Handed, for instance, lived in a hogan with only his adoptive parents (his mother's older sister, Abaa, and her husband, Old Man Hat) for much of his youth. At certain periods, other family members, such as Old Man Hat's second wife and her brother, also shared their home, but this arrangement (and the marriage) did not last long (Dyk 1967:16–18). The size and composition of the residence group Left Handed lived in varied over the course of his narrative. At times he shared a residence site with several families including his adoptive parents, Old Man Hat and Abaa, his sister's (or clan sister's?), Moving On's nuclear family, his clan "father's," Slim Man's nuclear family, and Slim Man's adoptive mother's extended family (Dyk 1967:22). At other times, as a young adult, he lived with just his wife and aging mother (Dyk and Dyk 1980). Beyond the residence group was a variable cluster of adjacent cooperating residence groups. These included some of the same people that Left Handed had at times shared a residence group with (such as Slim Man), as well as the family of Old Man Hat's younger brother, Choclays Kinsman, Old Man Hat's clan sister, Woman Who Walks Alone, and others.

The number and composition of this group varied. When Slim Man referred to five families living "right close to each other" and "helping each other along" (see earlier quotation), he was referring to this sort of cooperating cluster, though it is unclear if some of those families actually shared a single residence group. It is clear that even over the relatively short period covered in Left Handed's narrative, the composition and size of these clusters fluctuated a great deal. Overall, the structure of these groups appears to have combined elements of kinship, spatial proximity, and cooperation.

It is likely that some of the ambiguity surrounding supraresidence group organization in Navajo society represents actual variability in social unit composition in response to the changing circumstances under which Navajo society operates (Aberle 1963; Levy et al. 1989). Such a suggestion derives from studies specifically devoted to Navajo social organization and from more general considerations of cultural adaptation.

Downs (1964:73–77) has proposed that middle-level groups ("outfits") may have existed on a large scale prior to the decrease in herd size imposed by the U.S. government's stock reduction program of the 1930s (see chapter 2). Following stock reduction, as well as the substitution of tribal government services for locally organized action (e.g., Williams 1970), the large outfits declined in importance due to the decreased need for regular large-scale interresidence group cooperation. Downs (1964:75) suggests that the decrease in defensive requirements brought about by the end of warfare in the area may have had a similar (earlier) impact on middle-level organization. Kelley (1982b:94–95, 1982c, 1986) has proposed a more complex process. Like Downs, she indicates that supraresidence group organization was fostered by the requirements of a livestock economy (particularly the maintenance of land access). Kelley's description suggests, however, that outfit organization could be disrupted by increased market involvement due either to the growth of very large-scale herds, the owners of which sought to monopolize the outfit's land base, or, alternatively, by the collapse of the pastoral economy and shift to wage and market dependence as an alternative to livestock raising. Ross (1955:138–42) has described the gradual fragmentation of an outfit under the impact of changing economic conditions. He attributes the breakup to a combination of economic factors (loss of sheep herds and construction of a government irrigation project with very small farm plots for each family) that made it impossible, as well as unnecessary, for families to maintain previous large-scale cooperative activities (Ross 1955:181–82). Lamphere (1977:103) and Levy (1962) have discussed the possible role of population growth in the disruption of discrete middle-level units over the last fifty years (see also Witherspoon 1975:108–10). Levy (communication cited in Lamphere 1977:103) has suggested on the basis of ethnographic data that such a transition in social organization may be recognizable in a breakdown of clustering in Navajo settlement patterns.

The Navajo Singer Frank Mitchell (1978:42) suggested that cooperative activities among the families of a region broke down as people came to expect pay after the introduction of public wage-paying projects in the mid-twentieth century:

> One thing that kept the People in the whole area together was that if any of them decided to move away and start on their own, they knew that sooner or later they would go hungry. If they stayed together, they knew that if they ran out of food other people from the families nearby would always have something to help out with. That was one thing that kept us close together. If one of us needed help, there was always somebody to offer it.
>
> When the hoeing season came, there would be groups of men who

would always get together and come out on horseback and hoe. . . . All of the people in the area did the same thing. They would go to one place and help. . . .

Today the People do not do that. The Ten Days Projects have ruined us. Now it has gotten into the minds of some people that if they do a little work they should get paid for it. Back in those days when I was a boy, people used to help each other all the time.

On a more general level, Sahlins (1972) has discussed the characteristics of preindustrial domestic economies. He has suggested a special case of his preindustrial economic model applicable to societies operating as peripheral inputs into larger market economies (Sahlins 1972:224–27), a case that should apply to the Navajos. In general, Sahlins suggests that the size of cooperative units in domestic economies increases with increased economic complexity. Sahlins suggests, however, that involvement in the market economy breaks down the scale of cooperation, particularly cooperation in the production of the principal market commodities. After around 1870 when the trading post system began to emerge, Navajo sheep production was organized at least in part for market exchange, and the scale of market involvement in the sheep industry increased during the late nineteenth and early twentieth centuries (see chapter 2). Following Sahlins' model, such a development of production for market ought to result in a decrease in the scale of cooperation.

With the decrease in Navajo reliance on pastoralism imposed by stock reduction, the Navajo economy changed in two ways. First, the overall degree of reliance on the sale of livestock products diminished, and second, reliance on external (market) sources of food and other resources probably increased. The former change should decrease the factors identified by Sahlins as being associated with atomization in societies operating on the fringes of market economies. Thus, following part of Sahlins' argument, the poststock-reduction period should have been a time of reversion to some form of tribal cooperative arrangements. However, increased dependence on the market for crucial resources may mark the destruction of the basis of tribal organization (e.g., Marx 1977:344), and thus the poststock-reduction period might involve the transition away from a "domestic" economy altogether.

Sahlins' model of tribal economics, as well as the particular interpretations of the history of Navajo social change cited previously, thus provide a basis against which at least the prestock-reduction period of Navajo social and economic development may be examined. Applied to the late nineteenth- and early twentieth-century Navajos, the implications of Sahlins' domestic production model appear to be at odds with ethnographic evidence concerning the emergence of economic cooperative (middle-level) groups. Predictions generated by his model for the period after stock reduction are ambiguous, because Sahlins does not discuss the processes involved in the major transformation of a tribal economy that is in growing articulation with a central market-based economy.

Herein lies the strength of the detailed Black Mesa Navajo archaeological record. Its time depth permits a diachronic study of the changes in economy, demography, and social organization undergone by a society in a largely preindustrial context. The comparative ethnographic cases (chapter 8) allow a similar but synchronic examination of patterns among these variables.

Specifically, researchers of nonunilineally organized (cognatic) societies, of social networks, and particularly of pastoral societies find numerous examples of middle-level forms of social organization. They frequently recognize that middle-level social units offer a great degree of flexibility, allowing the basic building blocks of a society (the households) and the larger political organization (community or tribe) to remain stable, while adjusting to the fluctuating needs of land availability, population distribution, and so forth. They also note a wide range of types of middle-level units, and postulate relationships between this range and changing economic or demographic conditions. Examination of the Navajo archaeological record allows tracking the relation among social units and economic and demographic conditions over a long stretch of time.

The aim of this study of social dynamics is to assess the existence of cooperative units larger than the residence group, and to test the alternative views, outlined in this chapter, regarding the history of such large-scale cooperative units. The analysis of change, as proposed here, explicitly neglects the issues of "acculturation" in the sense of distinguishing "native" actions from "external" pressures. The subject of interest is the transformation of a cultural system under conditions of economic and demographic change, not the historical origins of particular aspects of that transformation.

The analysis of social change on northern Black Mesa in the following chapters is intended in particular to test three ideas that have appeared in the literature regarding the organization of social units:

1. Increasing population density results in competition and decreased interresidence cooperation (cf. Lamphere 1977:103; Levy 1962). This is particularly likely in a land extensive economy such as animal husbandry.

2. Increased pastoral production encourages economic cooperation for certain activities (e.g., shearing and lambing in the case of sheep pastoralism), which require short bursts of extra labor force, but not full-time aggregates of large production units. In addition, differences should exist in the importance of such cooperation depending on the season. This hypothesis derives from the suggestion that the breakdown in cooperative units in the poststock-reduction period was, in part, a result of the loss of the need for mutual assistance among the remaining owners of small herds (Downs 1964: 73–77; Kelley 1982b, 1982c, 1986; Ross 1955:138–42).

3. Increased involvement in a market economy may take several forms: (a) increased pastoral production for market sale intensifies the factors noted in (2), or, alternatively, in (1) because herd sizes are expanded (cf. Netting et al. 1989); (b) increased market involvement with decreased domestic production (a situation based on wage or public assistance funds) eliminates the impetus for interresidence cooperation such as discussed in (2). In this second case, the irregular availability of wages and public funds encourages *intra*site population concentration for the pooling of fluctuating economic resources; constraints on livestock concentration at a single site are also decreased. Thus, expansion in the size of social units at the basic residence group (camp) level is expected (Aberle 1981a:22; Jorgensen 1971:78–79, 1972:114–15, 160–61; Kelley 1986:13, 166; Levy et al. 1989:352–53; Wilk and Netting 1984:10). In this study, I do not examine (c) a third situation of market involvement—the development of a *reliable* and adequate wage-based economy, because this has not characterized northern Black Mesa in the time period I consider. Such a development, however, would be likely to break the economic bonds tying domestic units together and encourage the development of independent nuclear families (cf. Aberle 1989:410; Goode 1963; Levy et al. 1989:356).

To investigate these propositions using archaeological data, it is necessary to formulate a model linking changes in social unit size and function with archaeologically observable phenomena. The approach that I follow in this study is based on the expectation that cooperating residences are likely to form spatial clusters to make joint activities easier. Levy's description of outfit settlement patterns provides a basis for suggesting such a settlement pattern.

Sahlins (1972:96–98) also makes an argument for the spatial correlates of domestic economic systems. Following Levy's suggestion, Navajo middle-level groups may form clusters of cooperating residence groups occupying contiguous blocks of land. The disintegration of these units should destroy this pattern of land use, and allow us to recognize a decrease in spatial clustering among contemporary settlements.

This spatial model is based on the expectation that certain cooperative activities favor or require proximity (cf. Stone 1991). Thus, social units above the level of the residence group (as well as the residence group itself) may be recognized by the spatial distribution of their members.

Not all group activities have spatial correlates. Lamphere (1970:43) has pointed out that the organization of Navajo religious ceremonies ("sings") results in shifting, ego-centered cooperative patterns. Although they involve cooperation among individuals from different residence groups, Navajo ceremonies operate at sporadic intervals and in shifting locations, not fostering the formation of stable social aggregates. A similar argument may apply to some other activities. Traditional Navajo group hunting, for instance, centers around individual hunt leaders who are familiar with hunting techniques and ceremonies (Dyk and Dyk 1980:19–43; Hill 1938). Furthermore, the requirements of hunting cooperation do not include spatial proximity of residence groups from which participants are drawn, because the hunts are carried out several days' travel distant from residences.

Some activities *do,* however, involve local cooperative efforts and require spatial proximity of participants. Facets of pastoral production are examples. Sheep shearing requires a burst of labor constrained by seasonal timing and by the limited mobility of the herds. This activity often involves interresidence group cooperation. Farming activities, particularly planting, hoeing, harvesting, and storage similarly involve seasonally regular, spatially constrained cooperation (numerous examples are cited in Dyk 1967 and Dyk and Dyk 1980). By this reasoning, settlement groupings should change through time as patterns of cooperation vary. Furthermore, these changes should vary among different classes of sites (such as settlements associated with farm fields versus sheep camps, for instance) and under the impact of different economic factors.

This argument applies to the occurrence of archaeologically visible settlement clusters, and to the occurrence of middle-level social units. That is, under some conditions of cooperation, middle-level units are important, and under others they are not. Thus, in the discussion of the Black Mesa Navajo case, I examine the economic and demographic correlates of archaeological settlement clustering. In the comparative discussion in chapter 8, I examine the economic and social patterns of ethnographically studied systems in which middle-level units are prominent.

To briefly anticipate the results of this study, the major points may be summarized as follows: In chapter 5, I describe ethnographic evidence showing that social relations may be recognized through the analysis of spatial patterns. Specifically, spatial proximity among residence groups *is* associated with comembership in supraresidence group social units. The ethnographic data do not, however, provide evidence of a simple correspondence between the existence of supraresidence group units and spatial clusters of sites. This indicates that some types of supraresidence group social units can exist without being represented in the spatial arrangement of sites, and conversely the presence of clusters obviously can reflect a variety of factors other than social relations. This facet of the study is inconclusive, however, because the range of conditions and social arrangements represented in the available ethnographic samples is limited. The conditions represented by the Black Mesa archaeological sample of the nineteenth and early twentieth centuries, for instance, are not adequately documented ethnographically. Thus, the possibility remains that social units existing under these conditions (a sparse population with large, prestock-reduction herds) *do* show the spatial correlates lacking in the ethnographic samples. Archaeological data and ethnohistorical information are the only ways of investigating patterns in these earlier periods.

In order to examine this possibility, in chapter 6 I describe changes in Black Mesa archaeological settlement. I examine how these changes relate to the economic and demographic factors proposed earlier to explain changes in social unit size and composition. By combining archaeological data with historic and ethnohistoric sources of information, I gain greater time depth for the study of change than is typically available in purely ethnographic studies. In this respect, the archaeological data I use offer a unique opportunity to examine long-term patterns of change that are difficult or impossible to examine ethnographically.

The results in chapter 6 offer encouragement for archaeological and ethnoarchaeological study of the issues raised here. First, many aspects of changes in economics and population within the study area appear adequately documented by the combined archaeological and ethnohistoric record. Although I note certain limitations and biases in the measurement of these variables, a reasonably clear picture of local patterns emerges from the analysis.

Second, the measures of site composition and spatial relations among sites provide results compatible with the hypotheses outlined previously. Specifically, population increase correlates with interresidence group dispersion (which I argue represents a breakdown in middle-level cooperation), high livestock levels co-occur with interresidence group clustering (which I suggest represents the formation of middle-level cooperating groups), and high market involvement *without* major livestock dependence correlates with the formation of large residence groups.

As suggested in the discussion in chapter 7, the results of the archaeological study are by no means conclusive, but rather generate as many questions as they answer. A shortcoming of the analysis is a lack of sufficiently detailed ethnohistoric data with which to independently evaluate the interpretations of the archaeological patterns. However, the results provide an example of the potential of archaeological data for investigating questions of fundamental anthropological interest, and for use of archaeological time depth to investigate ethnographically undocumented facets of culture change.

The discussion in chapter 8 further suggests that both the kinds of social units found among the Navajos, and the factors that influence changes in these units, may have relevance to a fairly wide number of cultures. Middle-level social units are a critical feature of adaptation in societies requiring flexibility at the local level. Such units include cognatic groups such as ramages and kindreds, as well as more amorphous social networks. These sorts of units are found in a variety of societies, most notably (but not restricted to) pastoral societies such as that of the Navajos. The Navajo case is not unique.

Thus, a focus on any single level of social organization is likely to be seriously flawed if it ignores other levels. Students of social organization must consider not only changes in household and large-scale social units, but the impact of fluctuations in middle-level social units as well.

2

The Black Mesa Navajos

Navajo life must be understood in the context of the environment and history that have molded it. The Navajos have experienced tremendous variability and change, as well as physical adversity. It is this flux and challenge that have shaped the organization of social units and the patterns of interaction among the Navajo people. Although numerous general histories of the Navajos are available (e.g., Bailey and Bailey 1986; Correll 1976; Hester 1962; Iverson 1981; Vogt 1961; Young 1978; see Correll et al. 1969 and 1973 for additional references), the impact of historical events has been different in different parts of the reservation. The Navajo archaeology of northern Black Mesa must therefore be examined in relation to the particular environment and events that affect life there.[1]

Although Black Mesa is located near the geographic center of the Navajo reservation (fig. 1.1), it forms part of the relatively sparsely populated western Navajo country (Goodman 1982:63). It is here that the Black Mesa Archaeological Project (BMAP) study area is located (fig. 2.1). Until the late 1960s and the development associated with coal mining on the mesa, the area was one of the more rural and isolated portions of the reservation (Downs 1964:6; Russell 1981a:3–4; Van Valkenburgh 1941:10).

Black Mesa is a large highland (ca. 120 km east-west by 80 km north-south), ranging in elevation from a high of about 2500 m (8210 feet) at its northern rim to a low of less than 1830 m (6000 feet) at its southern end. The mesa is an imposing landform, standing more than 300 m (1000 feet) above the surrounding lowlands at its northern edge. It inclines to the southwest, projecting along its southern edge in a prominent series of fingers (including the well-known Hopi mesas). The bulk of the mesa is composed of alternating thick beds of sandstone and thinner bands of shale, along with the coal beds that are responsible for the current mining activity and the associated archaeological work by the BMAP (Nichols and Karlstrom 1983:3).

The drainage system on the mesa runs northeast to southwest, emptying into the Little Colorado River through a series of large seasonal streams—Moenkopi, Dinnebito, Oraibi, and Polacca washes. These drainages fan out in a dendritic system with its head near the north rim of the mesa. Moenkopi Wash and a small part of Dinnebito Wash pass through the BMAP study area (fig. 2.2).

The climate of northern Black Mesa is semi-arid. Maximum mean annual rainfall is 50 cm (19.7 inches) at the north rim (north of the study area) and decreases to an average of about 25 cm (9.8 inches) in the southeastern corner of the BMAP study area (Nichols and Sink 1984:7). Shallow subsurface water is available in the washes and was present in several springs that have dried out in recent years (Nichols and Smiley 1984:7), but water remains a limited resource.

The frost-free period in the study area typically runs about 120 days, and there is considerable variation in the dates of first and last frost (Nichols and Sink 1984:7). The combination of low rainfall, frost, and cool temperatures during the growing season limit the reliability and yield of agriculture (Russell 1983b:25). Many local residents harvest their corn crop green rather than waiting for full maturation (Russell n.d.). Black Mesa soils formed in the alluvial deposits of the stream valleys are fertile (Karlstrom 1983:330); agriculture is limited primarily by rainfall and the short growing season.

Vegetation varies with elevation, topography, soils, and water availability. The most widespread vegetation is a pygmy piñon and juniper forest that covers the upland slopes. The wash valleys and upland basins support a more open cover of sagebrush, saltbush, snakeweed, and grasses or forbes (Nichols and Sink 1984:7). The piñon stands in parts of the BMAP study area periodically produce large numbers of nuts, which attract collectors from off the reservation, as well as local inhabitants (Russell n.d.). The forest cover also provides an abundance of firewood that is used locally and collected by inhabitants of the surrounding region (Gumerman 1970:11). From the point of view of Navajo economics, the grasses and shrubs are also a crucial resource, providing graze for livestock. Game is relatively sparse on the mesa (Gumerman 1970:11). Overall, the Black Mesa area differs from the surrounding country in its higher elevation, cooler and shorter growing season, slightly

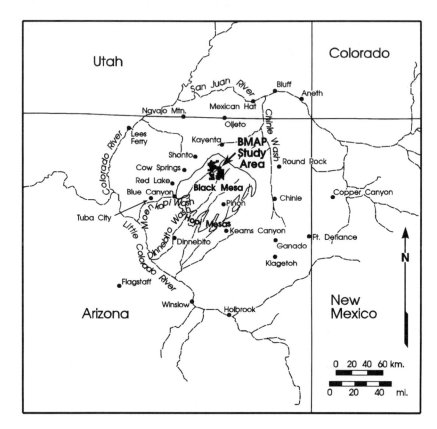

Figure 2.1. Locations Near Black Mesa Referred to in the Text

higher precipitation (but still semi-arid and topographically not well suited for simple irrigation) and forest cover with associated resources (particularly wood for fuel and construction, and piñon nuts).

The BMAP study area within this upland habitat is the home of several dozen Navajo families. The Navajos have a long local history but are ultimately descendants of long-distance travelers. The Navajo (as well as Apache) language is a member of the Athapaskan language family, which links the Navajo to populations of western Canada and interior Alaska. Current archaeological and ethnohistoric evidence suggest an Athapaskan entry into the Southwest around A.D. 1500 (e.g., Brown and Hancock 1992). The area of earliest known Navajo settlement in the Southwest lies in the northwestern part of New Mexico, the area identified in Navajo tradition as the old

Navajo country or "Dinétah" (Hester 1962; Reeve 1957; Schroeder 1974). By the late seventeenth or perhaps even late sixteenth century, Navajos were in at least sporadic contact (through trading and raiding) with the Hopis at the southern end of Black Mesa (e.g., Brugge 1983:491; Hester 1962:21, 77–79). The major area of Navajo occupation, however, remained in the Dinétah until warfare with the Utes in the mid-eighteenth century pushed the Navajo southwestward toward the Canyon de Chelly area (Hester 1962; Reeve 1960).

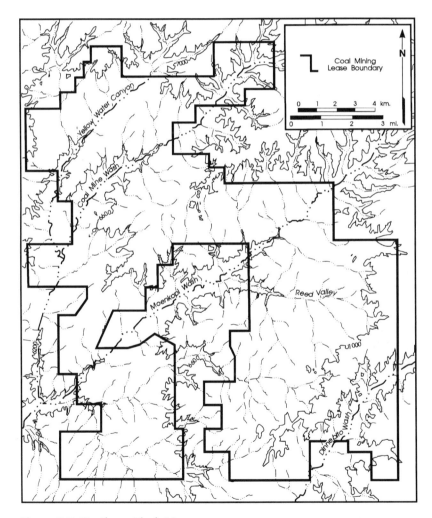

Figure 2.2. Northern Black Mesa

Although the original Navajo settlers in the Southwest were probably hunter-gatherers, they developed a mixed farming economy early on; in fact an early seventeenth-century Spanish account interpreted the name "Navajo" as meaning "large planted fields" (Benavides 1952). Of even more critical importance for the future Navajo way of life was the acquisition of livestock, particularly sheep. The Navajos probably began to get sheep from the Spanish in the seventeenth century. By early in the eighteenth century sheep and horse bones as well as corrals were present on Navajo archaeological sites in the Dinétah, and livestock is mentioned alongside farming in Spanish documents (Carlson 1965; Hill 1940b; Marshall 1991). Stock, however, remained of limited importance throughout the eighteenth century (Bailey and Bailey 1986:16–17).

Past archaeological research suggests that Navajos were living in substantial numbers on eastern Black Mesa by the mid- to late eighteenth century, and on central and northern Black Mesa by the early to mid-nineteenth century (Kemrer 1974:129–31). BMAP tree-ring sampling, which produced reliable dates extending as early as the 1830s, supports this interpretation (see chapter 6). The absence of definite pre-1830s dates in the large BMAP sample supports the view of a gradual northward (or northwestward) spread of Navajo settlement into the area, with slightly earlier dates coming from the central part of the mesa (see Stokes and Smiley 1964).

The timing of the move onto isolated and rugged Black Mesa coincides with a prolonged period of Navajo-Spanish (and later Navajo-Mexican and Anglo-American) warfare that began in 1804 and escalated around 1818 (Bailey 1980; Brugge 1964; Reeve 1960; see also Kemrer 1974:132–35). The historical sources concerning Black Mesa in the early nineteenth century referred to the area as Mesa de las Vacas (Van Valkenburgh 1941:10), and come from Spanish or Mexican military expeditions against the Navajos. In August 1823, part of a Mexican force traveled across Black Mesa from south to north and also went around its western and northern flank. The members of the expedition located a few Navajos and killed those they were able to catch. They also captured Navajo sheep, goats, and cattle, and reported seeing Navajo mules and horses and the tracks of still more livestock (Brugge 1964). Hostile forays continued throughout much of the second quarter of the nineteenth century. Mexican forces were in the Black Mesa area again around 1840 (Bailey 1980:160) and the region was a prime target of Mexican slaving expeditions in this period (Bailey 1966:79).

The Mexican accounts indicate considerable Navajo wealth in livestock, though little about the Navajo occupation of northern Black Mesa beyond its use as an escape route north, away from the enemy forces. The descriptions of substantial numbers of livestock, however, indicate a critical transformation in the Navajo economy. Although farming remained important in some regions, it was during this period of warfare in the early nineteenth century that herding apparently became a central part of Navajo adaptation in many areas (Bailey and Bailey 1986), including Black Mesa.

The threat of warfare involved not only people of European ancestry, but other Native American tribes as well. Navajo tradition refers to battles between Utes and Navajos on and around Black Mesa (Correll 1972, cited in Russell 1983b:15–16; Dyk 1967:64–66). A metal projectile point found on Black Mesa at a site where such a battle was said to have occurred (just south of the BMAP study area) substantiates these accounts (Russell 1983b:16). Given these unsettled conditions, it is likely that Navajo occupation was irregular from year to year and season to season. Northern Black Mesa probably served as a hideout from Euro-Americans and Utes, a travel route for trade with the Hopis to the south, and perhaps, as in later years, a winter settlement area.

Hostile activity in the area continued intermittently into the second half of the nineteenth century after the United States gained control of the region from Mexico. An Anglo-American force crossed the north-central end of Black Mesa in the fall of 1858 (Bailey 1980:201; Van Valkenburgh 1941: 113). This expedition reported most of the area deserted, although this probably represents Navajo evasion of the force more than any characteristic of the regular seasonal settlement pattern. Continued tension is indicated by a Navajo killing of a Mormon traveler west of Black Mesa near Red Lake in 1860 (McNitt 1962:90; Shepardson and Hammond 1970).

During the early 1860s, hostilities between Navajos and the United States intensified. Finally, the United States embarked upon a systematic campaign to pacify the entire tribe by capturing and imprisoning all Navajos. The military's plan was to transport the entire tribe to a concentration camp at Fort Sumner in eastern New Mexico and establish a permanent agricultural community there. U.S. forces began to cover much of the Navajo territory, killing those who resisted and destroying fields and herds, in a largely successful effort to force Navajos to surrender. During this period the area on and around Black Mesa continued its role as a remote hideout for Navajos escaping their enemies. A number of families successfully evaded the U.S. troops and remained in the area through the period of government incarceration at Fort

Sumner from 1864 to 1868 (Adams 1963:39; Bailey 1980:253–54; Brewer 1937:611; Downs 1964:6; Dyk 1947:13, 1967:4; Henderson 1982:115; McPherson 1988:9–10).

Finally, in 1868, a treaty with the U.S. government resulted in the freeing of the surviving Navajos at Fort Sumner. The treaty created a reservation that covered a portion of the original Navajo territory. Black Mesa fell outside the reservation boundaries, but it was nevertheless quickly resettled by the returning captives, who joined those who had remained during the Fort Sumner period (Dyk 1967:4). The archeological record of northern Black Mesa shows a jump in site construction during the 1870s, marking the return of the refugees. The latter half of the 1870s and the succeeding decade is also the first period for which detailed accounts are available concerning Navajo settlement on and around Black Mesa. These descriptions are in the autobiographies of Left Handed (also called "Son of Old Man Hat"), Old Mexican, and Frank Mitchell, Navajos who lived on or near Black Mesa at various times during the 1870s or 1880s (Dyk 1947, 1967; Dyk and Dyk 1980; Mitchell 1978; see also Russell 1981a and 1983b for much of the discussion that follows). By the end of the 1880s, ancestors of most of the family groups currently in the BMAP area were present in the region (Russell 1981a:54 and n.d.).

Navajo settlement on Black Mesa during this period was most common during the fall and winter (Russell 1981a, 1983b; see also Van Valkenburgh 1941:113). This was true in the southern part of the mesa, where trade with the Hopis was among the factors encouraging Navajo settlement (Dyk 1947:13; Mitchell 1978:39–41), and in the higher northern part of Black Mesa where the supply of winter graze, firewood, and water (in the form of snow) encouraged settlement. In addition, the tree cover provided by upland areas such as Black Mesa created sheltered spots with accessible graze free of snow (Dyk 1967:117, 288; Jett 1978; Russell 1983b:58). During the summer, the typical pattern was for the families who wintered on northern Black Mesa to move onto the adjacent lowlands, leaving livestock that did not require daily care (cattle and excess horses) unattended on Black Mesa (Dyk 1967; Dyk and Dyk 1980; Hegemann 1963:320).

This pattern was not universal. Russell (1981a:51) reports one elderly pair of informants who stated that their parents summered on the mesa and wintered off of it. Another informant (Russell n.d.: interviews 6/7/75, 6/8/75) pointed out summer sites in the BMAP study area—an agricultural field and a Nda ("Enemy Way" ceremony) location—that may date to this period. Still another elderly informant indicated that his parents had moved off the mesa in the summer, but his grandparents had lived year-round on the mesa (Russell n.d.: interview 6/7–8/76). Furthermore, the names of some particularly rich individuals—Who Has Mules and Choclays Kinsman in particular (Dyk 1967; Dyk and Dyk 1980)—appear to have been closely associated with Black Mesa in a manner suggesting extended periods of occupation. Two grandchildren of Who Has Mules indicated that their grandfather lived year-round on the mesa (Russell n.d.: interviews 6/10/76, 6/3/80). The archaeological record of Navajo occupation on top of Black Mesa thus incorporates variable portions of family settlement rounds depending on the particular family and period considered (see discussion in chapter 5).

Aside from individual variation in seasonality patterns, the major factors causing variability in movement were climatic fluctuations. A period of drought began in the mid 1800s, culminating in peak drought conditions in the mid- to late 1870s and again around 1900 (Dean 1982: fig. 1). The first of these drought peaks corresponded to a period in which Left Handed described his family's urgent search for water and graze. This drought disrupted Left Handed's family's typical pattern of seasonal movement. During the drought they wintered near the San Juan River by Navajo Mountain and spent the summer near Hopi (Dyk 1967: 104, 111, 129, 132). The account of the mid-1870s up to 1890 appears to record only two major deviations from the general seasonal pattern of movement (Dyk 1967; Dyk and Dyk 1980), though an additional, even more dramatic, disruption in settlement is suggested by the archaeological data from the time of the second drought peak in 1900 (see chapter 6).

The summer range along the base of northern Black Mesa was not uniquely Navajo; Paiute groups had lived in the area alongside Navajos since at least the 1820s (Brugge 1964:226). During the period of drought in the late 1870s, Left Handed mentioned a confrontation over land with one of the Paiute neighbors, emphasizing the stress characteristic of the time (Dyk 1967:111). Paiutes continued to live in the area into the twentieth century, however, increasingly becoming absorbed into the growing Navajo population (Dyk 1967:10; Shepardson and Hammond 1970:33–34, 37). Utes, previously a major threat to the Navajos, appear to have served merely as sporadic trade partners during most of this period, and they are not mentioned often (Dyk 1967:344, 511).

An event of major legal significance for the area, although with no direct local effect at the time, was the establishment of the 1882 and 1884 reservation extensions (an area that includes what came to be called the Navajo-Hopi

Joint Use Area as well as the Hopi reservation) (Goodman 1982:57). These additions recognized the fact of Navajo occupation on and north of northern Black Mesa, and the combined Hopi and Navajo occupation to the south. A minor prospecting boom accompanied growing Euro-American knowledge of the area, culminating in two killings (one by Paiutes in 1880, one by Navajos in 1884) of pairs of prospectors just north and east of Black Mesa. Although a military force entered the area in 1884, these events did not escalate into warfare, nor did mineral prospectors overrun the area (Dyk 1967:168–96; Gilmor and Wetherill 1953:13–14, 133–35; McNitt 1962:177–85; Shepardson and Hammond 1970:30; Van Valkenburgh 1941:38). The region remained in relative isolation.

The major economic characteristics of northern Black Mesa through the mid-twentieth century began to develop during the late 1800s. Navajo sheep and goat herds, decimated by the scorched earth warfare of the early 1860s, were reestablished at a minimal level as a stipulation of the 1868 treaty. Navajos returning to the Black Mesa area were probably able to supplement their stock with purchases from herds owned by Navajos who had escaped the 1864 round-up (Dyk 1967:4). Initial herd sizes were small, but they grew rapidly. Navajo families avoided butchering their animals, permitted year-round breeding (i.e., the males remained with the herd year-round), and used labor-intensive care for lambs and kids that were born during harsh weather. They also continued to trade and in some cases raid to acquire new animals (Bailey and Bailey 1986:39–40; Dyk 1947:18, 1967:67; see also Downs 1964:36). Year-round breeding appears to have stopped by the late 1880s or around 1890 (Dyk 1947:30; Dyk and Dyk 1980:152), but by then some herd sizes were up in the hundreds or, in certain cases, more than a thousand (e.g., Dyk and Dyk 1980:376, 447). Horse herds also grew very rapidly. A few rich men in the Black Mesa area claimed to own herds of a thousand or more by the late 1880s, although horse herds numbering in the tens seem to have been more typical (Dyk and Dyk 1980:266–67). Anecdotal references suggest that around this time livestock herds in the Black Mesa area were larger and in better condition than were herds in at least some areas to the north and east (Dyk and Dyk 1980:266, 351, 357), although this may merely reflect local climatic fluctuations.

Cattle herds were present in the Black Mesa area in the 1820s (Brugge 1964; note also the nineteenth-century name of Mesa de las Vacas for Black Mesa) and perhaps as early as the 1770s (Escalante 1976:106). After the Fort Sumner period, however, cattle herds were not reestablished until the early

1880s, when Mormon settlers sold them to the Navajos; again herds increased dramatically in size thereafter (Dyk 1967:155–88ff).

Navajo agricultural efforts suffered a series of severe setbacks in the first years after the return from Fort Sumner (see Underhill 1978:167 and Brugge 1980 for a list of environmental catastrophes during this period; see also Mitchell 1978:3 for a perhaps exaggerated account of nonagricultural Navajo subsistence). By the 1880s, however, successful fields of corn, squash, pumpkins and melons had been established on the lowlands around northern and northeastern Black Mesa (Dyk 1967; Gregory 1917:130–31).

The subsistence base of the Navajos around the BMAP study area in the mid- to late nineteenth century thus combined a substantial seasonal investment in agriculture and livestock. The importance of farming varied among individuals and from year to year (see Dyk 1947, 1967; Dyk and Dyk 1980). Sheep and goats were the major stock animals, but horses and cattle were also kept in varying numbers. Farming and stock raising were supplemented by occasional fall deer hunts in the mountains of Utah or the San Francisco Peaks near Flagstaff (Dyk 1967:219; Dyk and Dyk 1980:19–42, 400–402), as well as small-scale opportunistic hunting of small game such as rabbits (Dyk 1967:71–72; Dyk and Dyk 1980:57). Gathering of wild plant resources, a significant factor in the area in the early twentieth century (Russell 1983b: 22–23), was undoubtedly also carried out in the mid- to late nineteenth century (Bailey and Bailey 1986:49). However, the lack of references to this activity in the contemporary local sources (Dyk 1967; Dyk and Dyk 1980) suggests that it was of limited importance in the northern Black Mesa economy, even during periods of environmental stress.

In addition to the factors of domestic consumption, the economic significance of trade developed in this period from a seasonal sideline to a major focus of Navajo activity. Intertribal trade, particularly with the Hopis, had a long history, and as noted previously, the Hopi trade was one of the factors influencing Navajo winter settlement on southern Black Mesa. Navajos exchanged their mutton, goat meat, sheep and goat pelts, piñon nuts, firewood, and rabbits for Hopi corn, corn meal, piki, melons, apples, peaches, beans, and pottery (Dyk 1967; Mitchell 1978:38–39; Russell 1983b:15). Navajos also traded with the Ute, Apache, and undoubtedly the Paiute (Dyk 1967; Dyk and Dyk 1980).

A relatively new factor, however, was the availability of regular Euro-American trade. Trade with non-Indians had existed on a limited scale by at least the eighteenth century, with Navajo woolen textiles exchanged for Spanish manufactured goods (Amsden 1934:133; Reeve 1960:228). The trade that emerged in the 1870s and 1880s, however, became more central to the Navajo economy. Access to Euro-American goods in the period following the release from Fort Sumner began with the distribution of livestock, food, and seeds at Fort Defiance (Underhill 1978:154–59). These distributions (in later years Navajos paid for the goods with labor), along with supplies of farm implements, other tools, and wagons, continued to be provided in limited quantities into the early twentieth century (Dyk 1947; Underhill 1978:173).

Starting around 1871, however, a successful effort at marketing Navajo products through trading posts began at Fort Defiance (Utley 1961:7). A year later, an informal trading post developed at Lee's Ferry to the northwest of Black Mesa on the Colorado River; after 1874 this was developed into a larger operation (McNitt 1962:98–99; Utley 1961:7). Additional posts on and near the western reservation included Keams Canyon (ca. 1875), Ganado (early to mid-1870s), Red Lake (ca. 1881), Blue Canyon (mid-1880s), Round Rock (by the late 1880s), Chinle and Tuba City (mid- to late 1880s), and Cow Springs (early 1890s), as well as Oljeto, Kayenta, Pinon, Dinnebito, and Shonto (early twentieth century) (Dyk and Dyk 1980:356; James 1976; Kelley 1977:251–53; McNitt 1962:161, 265–74; Russell 1981a:35; Utley 1961).

Keams Canyon seems to have been the first post to gain major importance among the inhabitants of northern Black Mesa, although visits to Fort Defiance, Ganado, Blue Canyon, an unnamed post near Chinle Wash, and even Aneth and Bluff, Utah, were also made in the 1870s and 1880s (Dyk 1967; Dyk and Dyk 1980). The initial pattern of trading involved spring and fall trading trips; the fall trip often combined trade at the Hopi villages with the visit to the Keams Canyon trading post (e.g., Dyk 1967:36–37, 71–73, 99–102, 121–22, 229–36, 247–48, 297–300). The spring trips—sometimes an early and a late spring trip were made (Dyk and Dyk 1980:500, 529)—usually involved the sale of wool and skins, although two references to the movement of the entire herd to the posts suggest the possibility of sales of lambs as well (Dyk 1967:71–73, 99–102; see also Mitchell 1978:60 for a reference to early limitations on the market for sheep). By the 1890s, livestock sales were a major trade factor in parts of the reservation, and in the early 1900s efforts were being made in some areas to curtail excessive sales of Navajo breeding stock (Dyk 1947:111, 112, 113; Utley 1961:14). In other areas, including Black Mesa, however, records suggest that sales of livestock were negligible until around 1920 (Pinon Trading Post sales records in the Hubbell Papers) or the 1930s (Adams 1963:158; Kelley 1982b:61). Other items involved in the trade included piñon nuts, buckskins (and other wild animal skins), and Navajo blankets (Utley 1961:14). Based on subsequent patterns and accounts in Dyk (1967) and Dyk and Dyk (1980), Navajo agricultural products were probably not a significant trade item in the region (Hubbell Papers; Russell 1983b:25).

Navajo purchases at the trading posts included flour, coffee, sugar, baking powder, salt, tobacco, crackers, candy, cloth, blankets, tools, pots, dishes, matches, gunpowder, and (rarely) clothing (Dyk 1967; Dyk and Dyk 1980; Hubbell Papers, Ganado store inventory for 1890; Russell 1983b:29). As the Navajos became accustomed to these items and as their herd sizes increased over the course of the 1870s and in subsequent years, trading trips became slightly more common, and were increasingly viewed as necessities rather than luxuries (e.g., Dyk and Dyk 1980:500, 529; Russell 1983b:29). Despite the continued existence of a primarily barter economy, money was available and formed part of Navajo-trader and Navajo-Navajo economic as well as social transactions (Dyk 1967:248; Dyk and Dyk 1980: 271, 278–79, 281–82, 324, 328, 338–40).

Social units represented in the accounts of northern Black Mesa from the 1880s appear to have consisted of nuclear and extended family residence groups. These often formed the short-term seasonal clusters of kin- or clan-related residence groups that provided mutual assistance (as described in chapter 1). Prominent local figures during this period included Slim Man and Hoskinini (translated as "Giving Out Anger"), whose main ranges appear to have been north and northeast of Black Mesa. Who Has Mules (or "Many Mules"), and perhaps Choclays Kinsman lived on northern Black Mesa (see Dyk and Dyk 1980:266; Gilmor and Wetherill 1953), and residences associated with Who Has Mule's family are identified in the BMAP site records. Some of these prominent individuals seem frequently to have formed nuclei for the clusters of cooperating residence groups.

At that time, land use was flexible and no exclusive claims to range were honored. Still, repeated references to the potential for conflict suggest that even in this period some sense of restricted land use rights existed (e.g., Dyk 1967:111, 129–30; Dyk and Dyk 1980:84, 354, 470, 472). The large horse and cattle herds of the richer individuals roamed unrestricted, although at the cost of occasional theft by poorer neighbors. The large herd owners also employed herders to care for their sheep and goats. These herders were sometimes slaves and in other cases probably poor or young relatives (Dyk 1967:109, 217; Dyk and Dyk 1980:432, 440, 447).

The 1870s and 1880s were the beginning of an era of a strong livestock economy and relative prosperity that characterized the first period of abundant sites in the BMAP archaeological record. Many of the trends of this period continued into the late nineteenth and early twentieth century. These included a growing availability of trading posts and growing populations. Several additional factors developed in this later period.

Environmental change was one major characteristic of the late nineteenth century, and that change has continued up to the present. Large-scale arroyo down-cutting began around 1884 in Tsegi Canyon and developed rapidly throughout the surrounding lowland valleys. The result was the formation of the deep arroyos characteristic of the area today, elimination of a series of natural lakes that had existed along Laguna Creek just north of Black Mesa, and lowering of water tables in areas of prime agricultural alluvium (Gregory 1917:130–31). Notably violent storms in 1912 caused extensive damage to agricultural areas in the flats north and northeast of Black Mesa. These storms destroyed a successful Navajo irrigation farming area at Baby Rocks, east of Kayenta (Van Valkenburgh 1941:51).

Such destruction of valley farm land undoubtedly increased local population pressure on available land and water supplies. Russell (1981a:51) reports that one informant's family stopped their summer migrations off the mesa around 1910 to 1915 because they were denied permission to cross the grazing areas of other families. Russell suggests that around this time seasonal movement off the mesa in general began to decrease in frequency. This marks the beginning of a significant change in subsistence pattern and a formalization of land use rights (Russell 1981a:51). A change of this sort occurred in many areas of the reservation beginning around this time (Blomberg 1983:53, with references; Kelley 1982b:173).

This change in settlement pattern is visible in the archaeological record. Blomberg (1983) demonstrates an increased number of herding and storage facilities as well as other features on habitation sites in the BMAP sample; these increases begin around 1925. She interprets this as evidence of decreasing mobility. Analysis of the seasonality data on BMAP sites suggests a drop in the proportion of winter season sites relative to sites of other seasons over time (see chapter 6), although the pattern is not uniform across the study area.

Accompanying the decrease in summer habitation off of the Mesa was a shift to a smaller-scale settlement pattern restricted to the mesa top. Summer residence and farming was typically in the major alluvial washes and winter occupation in more wooded uplands. This involved relatively minor seasonal altitude movements (Russell 1983b:57–58).

Throughout the late nineteenth and twentieth centuries, overall Navajo population continued to rise rapidly (Johnston 1966). The only significant break in this growth occurred when the flu pandemic in the fall of 1918 caused very high mortality among the Navajos (Reagan 1922; Russell 1983b:36). Almost every family in the area experienced deaths and at least one family in the eastern BMAP area died out entirely (Russell 1981a:52). A number of sites in the BMAP sample contain burials from this catastrophic event. Tribal-wide population recovered by the mid-1920s (Johnston 1966) and it is likely that the same is true of the BMAP area.

The possible shift to increased farming on Black Mesa rather than in the lowlands probably decreased the potential for agricultural productivity and the range of crops grown (because, as noted previously, the short growing season and unpredictable distribution of rain on Black Mesa frequently threaten crops such as corn). It is likely that an increase in reliance on live-stock and trade for agricultural products or trading post goods accompanied this shift.

The 1920s marked the beginning of an increase in the use of Euro-American trade goods, as indicated by artifacts recovered from sites in the area (Holley et al. 1980:314; Myers and Russell 1983:221). Trading posts were readily accessible during this period. One post under Navajo ownership even operated briefly within the BMAP study area in the 1910s, a further indication of increased Navajo involvement in the market economy (Rocek 1984a). Trading post operators continued to purchase sheep, goats, wool, mohair, sheep and goat skins, rugs, and piñon nuts (Hubbell Papers; Rocek 1984a). Wool was typically the single most important item in terms of total economic value, followed by livestock, rugs and blankets, and finally skins and pelts (although this order varied from year to year and post to post). Piñon nut sales fluctuated from negligible to (rarely) rivaling wool as an income source. Corn, firewood, and various native crafts aside from blankets were minor items in the trade. These observations are based on Utley 1961:14; and on a preliminary examination of ledgers from Ganado (late nineteenth century), Pinon (ca. 1917–1930s), Dinnebito (ca. 1930), and Black Mountain (early 1930s) trading posts (see Hubbell Papers). Credit accounts and pawn served to even out the seasonal fluctuation in Navajo income, as well as to tie

Navajos to particular posts (U.S. Trade Commission 1973:18–26). Fluctuations in national economic conditions also had an impact on local market conditions; low wool prices in the early to mid-1890s and in the early 1920s noticeably hurt the Navajo economy (Brugge 1980:150–52, 313, 316, 318; Dyk 1947:58; U.S. Bureau of the Census 1975:517–20).

In addition to greater involvement with traders, the early twentieth century was a period of increased, if still limited, U.S. government presence in the region. Schools were established at Keams Canyon (1887), Blue Canyon (1895, closed in 1901), Tuba City (1901 or 1902), and Kayenta (1914) (Bailey and Bailey 1986:169; Underhill 1953:227; Van Valkenburgh 1941: 13, 164; Young 1961:62). Hospitals were built at Tuba City (1911) and Kayenta (1927) (Underhill 1953:278). Sheep dipping, introduced into the eastern reservation around the turn of the century (Brugge 1980; Dyk 1947: 127, 130), was available on a limited basis near Black Mesa by about 1920 (Kelly 1970:106–7; Roessel 1974:197).

Some improvement of water facilities also occurred on the reservation in the early 1900s. Reservoirs were in existence on Black Mesa by the early 1900s (Mitchell 1978:82), but their location is uncertain. A map from 1916 shows wells on the southern end of Black Mesa near the Hopi villages and one tank on its western end, southwest of the BMAP area (Gregory 1917: Plate 1). The government sponsored well and reservoir construction on the reservation in the 1920s, along with efforts at stock improvement, control of excess horse populations, and further efforts at promoting sheep dipping (Kelly 1970: 104–12). In the late 1920s large numbers of horses were destroyed at government direction in response to an epidemic of Dourine, an incurable, sexually transmitted horse disease (Aberle 1966:58). Some Dourine outbreaks and destruction of horses occurred at least as early as 1919 (Hubbell Papers: box 522, folder 4).

Government efforts to improve range conditions resulted from the recognition of a growing overgrazing problem on the reservation. References to overgrazing date as early as 1883, and the 1894 report by the Navajo Indian Agent suggested that the Navajo land base was insufficient. References to this inadequacy became common after the first decade of the twentieth century (see, e.g., Iverson 1981:11, 17, with references; Kelly 1970:104–5).

Data on Navajo livestock holdings during this period suggest a peak in herd size around 1880 to 1890. A particularly harsh winter in 1894–1895 and episodes of drought in the 1890s and early 1900s slowed this growth, and probably reduced overall holdings to a low around 1895 or 1896 (Bailey and

Bailey 1986:100–105). At the same time, erosion that was caused by or coupled with the effects of overgrazing reduced range productivity. Sheep and goat populations grew again in the early twentieth century, but at a slower average rate than previously, and partially at the expense of horse populations. During this same period, the Navajo population continued to grow rapidly. Thus, after the 1880s average per-capita livestock holdings leveled off and began to decrease (Aberle 1966:30–32; Bailey and Bailey 1986:104; Kelley 1982b:30; White 1983:219–22).

Historical information on livestock holdings specific to the BMAP area are not available for the late nineteenth century, but data from the period immediately following suggest that per-capita sheep holdings in the overall Black Mesa area were comparable to the interregional mean (Bailey and Bailey 1980:1437, 1433; Russell 1983b:31), and thus the reservation-wide figures may roughly reflect local factors (but see discussion that follows). Preliminary analysis of material recovered from BMAP sites suggest a slight peak in the number of artifacts on sites dating prior to the late 1890s, perhaps reflecting the period of maximum wealth in herds. This also matches the archaeological evidence discussed in chapter 6 that shows a peak in livestock holdings in the 1890s followed by a temporary decline and then a rebound.

Overall, the late nineteenth century appears to be the culmination of a livestock-based economy for the Navajo, over the entire reservation and in the BMAP area specifically. This is the period best matching the conditions expected to encourage middle-level cooperative units, and it is this period that shows the maximum clustering among archaeological sites in analyses described in chapter 6. This prosperity collapsed with the loss of livestock in the 1890s and a fall in wool prices in the Panic of 1893, and was never fully regained (Bailey and Bailey 1986:100–105). Again the archaeological record shows a decrease in site clustering in the 1890s, never regaining the level seen for preceding decades. The economy made a partial recovery in the early 1900s, and the Navajos began a process of re-establishing the successful pattern of the preceding period. On the reservation as a whole, the early twentieth-century economy involved more intensive sales of lambs (rather than wool as a primary commodity), substantially lower per-capita livestock holdings, and a closer dependence on the market for basic goods (Bailey and Bailey 1986). The isolated Black Mesa area probably participated less in this trend toward intensive interaction with the national economy, though the market was clearly an important part of the local economic pattern. Again, the archaeological record appears to track this pattern, with a slight recovery in clustering in the first third of the twentieth century (see discussion in chapter 6).

With the coming of the Great Depression, the move toward tighter integration with the national market and political system accelerated dramatically, and fundamentally transformed the Navajo way of life. Prior to the Depression in the 1930s, federal programs had a limited effect on select segments of the Navajo population. Federal involvement was probably slight in an isolated area such as northern Black Mesa. The explosion of government programs during the New Deal era, however, had a major impact on virtually all Navajos.

By far the most important program was livestock reduction. As a result of overgrazing on the reservation and a concern for the long-term effects of continued erosion of the Navajo range (as well as concern over the effects of silt derived from this erosion on Boulder Dam), the federal government exerted increasing pressure for drastic cuts in Navajo livestock populations. The initial efforts in 1934 and 1935 were "voluntary" in the sense that no formal coercion was authorized (although some did occur); efforts after 1937 were based on rigorously specified grazing levels and legal action against those who exceeded them. Stock levels were set in sheep or animal "units" reflecting approximate graze consumption per animal; sheep and goats were defined as one unit each, cows were four units, and horses five. In addition to the reduction of the livestock population, government programs of this era included an increased effort at stock improvement, sheep dipping, erosion control, reservoir construction, well drilling, and the construction of irrigation projects. Many of these projects were carried out with local labor hired with Soil Conservation Service (SCS) and Civilian Conservation Corps (CCC) funds, thus providing temporary jobs throughout the reservation. (For details of the sequence of events of the stock reduction period see Aberle 1966; Roessel 1974; Sasaki and Adair 1952; Spicer 1952; Young 1961:150–78; and White 1983:250–314.)

After 1937, the administrative basis of stock reduction was a set of nineteen grazing districts that covered the reservation as well as adjoining Navajo and Hopi land. Much of the information concerning this period is available in summary form by grazing district. The BMAP area straddles the boundary between Districts 4 to the south and 8 to the north (it also includes a small piece of District 2). The sample of sites examined in this book falls largely in District 8. District 4 covers most of Black Mesa and so may be more representative of the BMAP area elevation and soil characteristics (cf. Russell

1981a:38). The District 8 data, in contrast, reflects an area of low population density comparable to that seen on northern Black Mesa, making it quite different from the relatively crowded conditions farther south in District 4 (Goodman 1982:62). In addition, the District 8 livestock figures are of relevance in the stock reduction period, because enforcement of reduction policy was applied by district; hence District 8 regulations applied to most of the sites in the study sample. Given the BMAP area's peripheral position to the two districts, data from both districts are of interest.

Two studies gathered district-wide statistics, one in 1936, and the other in 1940 (Bailey and Bailey 1980 and Kunitz 1977; see Rocek 1985 for details of the data cited here). In 1936, District 4 was by far the poorest region of the reservation in overall per-capita annual income ($70.28 compared to an inter-district mean of $132.76, including all income in sales as well as estimated use-value of home consumption) and in per-capita wage income in particular ($5.35 compared to $45.54). Per-capita livestock holdings (21.2 animal units) were near average, and the percent of total income derived from livestock was higher than average (49 percent compared with 35 percent). The absolute value of per-capita income from livestock was well below average, however, because income-per-animal unit was very low. Reliance on agriculture was higher than average (31 percent as opposed to 22 percent), although agricultural income was low. The order of economic importance of the primary sources of subsistence was livestock, agriculture, and finally wage labor (Kunitz 1977; Russell 1983b:31–33). These statistics correspond with a serious undersupply of land, limited livestock productivity (perhaps also limited access to markets), a very limited supply of jobs, and overall poverty.

The District 8 figures suggest a less extreme situation. Total per-capita income and reliance on wage income were near average. These values are probably distorted by wage opportunities at Kayenta, Dinnehotso, Mexican Hat, and towns along the northern border of the reservation. These communities were included in District 8, but all lie north of the BMAP study area. Wage opportunities in the study area itself were probably substantially lower. Like District 4, District 8 livestock holdings were near average, but livestock income was below average. Reliance on agriculture was also near average, lower than the level indicated in District 4. The ranking of income sources in District 8 was wage income first (but see previous comments), then livestock, and, finally, agriculture.

Overall, if the high wage levels in District 8 are discounted, the data from the two districts together suggest that occupants of the study area probably had low total income, near-average livestock levels, and low livestock income (but perhaps medium to high percent dependence on livestock).

The major impact of stock reduction reached Black Mesa (at least the south-central part of it) near the end of the 1930s and in the 1940s (Downs 1964:19). So, the region missed the full impact of the "voluntary" stock reduction programs of the early 1930s, which hurt small herd owners the most. These programs worked through constant percentage cuts in herd size, which permitted the culling of large herds but cut into the breeding stock of small ones (Henderson 1989; Kelley 1986; Spicer 1952:193–94). The delayed impact of the program on Black Mesa may have allowed the leveling of herd sizes rather than the destruction of small herds as happened elsewhere. However, District 4 was judged to be one of the most seriously overstocked areas of the entire reservation, and a maximum permit level of 72 sheep units (compared with an overall average among reservation grazing districts of 175) was imposed. Although the District 4 reduction requirements were never reached and were subsequently relaxed, the impact of attempts at such severe cuts must have been catastrophic (Young 1961:155–56, 168, 171). District 8 was assigned a less draconian level of 154 maximum sheep units per permittee, and thus suffered less drastic cuts.

In addition, the Depression had a serious impact on Navajo subsistence, as wool and sheep prices fell to one half or less of their pre-1930 levels and did not fully recover until the early 1940s (U.S. Bureau of the Census 1975:517, 582). Thus, when low depression prices were combined with government pressure (and financial inducements) to sell stock, the Navajos made major cuts in their herds. The delay in the onset of reduction on Black Mesa may have encouraged particularly severe cuts, because the program started before the 1940s recovery began but after the Navajos had undergone nearly a decade of the Depression and were desperate for income (Downs 1964:20). Blomberg (1983:53) notes a correspondence between the late onset of stock reduction and further increases in the archaeological evidence of growing sedentism on sites of the 1940s and later.

As elsewhere on the reservation, stock reduction decreased District 4 per-capita livestock holdings (16.5 animal units). By 1940 livestock production dropped even further than it did in most other districts, so that livestock income ($20.99) was the lowest of all grazing districts. Reliance on livestock as a percentage of total income per-capita remained only slightly above average (50 percent compared with 47 percent). Wage income remained low ($6.26),[2] but its relative importance had doubled at the expense of both live-

stock and agricultural income. Total annual per-capita income ($42.32) re-
mained the lowest on the reservation. The order of economic importance of
subsistence activities in District 4 remained the same, but the gap between
wage labor and agriculture had greatly narrowed, and the importance of livestock had begun to decline. This was the beginning of a trend characteristic
of recent Navajo economic history (Bailey and Bailey 1980:1439–45).

District 8 wage opportunities fell sharply from 1936 to 1940, probably as
a result of the loss of CCC and SCS jobs. Still, per-capita wage income
($24.14) and reliance on wages (33 percent) were well above the reservation
average ($20.70 and 25 percent respectively). Again, these figures probably
reflect employment in the portions of District 8 north of the study area rather
than conditions in the study area itself. Because of the less stringent stock-
reduction levels in District 8, livestock decreased slightly less than in many
other districts, so that per-capita stock holdings were slightly higher than the
mean (19.3 animal units compared with 16.6). Despite this, total annual income ($72.98) remained low. Agricultural production was much lower than
reported in 1936. The order of importance of income sources was livestock,
wages, and finally agriculture.

The District 4 and 8 data combined suggest that the region surrounding the
BMAP study area remained poor even by the impoverished standards of the
reservation. Livestock provided a slightly higher than average percentage of
income. Wage labor opportunities during this period included the temporary
CCC and other government jobs, as well as a few jobs made possible in the
late 1930s by the opening of a small coal mining operation within the BMAP
area. Off-reservation jobs were not widely available or used through the 1930s
(Russell 1981a:30–31).[3]

Despite the region-wide figures suggesting a decrease in agricultural production, data collected by Russell (n.d.) suggest a peak in the establishment
of new fields in this period (see chapter 6). These figures may be distorted by
informant memories, because many of the informants were in their prime or
young adulthood in the 1940s. The fields may, however, actually represent a
local increase in agricultural activity in an effort to compensate for livestock
losses (see Kelley 1982b:102, 1986:136). A 150-acre Indian Service irrigation project was in operation at Kayenta during this period, and some of the
inhabitants of the BMAP area also made seasonal use of plots there (Russell
n.d.: interviews 6/10/76, 6/15/76; Van Valkenburgh 1941:83).

As in the period preceding stock reduction, hunting and gathering were
minor components of the local subsistence base. Prairie dogs, the most com-

monly hunted wild animal, were poisoned on a large scale as part of the range improvement effort during the stock reduction era. Therefore, even this limited food source was diminished (Russell 1981a:13-14).

Noncommercial trade with the Hopis continued through this and the succeeding period, although at diminishing levels. More of the goods formerly involved in this trade presumably were routed through the trading post system (Russell 1981a:28-29).

Overall, the economic impact of the stock reduction period was dramatic. As livestock and region-wide agricultural production fell and as wage labor availability rose, a large increase in purchases of meat and other formerly home-produced food items was noted at some trading posts (White 1983: 265). The end of the Depression and the start of World War II opened job opportunities on and off the reservation (Boyce 1974:103; Young 1978:120). Although few men from the BMAP area served in the armed forces (Russell 1981a:30), income from other sources became available. Thus, the trend toward increased wage dependence at the expense of livestock and agriculture continued. Sites in the BMAP sample dating from the late 1930s onward typically have a large number of purchased Euro-American goods on them.

Active efforts at stock reduction ended in 1948 (White 1983:309-10). Still, in the late 1940s economic crisis hit the reservation due to the post-war drop in employment and the greatly diminished livestock base. The collapse encouraged a reassessment of federal policy. Nationwide publicity accompanied relief efforts to prevent starvation among the Navajos, as well as efforts to reverse neglect of health and educational services during the war years (Boyce 1974:220-41; Underhill 1978:251-53; Young 1961:560-61).

Tribal-wide livestock populations began to grow again in 1953 (Iverson 1981:54; Young 1961:71). Livestock and wool prices remained high until about that same year (U.S. Bureau of the Census 1975:519), encouraging a continued significant reliance on livestock income. Per-sheep wool and meat production had also been greatly improved by stock reduction era programs, so that total reservation financial returns on livestock at mid-1940s prices actually increased despite the decrease in stock population (Spicer 1952: 198-99).

After 1953, however, livestock prices collapsed, and wool prices also declined. Furthermore, as the livestock population began a slow climb, human population continued to increase rapidly. By the time total Navajo livestock holdings began to approach prereduction values in the 1980s (Reno 1982:32), human population stood at about three times its 1930s level (Goodman

1982:61). Thus, regardless of the financial potential of livestock, tribal per-capita stock holdings available for consumption and sale had fallen drastically.

By the mid-1950s, the relative importance of livestock to Navajo income had declined greatly. Data from 1955 at Shonto (located in Grazing District 2, just northwest of the BMAP area but off the mesa) show livestock making up less than 20 percent of the economic base (Adams 1963:137; Adams and Ruffing 1977:78; Russell 1983b:34). This may be compared against the 1940 District 2 level of more than 60 percent livestock income (Bailey and Bailey 1980:1439). Reliance on agriculture had also fallen drastically. The major increase was in the importance of wage work, which made up over 65 percent of the 1955 economic base (compared to less than 10 percent in 1940). An additional factor was the availability of direct government assistance in the form of welfare.

Russell (1981a; 1983b) notes the same factors operating in the BMAP area, with a major increase in the availability of jobs in the 1950s (primarily off-reservation railroad work). Job opportunities also included the continued operation of the local coal mine and the brief operation of a second one from the late 1940s to around 1950 (Russell 1981a:30). Sporadic jobs from tribal construction projects on reservoirs, wells, and roads were also available (Informant data 1981 for D:11:4216; Russell 1981a:31; Young 1961:172–77). Direct government assistance programs began to have an effect in the BMAP area in the 1950s and 1960s as well (Russell 1981a:32).

The BMAP area may have maintained a somewhat higher reliance on animal husbandry than the adjacent region, however. Except for older informants who remembered the prestock-reduction period, most informants in the BMAP area indicated a peak herd size some time in the 1960s (Russell n.d.:various). As of 1959, Districts 8 and 4 were judged to be heavily over-grazed (Kunitz 1977).

The increase in jobs on the reservation was not enough to compensate for population growth and declining income, and some younger inhabitants of the BMAP study area were forced to migrate to find jobs (Russell 1981a:31, 1983b:37). The peak in field construction noted in the preceding period ended by the early 1950s and in subsequent years a slightly increased number of fields were abandoned in the eastern BMAP area (data in Russell 1981a). One probable cause of the decline in agricultural productivity was headward erosion of the main washes. This process gradually destroyed the agricultural potential of an increasing percentage of the mesa-top alluvial land, as it had destroyed the lowland farm areas in preceding decades (Russell 1981a:12–13, 21). Migration for jobs also limited the number of people available for working the fields, although some use of fields at Kayenta continued through the 1960s (Russell n.d.: interviews 6/2/80, 6/3/80). Despite the reintroduction of deer onto Black Mesa during this period, hunting remained of little importance (Russell 1981a:14).

These conditions continued through the 1960s. An economic survey in the vicinity of the BMAP area in 1971 found very low per-capita income ($400), limited local employment possibilities, and a high rate of outmigration of the labor force (Kozlowksi 1972, cited in Russell 1981a:38–39). Agriculture continued to decline in importance in the 1960s (Russell 1981a:22). Data from Shonto during the same period also indicate low income, although not quite as extreme ($724 according to Adams and Ruffing 1977:71). The importance of livestock and agricultural income had fallen at Shonto since 1955, and federal aid (welfare) had grown in importance. Local jobs had become much more important than off-reservation jobs, with work available at a local school and on tribal projects. However, roughly 7 percent of the Shonto population had moved out of the area for an extended period to find work elsewhere (Adams and Ruffing 1977:15, note 19).

During the 1950s, road construction throughout the reservation dramatically improved the ease, speed, and reliability of transportation (Young 1961:133–45). As road conditions improved, motor vehicles began to be more widely used on the reservation, particularly during the 1960s (Chisholm 1981:155; Myers and Russell 1983:213). Some of this construction occurred in the BMAP area (e.g., informant data 1981 for D:11:4216; Russell n.d.: interview 6/7/76) and had several major effects. One was to encourage large-scale exploitation of the piñon nut harvest, which exhibited an apparent peak in the area in the late 1950s and early 1960s (Landreth and Hardenbergh 1985; Russell 1981a:316). Much of this piñon nut gathering involved people from outside of the immediate BMAP area who took advantage of the improved roads to gain access to the local piñon crop.

A more fundamental change (partially associated with the improvement of transportation) was a further decrease in the seasonal settlement mobility of area residents. During the 1950s and 1960s, the pattern of multiple seasonal habitations established in the 1920s began to shift to an increased use of year-round habitation sites, coupled with frequent travel to outlying herding and agricultural facilities. In some cases supplemental feeding of livestock was required to compensate for decreasing herd mobility (Russell 1981a:25–27,

1983b:57; cf. Rocek 1984c; Underwood 1985). During the late 1950s, federal government programs also encouraged range fencing, which further reduced mobility (Blomberg and Smiley 1982:20).

An era of new economic transformation in the BMAP area was ushered in in 1964 when Peabody Coal Company began leasing land on Black Mesa (Iverson 1981:105). Coal production began in 1970 and expanded two years later (Reno 1982:112). The impact of the mining and associated operations on the BMAP area has been great and dominates the final period covered in the BMAP archaeological data.

The financial effects of the mining include the introduction of a substantial number of high paying jobs. A survey conducted in the region in the early to mid-1970s (Callaway et al. 1976:67, 72, 80; Russell 1983b:35) found a large number of households with at least one member employed in mine-related jobs. A significant improvement in income ($1108) was evident relative to the 1971 Shonto and Black Mesa figures. Wage income accounted for 77 percent of total income, government assistance was next in importance, and livestock income made up only 6 percent of the total.

Researchers who conducted a 1977 survey that included the southern part of the BMAP area found a comparable level of per-capita income ($1267.66) (*Navajo Times* 1981b; Russell 1983b:35; Wood et al. 1982). Wage labor was again of overwhelming importance, but in this survey livestock income was a strong second, partially because of a short-term government program designed to provide an incentive for livestock reduction (discussed later in this chapter). This survey included a large area beyond the range of available mining jobs, and thus the relative importance of wage labor was lower. The relative importance of public assistance income was comparable to the 1971 study. Free government surplus food was used by over 65 percent of households. The survey found that only 45 percent of households farmed, and that median herd size included thirty-four sheep and/or goats, three horses, and one cow, for households averaging 5.6 individuals (these figures on livestock holdings were estimated just prior to the start of a livestock reduction program in 1976).

In addition to employment directly by the coal company, a variety of jobs in associated projects became available. Expansion of mining activities during the 1970s created additional opportunities. The BMAP itself provided local summer employment beginning in the mid-1960s, and with greatly expanded opportunities in the late 1970s up until the final season in 1983. These latter jobs provided employment for the young and elderly who were not eligible for mining or construction-related jobs (Russell 1981a:31–32). Due to the economic development outmigration slowed and to a limited extent reversed, as a number of former occupants or relatives moved back into the area in order to find jobs (Russell 1981a:31–32). A local economic boom is currently readily apparent in a proliferation of new trucks and of house construction (some built with coal company funds for relocatees off mined land).

Accompanying the mining activities was a development of facilities in the BMAP area: the paving of the main north road onto the mesa, construction of company showers (available for use by residents), construction of a company health clinic (also available for local use), and maintenance of local dirt roads.

Along with the economic benefits came a variety of hardships: the trauma and uncertainty of relocation, environmental destruction, disruption of agriculture and herding, increased theft and vandalism as a result of the growing population and improved access to the area, the effect of dust and fumes on people and livestock, and accidents associated with increased traffic. In addition, land disputes among households increased as the mine compensated displaced households for destroyed grazing acreage. A drop in the surficial water table and drying out of springs has also been noted by local residents and blamed on water use by the mining operation, although this is denied by the mining company (Iverson 1981:106; Russell 1981a:55–56, n.d.).

A second major factor affecting part of the BMAP area was the Navajo-Hopi Joint Use Area dispute, which crippled economic development in the southern part of the area for over a decade. Due to ambiguity regarding tribal rights to the 1882 reservation area, legal action between the Hopi and Navajo tribes first established joint use rights to the land that included the southern part of the BMAP area (1962), and finally divided the land between the two tribes in 1977. As part of the legal settlement, all Navajo construction on the disputed land was ordered halted in 1972 (local development had already been placed in limbo by the 1962 agreement), and a drastic reduction of around 90 percent of Navajo livestock was imposed. Although bitterly opposed, these decisions were gradually implemented, initially through the use of high incentive pay to encourage stock reduction (see earlier discussion) and later through confiscation of livestock in excess of permitted levels.

By November 1977, more than 45 percent of the livestock had been removed. The partition formalized in February 1977 included most of the BMAP area within the Navajo, rather than the Hopi, reservation and the construction freeze in the area was lifted (*Navajo Times* 1981a, 1981b;

Russell 1981a:40–41). Thus, after 1977 the economic condition of the southern BMAP area was permitted to stabilize, but with a drastically reduced livestock base that accelerated the trend toward abandonment of animal husbandry as a major subsistence item, and increased dependence on wages and federal assistance. Those Navajos caught in the Hopi-partitioned area suffered devastating emotional, as well as economic, hardship.

Data collected in 1975 through 1977 from the eastern coal lease area (Russell 1981a) and from the western lease area in 1980 (where mining had been in progress for a longer time) (Russell n.d.) give some indication of the recent trends. The earlier eastern data reflect many elements of the traditional pattern despite the disruption of the mining and the Joint Use Area dispute. Median herd size was about 100 sheep, 20 goats, 20 cows, and 3 horses for settlements averaging 10.5 members (the settlements in turn were composed of an average 1.75 households of 6.05 members each). Calculations using figures from those settlements with complete livestock data reveal a surprising 20.7 sheep units per-capita, a value near the 1936 District 4 average, and above the 1940 figures. A probable cause for these high apparent values, however, is suggested by the demographic profile associated with these data (Russell 1981a: Table 1), which reveals a drastic underrepresentation of individuals in the twenty- to forty-year-old range as well as in the zero- to five-year-old range. Obviously, outmigration remained a major factor despite the new jobs, and the per-capita sheep figures were inflated by the lack of tabulation of the absent population. In addition, the collection of these data preceded the later stages of the Joint Use Area stock reduction.

In 1980 the western BMAP area had a median of about 50 sheep, 12 goats, 15 cows, and 3 horses per settlement. Settlements averaged 8.75 people, made up of 1.50 households of 5.90 people each. Per-capita livestock holdings were 17.3 animal units. Thus, the later western figures show smaller social units, with less stock. These differences in part represent long-standing east-west contrasts (because informant estimates of "largest number of stock ever held" were higher in the eastern area). They also clearly reflect the direction of recent economic changes. Trends in social unit composition are less clear (see chapter 6).

An additional observation concerning local animal husbandry is evidence of a shift to the use of cattle. Informant estimates of almost all livestock holdings indicated a decrease through time up to the present. The major exception were cattle, which were at peak levels, or at least not minimal levels, when the data were collected in 1975–1977 and 1980. The chronological trend is again reflected in the slight east-west difference in herd composition. This shift was encouraged by high financial returns on cattle and by the ease with which cattle may be left in unsupervised herds compared with sheep and goats. The lower labor investment required by cattle permit a combination of wage labor and animal husbandry (Russell 1981a:23–24). The same trend toward larger herds of cattle characterized Shonto in 1971 (Adams and Ruffing 1977:74).

Agricultural production continued to drop in the 1970s in the eastern lease area as alternative sources of income became more important. Several settlements had not planted a crop since the mid-1960s (Russell 1981a: Table 5). Surprisingly, the western data showed a limited revival of farming, with small new fields along some of the large drainages (data in Russell n.d.). Perhaps the acquisition of tractors was increasing the possibilities for part-time farming by wage workers. On the other hand, a number of fields were destroyed by mining activity in the 1970s. The higher value assessed for land under cultivation also may have been a factor in increased farming activity (Richard Ford, personal communication 1984). Local weaving, other craft production, hunting, and piñon collecting were of very limited financial importance in the 1970s.

Thus, the BMAP area is now in the midst of a variety of transformations. On the one hand, it retains a significant animal husbandry economy, although with some modifications in herd composition and grazing strategy that contrast with practices of previous decades. The gradual opening of mined and recontoured land to grazing offers some additional but uncertain possibilities of a limited, sustained livestock economy. Culturally, the area remains unquestionably Navajo, with Navajo the commonly spoken language.

On the other hand, the influx of jobs, people, and construction has introduced a whole new range of economic and social conditions, ameliorating some hardships but adding a variety of others. The Joint Use Area dispute placed an additional strain on the area and truncated traditional economic patterns to the south. Religious affiliation of a majority of local inhabitants has shifted to Christian faiths, although traditional Navajo beliefs, in some cases coupled with the Native American Church, remain widespread as well (Russell 1981a:56).

The BMAP area can no longer be considered an isolated part of the reservation. It is clear that local autonomy (relying only upon access to trading posts for credit, supplies, and sales of stock, wool, mohair, skins and pelts, and blankets) is a thing of the past. Modern economic conditions are typified more by reliance on wage labor and purchases at the large supermarket that opened in Tuba City in 1983 (reached via pick-up or car on good quality paved roads). Social relations are undoubtedly changing with the solidification of land use boundaries, the relocation of homesteads, and the limitation on employment opportunities. The growth of the local population, as well as a desire for access to utilities, has led to the establishment of three small trailer parks in the area, as well as the rental of more traditional Navajo structures to mine workers (Russell n.d.). Some of these trends may signal the beginning of a shift to independent nuclear households, away from the cooperative residence group pattern.

Changes such as these, although perhaps not quite as rapid as in the BMAP area, are found throughout the Navajo reservation, and constitute merely the latest in the long history of fundamental transformations of Navajo culture (cf. Vogt 1961). The long-term stability and consequences of recent developments in the BMAP area, as on the reservation as a whole, remain unknown.

3

The Units of Navajo Social Organization

Even before the onslaught of recent changes on the reservation, Navajo society was constantly being reorganized. Any account aimed at describing "traditional Navajo culture" aims at a moving target, and must specify a particular time and region. Still, amid this variability there is much that can readily be identified as "traditional," a foundation around which variation develops.

Variation in Navajo social units fits this pattern. Descriptions of these units have sparked debate and controversy. As I argue in this book, this debate in part reflects social changes in response to changes in the conditions of "traditional" Navajo life. But in broader outline, most accounts of Navajo society *do* recognize similar basic patterns of organization and provide a starting point for describing them.

Navajo social units divide conveniently according to approximate scale, with "lower-level" units smaller than "higher-level" units (Lamphere 1977: 175; cf. Aberle 1981b:1; Adams 1983:396). In this scheme the individual and the tribe are the lowest and highest levels of Navajo social units respectively. The classification by scale is not absolute. For instance, there may be clans (a high-level unit) represented by only a single individual, and residence groups (a lower-level unit) with as many as fifty members (Downs 1965). The classification of levels refers to organizational position as well as to the typical size range of the units.

Four levels, termed (in order of rising scale) the "household," "residence group," "middle-level," and "community," conveniently delimit the range of social units of relevance here.[1] In addition, clan organization may be of a scale comparable to the "community" level, although it represents a quite different sort of unit (see later discussion). As in the discussion of comparable groups in other societies (chapter 8), the description that follows emphasizes the functional characteristics of these units rather than the specifics of their recruitment and composition.

The household and the "camp" or residence group are the two lowest level units above the individual. The anthropological literature concerning the function of these low level groups provokes little disagreement. The main variability concerns the specific criteria selected for defining them and the associated terminology.

Definitions of units at both of these levels typically use any of three major criteria: kinship, spatial relationships, or patterns of cooperation (the function of the unit). Thus, the lowest (household) level unit is often called the "family" or "nuclear family" or "biological family," and is defined in terms of kinship. Alternatively, the "household" or "hogan" is defined as a set of people sharing a single dwelling—this is typically a family. Finally, some definitions of the household are based on the occurrence of close daily interaction and the sharing of meals among its members—again, this typically corresponds to the family, residing in a single dwelling. Thus, despite the diversity of terms and distinct definitions employed, in most situations investigators with different criteria would still identify many of the same units. In the archaeological analysis used here (see chapter 5), the household corresponds to the dwelling.

In many cases, however, the correspondence of these differently defined units is not exact (Netting et al. 1984:xx, xxv–xxvi; Wilk and Netting 1984:2–3). Nuclear families with older children may occupy more than a single dwelling, relatives outside of the nuclear family frequently share a hogan, and the regular joint preparation of meals may occur in units other than a nuclear family. Thus, even where variously defined social units correspond fairly closely, it is important to recognize the exact basis used to identify these units, as distinct from the usual (but not defining) co-occurring characteristics. Similarly, these different definitions may be significant when comparing the results of different studies of social organization. Summary figures for mean household size, for instance, are likely to differ if computed as number of individuals per dwelling or per nuclear family (e.g., Laslett 1972).

The "camp" or "residence group" level typically consists of one or more household level units (households or families) combined. The families in the group are closely related, live close together, and cooperate in a variety of basic economic activities on a daily basis. Definitions of residence group level social units exhibit the same kinds of differences in emphasis as do the definitions at the household level. Some studies identify residence group level units on the basis of kinship, as extended families. Alternatively, spatial criteria are used—in this case the camp or "cluster" consists of a spatial aggregate of hogans, generally within "shouting distance" of each other. Another frequently used defining criterion is daily cooperation in basic subsistence activities, such as herding.

As with the household level, the same units would be identified in most cases regardless of the particular definition used, and many of the definitions implicitly assume that the different criteria define co-extensive units (e.g., that an extended family lives in a cluster of nearby hogans). The only significant disagreement in the literature is that of Witherspoon (1970), who has suggested that spatially defined units do not correspond to kinship or functionally bounded units. Most studies indicate that the kind of spatial "fuzziness" described by Witherspoon is not typical, however, and that different definitions of residence group level units usually produce comparable results (Adams 1983:394; Adams and Ruffing 1977:70). Still, as noted for the household level, the particular definition used in identifying residence group level units must be distinguished clearly, even when there is only minor variation in the units delineated by the different methods. In the archaeological approach used here, the residence group corresponds to the site, or site component (see chapters 4 and 5).

Most studies of Navajo social structure define two basic kinds of high level social units (just below the tribal level): clans (defined in terms of real and fictive kinship), and communities (defined in geographical and functional terms). In general, most workers identify clans in similar ways, but descriptions of geographical communities vary and attribute different functions to them.

Matrilineal clans are the basis for the organization of certain aspects of Navajo society, particularly marriage. The clans, in turn, are loosely organized into "clan groups." These are collections of clans that are considered to be in some way related and usually, like the clans themselves, are exogamous. Aside from the function of clans and clan groups in marriage prohibition, clan relatives are in a general way expected to provide hospitality and aid to each other (see for instance Slim Man's reference to shared clan membership quoted in chapter 1). In addition, historically, shared clan membership has often served as a basis for extending fictive kinship in establishing individual or group alliances. Because new clans have formed and old ones gone extinct through time, exact tabulations of all clans have not been consistent, but since detailed anthropological studies began around the turn of the century, there have been a total of around sixty-five clans and nine clan groups. (For a more extensive discussion of Navajo clan organization, see Aberle 1961:108–12; Kluckhohn and Leighton 1946:63–66; Reichard 1928).

In addition to clan divisions, workers in portions of the Navajo country recognize the division of Navajo society into geographical communities. In other areas, however, units defined by topographical barriers, traditional authority, patterns of cooperation and jurisdictions of various recent "community" institutions such as schools or tribal chapter[2] districts cross-cut in complex ways. In addition, settlement distributions may be nearly spatially continuous. In these cases, researchers recognize no consistent meaningful boundaries (e.g., Aberle 1961:107; Adams 1963:1; Kluckhohn and Leighton 1946:69).

Where identified, the geographical divisions have been called natural communities (Hill 1940a), local communities (Aberle 1961:106–7), bands, or simply communities (Kluckhohn and Leighton 1946:68–69). Traditionally, such communities were identified as largely self-sufficient economic units, under the nonbinding leadership of a local headman or headmen (Hill 1940a). This form of community level is analogous to an expanded form of some of the larger middle-level social unit described later. The degree to which the natural community functions in some meaningful way as a unit or recognizes a local leader is highly variable (Kluckhohn and Leighton 1946: 68–69; Shepardson 1963: 34–35). Increasingly, economic, political, and bureaucratic institutions (trading posts, grazing districts, school districts, and particularly tribal chapters) have taken on the role of focusing local political and social action (Aberle 1961:106–7). Some of the community level social functions have persisted independently of the political structure through the status of particularly prestigious ritual practitioners or other influential individuals. These may be called upon to settle disputes or perform other of the functions traditionally carried out by community level leaders (Adams 1963:65–66).

Above the household and residence group level and below the clan or community, middle-level social units cause the greatest disagreement and confusion among researchers in studies of Navajo social organization. As with the other categories of social units discussed previously, researchers have proposed a range of definitions for these units, including those based on kinship and functional criteria. Many definitions also specify spatial relationships.

Some degree of cooperation among member residence groups is commonly identified as a characteristic of middle-level units. Although the tasks for which cooperation takes place as well as the frequency of interaction vary greatly in different definitions, all agree that cooperation is less frequent than within the residence group. Other features include a degree of kinship among members, and possibly some spatial clustering or contiguity of the land owned by the residence groups making up the middle-level unit.

Unlike the relative agreement among different descriptions of the household, residence group, or community levels, however, accounts of middle-level units provoke debate concerning which definitions accurately describe the existing middle-level social groups, which definitions delineate equivalent units, or whether such middle-level units exist at all. A historical overview of definitions of middle-level units clarifies the issues.

Table 3.1 summarizes definitions of Navajo social units, with particular emphasis on middle-level units. The table is arranged in approximate chronological order, but this order is modified slightly to group the definitions into two basic categories. Most early descriptions of middle-level units focused on functional and/or spatial criteria (particularly cooperation in the group), leaving kinship as a secondary characteristic. Many subsequent studies have attempted to characterize these cooperating units more precisely by defining membership explicitly in terms of kinship, leaving function and spatial patterning as secondary factors. Finally, several studies (including some of the most recent literature) have described variation in middle-level units, the theme emphasized in this book. The focus of this study is on functionally recognizable units (in fact, my data do not permit me to directly address their social composition). However, as the following discussion suggests, some of the kinship-based definitions of middle-level units also identify functioning cooperative groups. Furthermore, the range of descriptions of *all* forms of middle-level units emphasizes the potential for variation and change over time in social organization at this level.

Kimball and Provinse (1942:22–23) were the first to describe a Navajo middle-level social unit. They identify the land-use community, a group larger and less clearly visible than the residence group. Land-use communities encompass "a number of *family groups* [residence groups]" that live on a contiguous area of land by right of inheritance and use. A defining feature of land-use communities is that they participate in occasional communal activities under a single leader. The activities typically involve land and water control (protection of land from encroachment, development of farm land, construction of water control facilities) and probably also the provision of food and facilities for ceremonies.

Kimball and Provinse explicitly defined the land-use community in terms of active patterns of resource use and organization of authority in communal activities, not in terms of genealogical or classificatory kinship relationships among the community members. Their goal in identifying land-use communities was to use them to effectively administer and monitor stock reduction-era regulations. They found that land-use communities typically covered more than 25,000 acres (10,125 ha) of contiguous land and, in some cases, as much as 80,000 acres (32,375 ha). As discussed later, this is considerably larger than the scale of some of the supraresidence group units identified by other students of Navajo social organization.

Kluckhohn and Leighton (1946) formulated the most widely cited definition of middle-level cooperative unit. Residence groups (which they identified as extended families) combined to form "outfits": "This Western term is used to designate a group of relatives (larger than the extended family) who regularly cooperate for certain purposes. Two or more extended families, or one or more extended families linked with one or more independent biological families, may habitually pool their resources on some occasions—say, planting and harvesting, or the giving of any major ceremonial for an individual member" (Kluckhohn and Leighton 1946:62). The outfit differs from the extended family (residence group) by its greater spatial dispersion and by the broader range of relations among its members. Although the members of the extended family live within "shouting distance" of each other, the outfit "may be scattered over a good many square miles," and it includes less closely related kin than the lineage members and in-marrying affines that make up an extended family. The defining characteristic of the outfit is the "intensity and regularity of the economic and other reciprocities" among its members.

Kluckhohn and Leighton indicate that outfits exhibit great variability in size, geographical distribution and makeup. Relatively rich families with large livestock holdings often form the nucleus, and the size of the group is related to the wealth of this family. Kluckhohn and Leighton equate some of the larger outfits, consisting of 50 to 200 people and occupying 12,000 to 80,000 acres (4,855–32,375 ha) of contiguous land, with land-use communities. They also give an example of smaller outfits from the Dennehotso Valley involving an average of four residence groups per outfit, and mention the occurrence of cooperation among groups of "two or more" residence

Table 3.1. Navajo Social Group Definitions[a]

Reference	Household	Residence group	Middle-level	Community
Kimball and Provinse (1942)	*family* — People living in single hogan. Family provides the basic biological requirements of its members. (20)	*family group* — Close consanguineal or affinal relatives, living at one locality, with a leader. Cooperate for seasonal labor-intensive activities; e.g., some livestock and farming functions, as well as sponsorship of ceremonies. (22)	*land-use community* — Contiguous family groups that occasionally participate in group tasks under a single leader. Typical activities relate to range use, agricultural development, water control, and defense of community [land?] rights. (22–23)	*greater community* — Local organization under the leadership of a prestigious individual. (24)
Kluckhohn and Leighton (1946)	*biological family* — Husband, wife, and unmarried children. This is the basic social and economic unit. (54)	*extended family* (also referred to as the "hogan group") — Ideally, a husband, wife, married daughters (with their nuclear families) and unmarried children, living within "shouting distance" of each other. Pool labor and economic resources for livestock, agriculture functions. (56–7, 62)	*outfit* — Families that "habitually pool resources on some occasions—e.g., planting and harvesting, or the giving of major ceremonials for a member. The families do not live within "shouting distance," but may occupy contiguous land, or may be dispersed. Relationships in the group include a "wider circle of kin" than the extended family. (62–3)	*local group or community or band* — Determined by locality, this unit cuts across kinship ties. Variable degree of cooperation, in some cases involving, e.g., sheep dipping or building and maintaining schools. Traditionally had a local headman. (68–70)

				larger community group
Collier (1966)	*hogan*	*camp*	*cooperating-group*	Variable, in some cases corresponding to a loosely organized extended cooperating-group that cooperates for some agricultural activities and recognizes a local prestigious individual as a leader. (38, 43, 53, 69–70)
	A hogan houses an elementary family (parents and unmarried children) and sometimes grandparent(s) and orphaned relatives. (24) Daily food preparation and consumption occurs in this unit. (27, 64)	Several families (hogans) within "earshot." (24) Considerale sharing of daily tasks such as wood and water hauling and sharing of food occurs in the camp. (26–7)	Closely interrelated (by consanguinity and affinity) camps, which live within about a half mile of each other. Camps cooperate, e.g., in herding, farming, and ceremonial activities. (53) These units are not identifiable in all cases— where not present their function is split between the camp and the larger community ("expanded cooperating-group") level. (69–70)	
Sasaki and Adair (1952)	*family*	*extended family*	*outfit*	
	Nuclear family, often with grandparent(s); they share a hogan. (100)	"Conjugal groups related through the female line," usually living within about a mile of each other; often within "shouting distance." They cooperate in farm work. (101)	Related extended families, herding and moving within a land area to which they share a common right, and which they defend against outsiders. This shared land use is the basis of the unit. Usually recognize an older individual as a leader. (102)	

a. Numbers in parentheses in columns 2 through 5 indicate page numbers from the references indicated. See text for an explanation of the order and selection of entries. This table is patterned after that of Lamphere (1977:176).

Table 3.1. Navajo Social Group Definitions (*continued*)

Reference	Household	Residence group	Middle-level	Community
Ross (1955)	*biological family* Husband, wife, and unmarried children. (185) *household* Group regularly co-operating in daily routine (e.g., cooking, eating, household chores); usually consanguineally or affinally related. (186)	*extended family* Cites Murdock (1949): two or more families, both joined to family of a parent. (186) *camp* Cites Collier: two or more elementary families who co-operate and live together (usually within earshot most of the year. (29, 185)	*outfit* Cites Kluckhohn and Leighton: group of relatives larger than extended family, regularly cooperating for some activities. (187) But also says outfit consists of individuals "related in a vague way, if at all," who engage in economic cooperation (97); Gives e.g., of outfit with affinal and consanguineal ties. (138–144) *cooperating unit* Cites Collier; cooperating unit is same as outfit; families (one or more camps) regularly cooperating in certain activities. (29, 185)	*local clan segment (LCS)* Cites Aberle's definition of the local clan element, but says LCS lacks ownership of land, leader, or similar characteristics. Function described by Aberle resides in lineages rather than LCS. (26–28, 118) *local group* Cites Bellah (1952): extended families living near each other, have recognized leader. (186) *band* Cites Bellah (1952): local groups in same area that occasionally combine for activities such as warfare. (185)

	[nuclear/biological] family	camp	outfit	community
Levy (1962)	Parents, unmarried offspring and sometimes additional dependents. Levy refers also to the definition of this unit in terms of co-residence in a single hogan. (782)	Defined on the basis of spatial proximity among the members' dwellings. (783) Members "cooperate in daily domestic, economic, and ceremonial" tasks. (784)	Levy lists previously published definitions of outfits and other middle-level cooperative groups. He emphasizes regular cooperation as the defining criterion; but he does not select a particular definition; he refers instead to the regional and temporal variability of outfits. He describes breakdown of spatial contiguity of outfits in his study area, and growing fuzziness of unit boundaries. (786–7, 791–2) He indicates that an outfit has a recognized leader. (794)	Topographically determined areas of settlement, which have recognized leaders. (789–90, 793–4) In many cases (particularly early in the history of settlement of a region), the community is coterminous with a local segment of a clan. (789–90)

Table 3.1. Navajo Social Group Definitions (*continued*)

Reference	Household	Residence group	Middle-level	Community
Downs (1964)	*family*	*homestead group*	*outfit*	(See text)
	A "matricentered descent group." Downs distinguishes this potentially larger unit from the nuclear family ("nuclear unit"). (71)	An extended family living close together (typically within 1/2 mile, or closer), in farming, wood and water hauling, organization of ceremonies, e.g., the arrangement of transportation, and sweat bathing. Extensive food sharing occurs; some families within the group regularly eat together. (77–80)	Downs cites Kluckhohn and Leighton's definition, but indicates that no such units exist in his study area, although they probably formerly did. (75) In his later publication, Downs (1965) adopts the terminology typically used by English-speaking Navajos, reserving the term "outfit" to refer to the residence group.	
Kluckhohn (1966)	*unit*	*extended family*	*group*	*band* or *community*
	People who live together (though not necessarily in one structure) and share food, chores, and to some degree, possessions. Often consists of a family. (366)	Two or more "units," at least one of which has both parents present. Units must share a lineal ancestor, and usually live within sight of each other or at least close enough for daily interaction. (317)	Geographically defined, consisting of two or more closely related "units" living within a few miles of each other in frequent interaction. Usually not all of the units are lineally related to a single common ancestor. (367)	Kluckhohn refers to the existence of some such unit and to the presence of a headman, but he does not define it except with reference to recent institutions such as tribal chapters. (369–70)

	household	residence group	outfit	resident lineage	community
Adams (1963)	People who regularly share food and eat together. Usually, but not always, share a single dwelling. (54)	Closely related households living close together (within "shouting distance") and sharing basic resources. (57, 102–3)	Defined by regular but infrequent sharing of resources among relatives more distantly related than an extended family. Sharing occurs e.g., for sheep dipping, shearing, lambing, long ceremonials, planting or harvesting. Outfits are large, less spatially integrated than the "group." Almost always have a recognized leader. (367–8)	Historical products of ancestral camp fissioning, associated with (with use right to) a contiguous land area. No necessary structure or function is present beyond shared ancestry and inheritance of use rights. As an incidental result of proximity and kinship, however, resident groups in a "resident lineage" often interact. (59–60, 104)	Adams indicates that at least in the case of Shonto "community," the boundaries are arbitrary and are of no geographical or social significance. (1)

Table 3.1. Navajo Social Group Definitions (*continued*)

Reference	Household	Residence group	Middle-level	Community
Aberle (1961)	*single hogan unit*	*extended family, cooperating unit, outfit*	*local clan element (LCE)*	*local community*
	People occupying a single hogan, typically parents with unmarried children. (108)	Extended family is a closely clustered set of consanguineally related families or individuals living in separate hogans but cooperating closely. Definitions of the cooperating unit and outfit indicate similar, but progressively larger groups; these may be tied by affinal as well as consanguineal relations. (108)	The members of a particular clan who live in a limited region, along with some of their close relatives. It is a loose unit of mutual aid and cooperation, under the leadership of an older clan member. The LCE head is distinct from the local community head, though this may not have always been the case. (108, 114) LCE functions include the settlement of disputes through the exchange of compensation, the organization of aid in the sponsorship of ceremonies, and the "monopolization" (and perhaps in former time ownership) of land. (113–5)	Defined variously as a geographic community centered on modern institutions such as trading posts or schools, and as a traditional, medium sized (60–200 people, after Hill [1940a]) territorial unit, weakly united around a local leader. (106–7)

	household	residence group or camp	sibling group	outfit	community
Reynolds et al. (1967)	The occupants of one dwelling, sharing and eating and sleeping together. Often consists of a nuclear family. (189)	Composed of a cluser (usually within "shouting distance"; typically less than 1/4 or 1/2 mile) of dwellings and corrals. The occupants cooperate, e·g·, in herding, cultivation, wood and water procurement, and the arrangement of transportation. (189)	Children of a single parent (and families of those children). Degree of integration and spatial contiguity varies with the wealth of the families: rich groups have contiguous land and pool their herds. Members cooperate in most of the activities discussed for "camp" cooperation, under the leadership of an older "resource controller." (192, 198)	A three-generation unit of grandparents, their married children, and married grandchildren. The camps of these individuals form a loose and variable cooperating association operating in a manner similar to, though less integrated than, the sibling group. (196–8)	Not defined. (196)

Table 3.1. Navajo Social Group Definitions (*continued*)

Reference	Household	Residence group	Middle-level	Community
Shepardson and Hammond (1970)	*nuclear family* Parents and unmarried children, eating, sleeping, and living together in a single hogan. Forms an economic unit and is the primary unit of child raising. (44)	*extended family* Typically three generations, consisting of two or more nuclear families living in separate hogans within "shouting distance." A unit of close economic and mutual assistance. The families share the leadership of an older male. (45)	*lineage* *maximal matrilineage* *localized matrilineage* *minimal matrilineage* (49–52)	*community* An interacting group of people making up a social system, persisting beyond the lifetime of its members, and reproducing itself, at least in part. (3)
	household The occupants of one hogan, typically a nuclear family. (46)	*camp* A cluster of one or more households in a distinct residence unit. (46)		
Witherspoon (1975)	*household* Normally consists of parents and children. Members eat and sleep together. (83–84)	*subsistence residential unit* A unit controlling a customary land-use area, organized around a "head mother," a sheep herd, and sometimes an agricultural plot. Members are matrilineal descendants of the "head mother,"	*outfit* A group of subsistence residential units composed of the families of descendants of an ancestral camp. (101) The outfit is like the group of the same name described by Kluck-	*community* Witherspoon denies the existence of well bounded geographic units, other than those associated with recent institutions such as trading posts and tribal chapters. (69)

	household	residence group	community
	or affinally related to her or her descendants. (72–3)	hohn and Leighton. Usually occupies a contiguous land area. Members cooperate for funerals, major ceremonies, or in times of great need; settlement of internal disagreements over land and mutual defense were traditional functions. They sometimes have a recognized head. (102, 108)	Lamphere suggests that the definition of social units is not the best way to assess Navajo cooperation at this level. (See text.)
Lamphere (1977)	People who regularly eat together. Usually a nuclear family living in a single hogan. (75) Members of the household share a great variety of basic domestic tasks. (83)	A nuclear or extended family living in a cluster of hogans. (78) This is the unit of joint management of livestock, grazing land, and agricultural fields. (83)	This unit is largely an artifact of anthropological necessity (bounding a study group) and of recent institutions (chapter, etc.). In practice, uses combination of boundaries of recent institutions, topographic features, and kinship ties, to define subject community. (14–8)

Table 3.1. Navajo Social Group Definitions *(continued)*

Reference	Household	Residence group	Middle-level	Community
Aberle (1981a,b)	*household* People sharing a single hearth, and hence sharing daily meals. Usually consists of a nuclear family. They normally occupy a single building. (1981a:23)	*camp* One or more households, who's members cooperate daily in herding, hauling wood and water, and often, farming. Some food sharing within the group. (1981:2) *cluster* One or more related households spatially separated from other households and cooperating, e.g., in herding and hauling wood and water. This unit is the same as the "camp" or "subsistence residential unit." Usually consists of an extended family. Assets are separately owned, but widely shared in the unit. (1981:23)	*coresidential kin group (CKG)* Residential aggregate, with a core matrilineage (primarily, but not exclusively, women) with the matrilineage members' spouses. The unit holds a territory "to some degree in common," the management and defense of which are CKG concerns. The CKG is not a unit of co-operation in basic [subsistence related(?)] activities. The CKG formerly served in defense and general conflict resolution. (1981a: 23–5; 1981b:2, 4)	

	household	residence group	cooperating kin group (CKG)
Adams (1983)	The inhabitants of a single hogan; usually a nuclear family. (394)	A cluster of hogans (households) usually with a corral and cornfield. The occupants are close kin. (394)	He repeats his (1963) definition of the "resident lineage," but emphasizes spatial proximity, in addition to shared ancestry. The CKG mainly functions to manage and defend grazing and farming land, though it may be involved in basic activities such as clearing farmland, hauling wood and water, and herding. (396, 407–8) He gives examples of CKGs involved in cooperation for agricultural and ceremonial activities. (399)

Table 3.1. Navajo Social Group Definitions (*continued*)

Reference	Household	Residence group	Middle-level	Community
	household	*residence group*	*cooperating groups*	*community*
Kelley (1986)				Refers to pre-Fort Sumner communal land using groups under leadership of a (usually wealthy) head-man. (31, 45–46)
Kelley and Whiteley (1989)	Ordinarily the occupants of one dwelling . . . exceptions include economically semi-productive people with dwellings of their own (e.g., teen-agers or older adults) who are part of most closely related household in same residence group. Building block of residence groups. (2)	Coresident families sharing homesite; cooperate in daily production. The fundamental land-using unit. (2)	Follows Collier (1966); contrasts cooperating groups that actually shared land and sometimes herds with looser outfits (1986: 3, 60; 1989:86–87, 121–123; Kelley personal communication 1985). *outfit* Land-using units composed of two or more residence groups, but characterized by *residual* land use claims from the original occupants rather than actual sharing of land. (1986:2, 48; 1989:86–87, 121–123)	
Levy et al. (1989)	*household*	*camp*	*network* After Lamphere (1977). Stress unstructured, situationally variable cooperation.	

outfit

After Kluckhohn and
Leighton (1946). Stress
cooperation among resi-
dence groups that only in
some cases have contiguous land.

land-use community

After Kimball and Prov-
ince (1942). Stress claim
to contiguous land area
based on ancestral rights
and continuous use.

localized matrilineage

After Shepardson and
Hammond (1970) and also
Aberle's (1981b) "coresi-
dential kinship group."
Stress claim to ancestral
land based on matrilineal
descent, though some-
times also including viri-
matrilocal lines. (359)

groups at Klagetoh, although they do not explicitly identify the latter as outfits (Kluckhohn and Leighton 1946:63).

Thus, like Kimball and Provinse, Kluckhohn and Leighton define the outfit in terms of the intensity of cooperation among its members. They add the observation that members are interrelated, but do not discuss particulars of kinship relationships. They expand the range of sizes and spatial patterns identified within outfits to include smaller units than those specified by Kimball and Provinse. Kluckhohn and Leighton suggest that the larger groups owning contiguous land identified by Kimball and Provinse reflect a special case of outfit formation around particularly wealthy individuals. Outfit cooperation also takes place to a lesser degree among residence groups that do not necessarily own contiguous land.

Collier (1966:43) gives the last of the detailed early descriptions of middle-level units explicitly defined in terms of joint activities among multiple residence groups. She identifies "cooperating-groups" as collections of camps (residence groups) whose members help each other in herding, farming and ceremonies. The residence groups of a cooperating-group typically lie within about half a mile of each other, and are closely interrelated by blood and marriage (1966:53).

In her study at Klagetoh, Collier identifies cooperating-groups averaging about 2.6 residence groups (19 members) each. At Navajo Mountain, however, she does not find middle-level units at the same scale as at Klagetoh, but suggests instead that the entire community of 135 functions as one large "expanded cooperating-group."

Collier (1966:69) concludes that the cooperating-groups at Klagetoh fall within the range of the outfit concept, though they are more closely integrated than required by the usual definition of outfits. These groups are at or beyond the small end of the range of outfit sizes described by Kluckhohn and Leighton, but do share a similar composition and function with that ascribed to outfits: cooperative activity among consanguinally and affinally interrelated residence groups, with a tendency toward close spatial contiguity.

The expanded cooperating-group is more difficult to classify. Collier (1966:69–70) suggests that it may correspond to various community level units such as the band described by Kluckhohn and Leighton, or Hill's natural community (see table 3.1). However, the Navajo Mountain expanded cooperating-group encompasses 135 members and covers a territory of around 80,000 acres (measured off of Collier's map [1966:15–16]; she does not give an exact figure); hence it falls at or near the maximum size range of outfits and land-use communities as defined by Kluckhohn and Leighton and Kimball and Provinse. The expanded cooperating-group exhibits limited integration around agricultural activities and the recognition of a local man as a leader on the basis of prestige (Collier 1966:29, 38). Thus, the expanded cooperating-group, with some weak outfit-like characteristics, is apparently coterminous with the community level.

Several subsequent Navajo community studies adopted the general outline of supraresidence group cooperative units presented by Kimball and Provinse and broadened by Kluckhohn and Leighton and Collier. These accounts describe some of the cooperative activities that outfit or cooperating units carry out jointly, including planting, harvesting, herding, lambing, shearing and sponsorship of ceremonies (Levy 1962; Ross 1955; Sasaki and Adair 1952). Some also emphasize communal leadership under an elder male spokesman (Levy 1962; Sasaki and Adair 1952), as well as communal land-use rights that are defended against outsiders (Sasaki and Adair 1952). Outfit members are "close relatives" (Levy 1962), or at least related to some degree (Ross 1955; Sasaki and Adair 1952). Examples of these units include an outfit centered around a core of about ten to thirteen adults at Fruitland (Sasaki 1960:156–63) and a large outfit consisting of roughly eight residence groups at Kaibito (Levy 1962:792).[3]

Researchers describing middle-level units in functional terms increasingly emphasized variability among these units. Kluckhohn and Leighton's (1946) original account of outfits mentions the numerous forms of these units. Levy (1962) explicitly emphasizes the variability among middle-level groups. He describes cooperative alliances among residence groups that vary depending on the particular activities involved, and that differ in intensity and scale between regions. He also suggests that outfits may have lost spatial integrity and social coherence over time. Downs (1964) suggests that outfits may have existed in his study area in the past, but disappeared over time.

Kluckhohn's (1966) final publication on the Ramah area gives the last major definition of middle-level Navajo social units deriving directly from Kimball and Provinse's and Kluckhohn and Leighton's emphasis on cooperation and spatial relationships (without regard to the particulars of kinship links). He emphasizes variability by defining two (sometimes coterminous) units, the group and the outfit. This pair of terms divides the old outfit concept into two cases. As defined in 1966, outfits are loosely organized structures with recognized heads and with periodic but infrequent cooperation in activities such as sheep dipping, shearing, lambing, sponsorship of ceremonies or agricultural tasks. Their spatial integrity is variable, but usually involves either a large area or noncontiguous land. The group seems to represent the case of the small outfit as formerly (Kluckhohn and Leighton 1946) defined, with geographical proximity (a few miles between units), and relatively close kinship among units (though usually not shared lineal ancestors). Kluckhohn does not specify the size of the various units, but indicates that out of a population of 625 people (Vogt 1966:173) there are seven distinct outfits (Kluckhohn 1966:368). He does not, however, indicate how much of the population does not belong to an outfit.

Beginning with many of the works published in the early 1960s, definitions of middle-level Navajo social units started shifting away from a spatial or functional emphasis, and more to an explicit specification of blood or marriage links within such units. This trend represents a shift in emphasis, but in general researchers implicitly or explicitly assumed a correspondence between the middle-level units defined in terms of kinship and the previously defined functional units.

Adams (1963) defines the resident lineage as the end product of the localized fissioning of families and residence groups through time; this results in a collection of residence groups composed of (bilaterally) related families. These families occupy a contiguous land area, the use rights to which they inherited from the ancestral group. Thus, of necessity the residence groups have a common interest in the land. Beyond this, however, members of the resident lineage interact as a consequence of their spatial proximity and because of the various kinship ties among them. The component residence groups do not form functional corporate groups, nor do all of them necessarily cooperate with each other. This definition minimizes functional criteria, while making an explicit statement of the kinship patterns associated with such a middle-level unit (families of people descended from a single ancestral family). It also implicitly introduces the concept of the formation of social units as the result of the developmental cycle of previously existing units (see Goody 1958 for a discussion of developmental cycles). Adams (1963:59) suggests that the resident lineage corresponds to the units identified by Kluckhohn and Leighton as outfits, although his account indicates a situation with a considerably lesser degree of integration than described by Kluckhohn and Leighton.

Several other kinship-based analyses of middle-level units identify them as the consequence of the developmental cycle of ancestral families. The terminology and precise definitions of kin-based middle-level groups has varied, though recent analyses by Aberle (1981a, 1981b) and Adams (1983) have settled on the CKG (Aberle's coresident kin group or Adams' cooperating kin group). Some descriptions identify middle-level kinship groups as corporate functional units similar to the cooperation-based definitions described above (e.g., Reynolds et al. 1967; Witherspoon 1975). Others, like Adams (1963, but cf. 1983) explicitly note a lack of most cooperative functions beyond a joint interest in communally inherited land-use rights (Aberle 1961, 1981a, 1981b; Shepardson and Hammond 1970). Recruitment for communal activity may, however, follow the same kinship lines that define these groups, making for de facto cooperation among group members (Adams 1963, 1983; Shepardson and Hammond 1970). In his early work, Aberle (1961) separates the limited-function, kinship-based middle-level units from cooperating units and outfits, which he considers essentially a continuum of expanded forms of the closely integrated residence group.

Lamphere (1977) does not find discrete middle-level units in her study community, and argues that Navajo culture lacks a concept or term for middle-level units such as outfits. (In fact reservation inhabitants, as opposed to anthropologists, frequently use the English term outfit to refer to the residence group [Adams 1963; Downs 1964, 1965]). She suggests that the delineation of such units does not best reflect the structure of Navajo interactions. Rather, Lamphere proposes that supraresidence group cooperation may best be understood as a process of selection and use of sets of particular relationships from a network of potential relations based on genealogical, spatial, or classificatory kinship proximity. From this perspective, cooperative groups are formed in a predictable, but variable way, depending on the task to be performed and the particular circumstances. Classification of particular cooperating sets as outfits obscures the underlying process of recruitment of assistance.

Most recently, two additional kinship-based discussions of Navajo middle-level units have again emphasized their variability. Kelley (personal communication 1985, 1986; Kelley and Whiteley 1989; see also Kelley 1982c) describes the outfit or coresidential kin group in terms quite similar to other recent kinship-based formulations (e.g., Aberle 1981a, 1981b). An outfit is primarily composed of the nuclear families of the matrilineal descendants of the original occupants of an area as well as descendants of the siblings of those earlier occupants. Others, such as patrilineal relatives and affines also have a potential attachment to the outfit, but this tie is weaker and less permanent. The outfit's main role is in the allocation of land use, which tends to be worked out among the component resident groups. Kelley shows through an analysis of historical records that outfits persisted from at least the early part of this century up to the present. But these units are significant only in the context of long-term residual land-use rights; they do not structure other forms of cooperation (Kelley, personal communication 1985; 1986; Kelley and Whiteley 1989).

Kelley (personal communication 1985, 1986:60; Kelley and Whiteley 1989:86–86, 121–23) also recognizes a smaller unit that may contain multiple residence groups. She suggests that these units may correspond to Collier's (1966) cooperating groups, and consist of the occupants of a single "customary use area," that is, those who share a particular plot of land. Such use areas are often occupied by only a single residence group, but two or more may share one; Kelley's data yield median values of two residence groups and a maximum of four (Kelley 1986:62, 126, 180). The unit often consists of parents and their grown children (with their families) living in separate residence groups. The occupants of these resident groups may pool herds, and multiple residence groups may join at a single homesite on a seasonal basis.

With this formulation, Kelley, like Kluckhohn (1966), suggests that there is more than one form of middle-level unit. In Kelley's formulation the units co-exist in a hierarchical relationship; outfits are composed of residence groups that use customary use areas, and some of these residence groups (those sharing a use area) form a cooperating group. Outfits are fairly subtle structures, visible only over the long run in the process of the reallocation of customary use areas over time. Cooperating groups may involve actual co-operative activities, such as joint herding.

Finally, Levy et al. (1989) reexamine middle-level social units, emphasizing regional and temporal variability. They examine four different types of middle-level units defined by other investigators. From Lamphere (1977) they adopt the concept of "sets" and "networks" of cooperation, involving situation-specific groups recruited among relatives and/or neighbors. From Kluckhohn and Leighton (1946), they take the definition of the outfit as a multiresidence-group cooperative unit that may, but need not, share a contiguous land area. They define this unit without reference to any specific kinship connection linking the residence groups. From Kimball and Province (1942) they adopt the land-use community, which consists of the occupants of a contiguous piece of land who share rights to the territory based on ancestral claims. Finally, they adopt Shepardson and Hammond's (1970) concept of

localized matrilineages, which they equate with Aberle's (1981b) coresidential kinship groups. In this case, emphasis is explicitly on a matrilineal kinship link, though some extensions may be included (such as the families of
married sons living in the husband's mother's area). These relatives cooperate
only in the defense and management of the matrilineally inherited land.

By accepting all of these alternative definitions of supraresidence group
units, Levy et al. (1989) indicate that middle-level units can vary in degree of
corporate function (ranging from the purely situation-specific composition of
shifting network cooperation to the cooperation-based outfit to the very subtle
latent land-rights claims associated with localized matrilineages), in composition (ranging from great flexibility in networks or outfits to the primarily
ancestry-based organization of the land-use community and the matrilineal
structure of the localized matrilineage), and in spatial organization (ranging
from the potentially noncontiguous layout of the outfit to the spatial integrity
of the land-use community or localized matrilineage). Levy et al. (1989) as-
sociate this variability with regional economic and environmental differences,
as well as varying patterns of social organization over time.

Of the four levels of Navajo social units examined here, variation in
middle-level units thus appears to cover the greatest range of forms. Still,
variation is possible at all four levels. Given the diversity of terms and definitions outlined previously (and in table 3.1), several major issues relating to
the composition and function of Navajo social units at each scale stand out.
Ignoring questions of semantics, these include:

1. Household level units. Despite variation in how these are defined, descriptions of the typical function or spatial distribution of these units raise
little substantive disagreement. The main questions are matters of scale: How
large are households? Most definitions of the household recognize a frequent
correspondence of the household to a coresident nuclear family, but also acknowledge potential flexibility in the inclusion of additional members. So,
variability in household size derives from two factors: nuclear family size and
the degree of independence of small social units outside of nuclear families.
The size of the nuclear family is a demographic question, depending upon the
rate of birth and death, and the age of migration out of the unit. The incor-
poration of household members from outside of the nuclear family relates to
the social and economic requirements of the minimal social unit, that is, the
degree to which the nuclear family household needs (or can sustain) additional
members, and the degree to which individuals outside of nuclear families can
maintain viable separate households.

As described in chapter 6, variability in household size is not one of the issues considered in this study. In fact, analysis of population in the study area makes the assumption that household size remained constant through time. Historical data suggest that variation in Navajo household size in rural communities such as the study area has been limited for the time period over which data are available (see chapter 6). Household size variation *is*, however, a significant possible source of flexibility in social organization, and interactions between variation at the household and higher levels is a fruitful area for future research.

2. Residence group level units. Much of the discussion of household level units applies to residence group level units. With the exception of studies of Navajos settled in urban or town communities (Aberle 1981a:30), all Navajo community studies identify residence groups composed of one or more households in roughly similar ways. As with households, questions regarding residence groups relate primarily to their size. Like household size, residence group size may be further broken down into two parts: the size of the component household level units (see above), and the number of households (or fragments thereof) that combine to make up the residence group. The degree of aggregation of households into larger residence group level units is a function of a variety of factors, including economic, environmental, and social determinants of group function and solidarity (e.g., Aberle 1981a). The examination of those factors that affect group size and composition is among the goals of this study, and is discussed in greater detail in subsequent chapters.

3. Middle-level units. As indicated previously, middle-level units are among the least understood aspects of Navajo social organization. Basic questions include the existence or nonexistence of middle-level units, their composition, size, function, and spatial characteristics. More specifically, studies of Navajo social organization raise the following major issues (see, e.g., Lamphere 1977:91; Aberle 1981b): (a) Can a unit larger than the residence group actually be identified in Navajo society? If such larger units exist, are there perhaps several levels of organization identifiable? (b) What is the composition of large cooperative units? Are they lineage-based, clan-based, collections of consanguineous and affinal kin, or a mixture of relatives and non-related neighbors? (c) What is the size range of such units? Do supraresidence group units of different size vary in characteristics other than scale? (d) What is the function of supraresidence group units? Do they serve for defense of claims to land use, for assistance in economic activities such as farming, shearing, lambing, herding, and sponsorship of ceremonial activities; for co-

operative communal effort under a tacitly recognized local leader; or for a combination of some of these functions? And (e) What is the spatial organization of Navajo social units larger than the residence group?

The alternative answers to these questions proposed by different studies of Navajo organization may in part relate simply to variation in definitions or methodology. As outlined in this chapter, the great range of characteristics ascribed to supraresidence group units allows for differing conclusions regarding them, independent of genuine variability in Navajo social organization.

In many cases, however, variability in descriptions of middle-level social units appears to reflect actual seasonal, regional, or temporal differences in Navajo social organization (Aberle 1963). As indicated in chapter 1, the focus of this study is the examination of certain of the factors responsible for Navajo social variation. In particular, by using a continuous archaeological record from a single locality, it is possible to examine evidence for change through time in Navajo social units. My approach to this question from an archaeological perspective limits the analysis primarily to the functional, cooperation-based definition of middle-level units. The characteristics identifiable with the available data include the relative prominence of middle-level organization (identified by spatial clustering among residence groups, or, for the purposes of this study, sites) and the size of the component residence groups and any supraresidence group clusters. As discussed in chapter 5, the scale of the BMAP study area and the spatial analysis used to identify social units in the archaeological record restrict this study to some of the smaller, more tightly integrated forms of social units described previously.

4. Community level units. Many of the issues already outlined for the lower levels apply to community level integration of Navajo society. Unlike these lower level units, however, there is little evidence that close community integration played an important role in Navajo society since at least the Fort Sumner period. The integration that has existed has tended to center increasingly around recent political, economic, or service institutions (federal or tribal government-imposed administrative units, trading posts, schools, etc.) for which a considerable literature exists (e.g., Adams 1963; Iverson 1981; Shepardson 1963; Williams 1970; Young 1978). Furthermore, the scale of community level organization is greater than the area of archaeological site data available in this study. Therefore, I do not examine integration at levels higher than the middle level.

However, some of the most widely used mechanisms for dealing with economic and demographic change lie within the realm of middle-level units (and to a lesser degree, residence groups) that *are* accessible to study here. This holds for the Navajo case in particular (hence the diversity of accounts of middle-level social units), as well as among other societies adapted to social flux (see chapter 8). This makes identification of these middle-level units and examination of their behavior over time a critical area for analysis of social organization.

4

Spatial Analysis of Navajo Social Units

To find archaeological evidence of change in Navajo social units we must first identify these groups in the archaeological record. This is a straightforward procedure for the lower level units. As outlined in chapter 3, the household (regardless of how it is formally defined) in practice often consists of the occupants of a single dwelling. For the purposes of this study, I define the household as the regular coresidents of a structure. Therefore, the archaeological equivalent of a household is obviously a dwelling. This definition will not always identify the same household units as some of the alternative ethnographic definitions (see chapter 3), but it yields a close approximation.

The archaeological record of a residence group is a site, or more properly, the portion of a site in use at a given time (a site component). The spatial distribution of Black Mesa Navajo structures and features makes delineation of sites fairly straightforward (see chapter 5). To identify residence groups, I break sites down into separate periods of site use (temporal components; see chapter 5 and appendix A). More specifically, I use habitation site components, which are defined as containing at least one dwelling and one sheep or goat corral (see appendix A). The units identified in this way would usually closely match residence groups identified by other definitions based on social relationships, land use, and so forth (see chapter 3).

It is not as easy to identify the archaeological equivalent of supraresidence group social units. Because researchers do not agree on the composition, function, or even the existence of these units, no archaeological marker would match many of the suggested ethnographic definitions. Given the types of data available in the archaeological record, spatial analysis is the most promising approach.

Several previous studies have examined intersite spatial patterns in Navajo settlement. Noisat (1978) used nearest neighbor analysis to evaluate the clustering of short-term use sites (camps) around habitation sites and the spacing of habitation sites relative to each other. He found a tendency for summer camps to cluster near habitation sites, forming what he termed "household clusters." He also noted a tendency for habitation sites to cluster near each other, and (significantly, with regard to the analysis here) for the clustering to be weakened over time within some environmental zones. Noisat interpreted the decrease in clustering as a result of the digging of wells, which permitted dispersal across the landscape. The finding also fits the interpretation of loosening interresidence group ties discussed further in this and subsequent chapters. Sessions (1979, cited in Gilpin 1986) also used nearest neighbor analysis and found camps clustered around habitation sites, but found a tendency for dispersion among the habitation sites.

In previous work (Rocek 1985, 1994) I used several spatial analytical techniques to examine Navajo ethnographic settlement patterns and relate them to

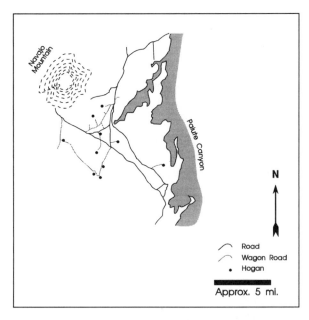

Figure 4.1. Navajo Mountain Summer Settlement Pattern, 1938

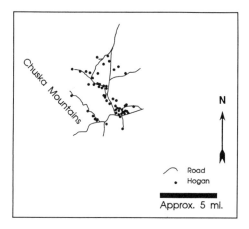

Figure 4.2. Copper Canyon Summer Settlement Pattern, 1966

social variables. This work, like the present one, was intended to examine middle-level units composed of two or more cooperating residence groups. My approach was based on the expectation that supraresidence group units tend to form spatial clusters to facilitate cooperation among the residence groups ("living right close . . . because we help each other," as Slim Man says [Dyk and Dyk 1980: 112]). Frequent cooperative activities (joint herding, sheep shearing, lambing, etc.) are most common in the smaller, more integrated forms of Navajo middle-level units—units such as Collier's (1966) cooperating groups. Spatial clusters are thus likely to correspond to some such form of relatively small-scale middle-level groups (Kelley, personal communication 1985). The spatial scale of the site sample (see chapter 5) also limits analysis to relatively small middle-level units.

Not the least important of spatial analytic approaches is a simple visual examination of settlement maps. My sample of ethnographic settlement patterns (Rocek 1985, 1994) consists of four groups of sites (located at Navajo Mountain, Shonto, Klagetoh, and Copper Canyon; see fig. 2.1), which are found in the western and eastern parts of the Navajo reservation and cover the time period from 1938 (at Navajo Mountain) to 1971 (at Shonto). Seasonal, environmental, and chronological variability are all represented, resulting in a wide array of settlement patterns. Figures 4.1 and 4.2, for instance, contrast the diffuse rural settlement of the western reservation settlement of Navajo Mountain in the summer of 1938 with the dense roadside clustering of Copper Canyon sites in the heavily populated eastern portion of the reservation in the summer of 1966 (the maps are at the same scale). Within the sample of four settlements, population density varies between nearly 7 to about .7 people per square km (17.7 to 1.7 per square mi), and mean interresidence group nearest neighbor distances range from 2.8 to .5 km (1.67 to .34 mi).

Aside from a visual examination of the settlement maps, I applied three quantitative measures of settlement patterning (Rocek 1985, 1994). First, a nearest neighbor analysis revealed moderate variability in patterning. The first nearest neighbor statistic ranged from .89 (most clustered, in the 1966 winter settlement at Copper Canyon) to 1.18 (most dispersed, in the 1938 Navajo Mountain summer pattern). All but two of the nine patterns have nearest neighbor statistics with values greater than 1.0, suggesting some degree of dispersion (see chapter 5 for further discussion of the nearest neighbor analysis). The exceptions to this generalization came from the settlement pattern in the densely populated eastern reservation of Copper Canyon in 1966 (fig. 4.2). There, both summer and winter sites were clustered along roads, reflecting a reservation-wide trend of recent decades for settlements to shift to accessible roadside locations (Jett 1980:108–12; Kelley 1986:156; Lamphere 1977:23).

A second spatial analytic approach, based on cluster analysis, showed a more complex pattern of variation (Rocek 1985, 1994). This technique allows the evaluation of settlement patterning at multiple scales. Nearest neighbor analysis simply provides an average of patterns among nearest neighbors. The cluster analysis, however, can examine cases where, for instance, clustering occurs on a macroscale but dispersion occurs on a microscale. Figure 4.3 illustrates this concept, showing simple clustering in the top figure, and "dispersed clustering" in the second. In the former cases, residence groups form three large clusters (the macroscale), and within the clusters (the microscale) residence groups also clump together. In the latter case, the microscale reveals that residence groups *within* clusters are dispersed away from each other, even though on a macroscale they are grouped together into three large clusters.

The cluster analysis, like the nearest neighbor approach, suggested that Navajo settlements tend to be dispersed at the microlevel. That is, Navajo residence groups tend to maintain a degree of separation from their neighbors. An examination of the correlates of the degree of dispersion was inconclusive, however, emphasizing the number of potentially significant variables. Within the ethnographic samples I examined (Rocek 1985, 1994), degree of micro dispersion did *not* correlate with population density, a finding at odds with the hypotheses outlined in chapter 1. In fact, there was a tendency (though

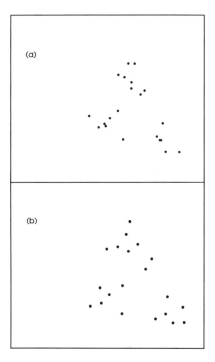

Figure 4.3. Example of Simple Cluster and "Dispersed Cluster" of Points

only among summer sites) for microdispersion to be highest in cases of low population density and high livestock dependence. Seasonal variation was inconsistent, with one community (Navajo Mountain) showing a slight degree of macroclustering in winter, and another (Shonto in 1955) showing macroclustering in summer.

The degree of neither macro- nor microclustering corresponded clearly with the presence or absence of supraresidence group cooperating units as reported by ethnographers. Of the four ethnographic settlement samples I evaluated (Rocek 1985, 1994), two (Klagetoh and Shonto) were described as displaying middle-level units. Shonto was the basis for defining Adams' (1963, 1983) resident lineage and cooperating kin group, and Klagetoh was the basis for Collier's (1966) cooperating group. Although both settlement areas displayed some tendency toward clustering at the macrolevel (particularly marked among summer sites at Shonto but very weak among the Klagetoh sites), neither case of clustering was more marked than that seen at Copper Canyon, the area that was the basis for Lamphere's (1977) suggestion that *no* middle-level social units exist. In fact, Copper Canyon, with its strings of sites hugging the roadways, had the most marked macroclustering of any of the settlement patterns. Furthermore, even when present, the evidence of macroscale clustering at both Shonto and Klagetoh suggested fewer and larger clusters than those identified by the ethnographers as cooperating social units.

Overall, then, the cluster analytic study serves to emphasize the complexities of such settlement comparisons among disparate communities scattered in time and location, and located in highly variable geographic areas. Clearly the tendency toward settlement along roads in recent times, differences in topography among settlement regions (for instance, the Shonto settlements were spread along the edges of deep canyon systems and the Copper Canyon sites were also heavily constrained by rugged topography), and the mass of additional factors shaping settlement render any simple comparisons among the settlement patterns from different regions and periods difficult to interpret. There is, however, another aspect of spatial analysis that offers more encouragement regarding the value of settlement studies.

As a final approach to the settlement analysis (Rocek 1985, 1994), I examined the two cases where ethnographers had identified multiresidence group social units, and evaluated the degree to which they could be approximated by spatial groups. Three sets of data are available for this evaluation: two at Shonto where separate summer and winter settlement patterns were recorded in 1955 and one at Klagetoh where year-round settlements were present in 1939. Again using cluster analysis (specifically, a variance minimizing agglomerative clustering procedure), I identified sites that could be grouped together based on spatial proximity. In each case, the number of groups formed by the clustering procedure was set to the same number as the number of multiresidence group units defined by the ethnographers.

I then compared the degree of correspondence between the purely *spatially* defined units formed by the cluster analysis with the *social* units identified by the ethnographers. Rand's statistic (Rand 1971) provides a measure of the degree of correspondence between these spatial and social classifications. The higher this statistic, the closer is the correspondence of the two classifications.[1]

Figure 4.4 compares the Rand's statistic measure for each of these three data sets (shown by the isolated case at the right end of each graph) against the distribution of Rand's statistic for randomized data (the distribution of points to the left in each graph). The Rand's statistic value for the actual

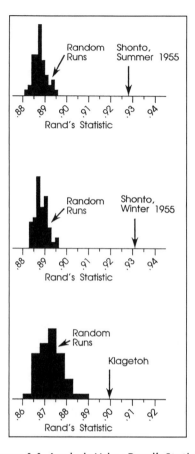

Figure 4.4. Analysis Using Rand's Statistic

settlement data clearly falls well outside the range of random patterning, indicating a far greater than random correspondence of spatial and social classifications. The correspondence of shared membership in supraresidence social units and spatial proximity at Shonto is perhaps of limited interest, because Adams' (1963) definition of "resident lineages" is partially based on spatial proximity, as well as genealogical links. The Klagetoh case is more interesting, in that Collier defined the cooperating groups functionally and apparently without reference to the location of member residence groups. Furthermore, the entire community was quite small (roughly 110 square km or 43 square mi), so that cooperation between residence groups in different parts of the community could and did occur. Nevertheless, as shown in figure 4.4, the correspondence of shared membership within the same cooperating group with spatial proximity is strong.

So, the analysis of the ethnographic settlement data provides a mixed indication of the potential of Navajo settlement studies. Navajo settlement patterns do display substantial differences among different communities. There is evidence of seasonal and temporal variation, and of the impact of changes in transportation networks. Demographic differences, as represented by population or settlement density, may also have an impact, although the nature of their effects are not clear and are confounded with the other differences between settlement regions. It is likely that the intercorrelation of a variety of factors such as economic conditions and local resource distribution, as well as population, contribute to the observed distributions.

Examination of the reflection of supraresidence group cooperative units in settlement patterns produced mixed results. The ethnographic data do not provide evidence of a simple correspondence between supraresidence group cooperating units and the formation of spatial clusters of residence groups. The range of cases available for ethnographic study does not, however, allow a full evaluation of the possibility of some such patterning under certain economic and demographic conditions. For instance, none of the ethnographic samples predates the stock-reduction period, when the undermining of functioning middle-level units is likely to have begun. Furthermore, the comparison of settlement patterns between different geographic regions clearly introduces additional sources of variability that are likely to swamp any simple spatial correlates of social differences between the areas.

Despite the lack of discrete spatial clustering, there is clear evidence for a correspondence between shared membership in supraresidence group social units and spatial proximity. Spatial proximity and social proximity clearly are not independent (see also, e.g., Stone 1991, 1992). This observation provides encouragement that under other circumstances, not represented in the ethnographic data, spatial patterns may reflect supraresidence group cooperating units.

The situation is far more complex than a simple one-to-one mapping of social relations onto spatial relations. Settlement patterns are the product of a range of conflicting social, environmental, and economic factors (see Douglas and Kramer 1992, with references and accompanying articles). But the ethnographic sample does not extend to the time depth that offers the best chance for recognizing middle-level units as spatial aggregates. This being the case, I turn to the archaeological record of Navajo settlement on northern Black

Mesa. My aim is to identify *some* of the causes of settlement variability over time. Based on the preceding discussion, it is clear that this variability reflects a range of interacting causes, only a few of which are discussed here. Examination of shifts in settlement patterns provide a source of ideas about changes in social relations among the Black Mesa Navajos (and other people in comparable circumstances) and also suggests some of the further research that would help to evaluate the hypothesized explanations for these changes.

5

The Black Mesa Sites

The Black Mesa Archaeological Project provides a unique record of Navajo life within the study area (fig. 2.2). Not only is the time depth of the data invaluable, but the large spatial extent covered by the BMAP makes possible the spatial analysis of settlement patterns.

The Database

BMAP historic sites data collection evolved over the course of the project. In the last several seasons, data were collected in three stages: (1) survey, during which sites were located and brief summary descriptions and sketch maps developed; (2) surface mapping, during which detailed site and structure and feature maps and descriptions were prepared, collections were made of wood (for tree-ring dating) and artifacts, and flotation samples from hearths and ash piles were taken; and (3) excavation (see Haley et al. 1983 for details of these procedures). The BMAP completed exhaustive (100 percent) surveys of most of the areas included in this study in the early 1970s. Excavation was limited to a small sample of sites. Surface mapping started as a limited sampling of sites in the early years of the project, but in the last several seasons expanded to include all but a small group of site types (excluded were presently occupied settlements, isolated features or fences, sites with known burials, and sites mapped or excavated in a previous season).

The resulting database includes information collected at two levels. All sites include survey data that describe the site as a whole. In addition, most sites (those that were mapped) include more detailed data broken down on a structure-by-structure and feature-by-feature basis. This detailed information provides functional and dating information about *components* of a site in addition to providing data on the entire site (see later in this chapter and appendix A). I use data from sites mapped or excavated primarily in the 1980 through 1982 seasons. The work during those three years covered large patches in and around the Peabody Coal Company Western Lease Area. These patches run south along Yellow Water Canyon and Coal Mine Wash, past the intersection of Moenkopi and Coal Mine Wash. An additional area extends into the northern and easternmost portion of the Eastern Lease Area, in the upper Moenkopi Wash and Reed Valley drainages (fig. 2.2). I selected this sample on a pragmatic basis: The data sets from the 1982 and immediately preceding seasons were the largest and most complete, and the 1983 data were collected too late to be included. To minimize spatial gaps in the 1980–82 data, I add sites excavated or mapped in earlier seasons. I also include the limited data available on surveyed but unmapped sites that lie interspersed among the mapped sites in the sample.

The result is a set of six study patches or subregions (fig. 5.1, table 5.1), within which I coded data for all known sites, either from 1980–82 site mapping or, when these are not available, from previous years' mapping or survey. In addition, I include a small number of mapped sites along Red Peak Valley in the southwestern part of the East Lease Area. The major regions that are excluded from the study sample are the southern part of the Eastern Lease Area (investigated by the BMAP in 1983 after my coding began), portions on the western fringe of the Western Lease Area (investigated prior to 1980), and several large portions of the Western Lease Area that were heavily disturbed in the early years of strip mining. These strip-mined areas were surveyed in the first few years of the BMAP, but the data from them are not sufficiently detailed, complete, or comparable to the more recent work to warrant their inclusion in this study. The few sites that I coded in these areas (because they were mapped in 1980–82) are included in the analyses of site characteristics, but are excluded from the spatial analyses in chapter 6. In all, the sample consists of 606 sites, divided into 750 components (plus an additional 22 site fragments that could not be included in any component).

The spatial analysis of the settlement sample is divided into the six subregions, within which the mapped sites along with supplementary survey data yield complete coverage. The subregions cover a total area of 134 km², located mostly on the 256 km² Peabody Coal Company lease area (Nichols and Sink 1984:3), but including about 6 km² of off-lease land as well. In a general way, the different regions reflect some of the diversity of the BMAP

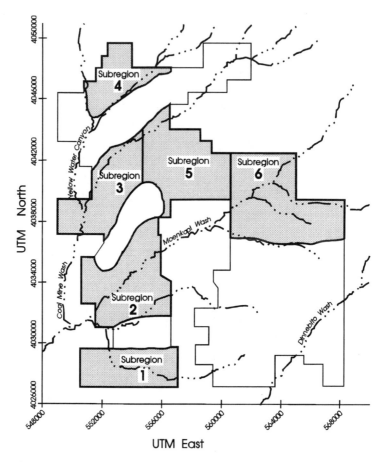

Figure 5.1. BMAP Study Area Subregions

study area, particularly with regard to topography. Subregions 1 through 3 represent the more southerly and westerly portions of the study area and tend to lie at lower elevations. Subregions 4 through 6 cover the higher areas closer to the mesa rim (table 5.1). Although the topographic division is insufficient to define fully distinct seasonal settlement areas, there is a correspondence of subregion and site season. The three higher elevation subregions (4–6) all have more than 30 percent winter site components, while the lower subregions (1–3) have lower proportions. As discussed in chapter 6, there are also inter-regional differences in the pattern of change in seasonal use through time.

Because the sampling of sites in these regions was exhaustive, the settle-ment data should not be subject to any great sampling biases. The major

Table 5.1. Geographic and Archaeological Properties of the BMAP Study Area Subregions

Subregion	Area (km²)	Perimeter (km)[a]	Average Site Elevation (m)[b]	Total Number Sites[c]	Number Habitation Sites[d]
1	16.48	18.12	1968	105	35
2	26.15	24.96	1963	180	36
3	20.37	19.78	1981	142	36
4	11.94	19.49	2078	79	19
5	24.87	22.32	2054	43	18
6	34.65	26.88	2076	198	68
—[e]	. . . . . .	. . . . . .	. . . .	25	7
3,5,6	79.89	62.40	. . . .	383	122
Tot.	134.46	124.97	. . . .	772	219

a. Approximate length of perimeter of subregion.

b. Average elevation of all site components in subregion. Includes all components, and therefore counts multicomponent site elevations more than once. Intended as rough indicator of subregion elevation.

c. Total number of site components. Includes components of all functional categories, and fragments of sites with unknown component affiliation which were assigned to separate "dummy" components.

d. Total number of habitation site components (defined as a component with at least one permanent dwelling and one sheep or goat corral).

e. Sites lying outside any of the subregions. These were not in areas for which systematic data were available, and are not included in the spatial analysis in chapter 6.

existing sources of bias are (1) the spatial distribution of the lease and of early coal mining, which together establish the boundaries of the subregions; (2) differential preservation of sites of different function and age; and (3) differential detail in data available concerning different site types. Given the good preservation of sites in the study area, the large and topographically diverse region covered by the lease areas, and the complete survey strategy employed by the BMAP, these factors are not too serious. In addition, because most of my analysis described in subsequent chapters is limited to substantial habitation sites (and does not include ephemeral camps), differential preservation should be only a limited problem.

Two additional limitations of the sample are important to discuss here. One is the size of the study area in relation to the scale of Navajo mobility. Navajo mobility in past decades covered a variable but in some cases very large range. For instance, Henderson (1983) describes wealthy families in the late nineteenth century occasionally migrating distances in excess of 150 kilometers. Even the smaller-scale seasonal round at Black Mesa in the late nineteenth and early twentieth centuries included annual movement on and off the mesa by many families. Thus, almost any archaeological study area would cover only a portion of the settlement round of most Navajo families who used the region (Roberts 1990).

This problem is compounded by change in settlement patterns, because the scale of settlement decreased over time. So, although sites of the early periods are likely to cover only a limited portion of the range of their occupants, some of the later sites may well represent a large part of a family's range. In any case, claiming to reconstruct "the settlement system" of the Navajos of northern Black Mesa with the BMAP archaeological site sample is unrealistic (cf. Roberts 1990). Change and interfamily variability in mobility add complexity to the factors shaping Navajo settlement choices and the archaeological record of site locations. Similarly, changes in the numbers of sites occupied per family over the course of a year may confuse the interpretation of spatial patterns (see chapter 7).

By restricting the analysis to settlement pattern by season, we *can* hope to assess patterns of intersettlement spatial relations among the families in the area in any given period. These patterns do not tell the whole story of these families' settlement, but they reflect part of it. Most interresidence group cooperative activities operate at a local scale regardless of the full range of seasonal migrations.

The second limitation of the BMAP site sample's spatial scale is its total extent in relation to the size of Navajo middle-level social units. As described in chapter 3, sizes attributed to Navajo middle-level units vary considerably. The largest, such as the larger of Kimball and Provinse's land-use communities, cover over 300 km², which is more than twice the total area included in my sample. The full spatial extent of social units of this size is thus outside the range identifiable in this study. As noted previously, however, seasonal interresidence group cooperative activities are unlikely to extend over the whole annual range. Furthermore, accounts of the more tightly integrated middle-level social units suggest a considerably smaller scale. Left Handed's (Dyk and Dyk 1980) references to the groups of cooperating residence groups imply quick travel between them, sometimes on foot instead of horseback. Collier describes twelve or thirteen "cooperating groups" in an area of about forty-three square miles (110 km²). At this scale, even the six subregions could contain a whole unit each, and the total study area may contain several units. Therefore, although the study area is likely to cut across the boundaries of some middle-level units, it covers a large enough area so that portions of several small or even moderate sized ($10-30$ km^2) middle-level cooperating units should be covered (if they exist in the area). Even when whole larger units extend beyond the study boundaries, a portion of their seasonal range may be covered.

Still, the available data may prevent a search for some of the largest possible middle-level units. Furthermore, the limited cooperation among large units renders their identification by spatial analysis unlikely in any case. The study region covers a sufficiently large area, so that one can seek out more closely cooperating moderate scale units that have seasonal settlement concentrations covering several tens of square kilometers. In order to search for this patterning, however, the raw BMAP site and structure and feature data require considerable preliminary interpretation prior to their use in spatial analysis. The details of the coding procedure are important, because interpretations based on archaeological data may be sensitive to the details of coding and these are often not described.

Coding Methods

The coding methods I describe here are only possible with mapped or excavated sites. Sites added to the sample that only have survey data cannot be fully analyzed. This lack of detail regarding surveyed sites is of particular relevance to settlements occupied at the time BMAP field investigations were in progress. Occupied sites were not mapped, and all data pertaining to them are based on survey. The missing information on occupied sites constrained some of my analyses (see chapter 6).

My coding strategy has two aims: reproducibility and accuracy. Reproducibility refers to the formulation of explicit coding rules yielding consistent results when applied to the same data. Accuracy refers to the effective use of available data to minimize incorrect coding interpretations. In practice, these two goals have to be balanced: A very simple and rigid (hence highly reproducible) coding methodology proves inappropriate in many individual cases, and may result in clearly incorrect interpretations. Conversely, a flexible "gestalt" coding approach may make the best use of the data, but is subjective and not reproducible. To balance these two goals I use data in a hierarchical fashion, ranking the reliability of different types of raw data, and placing correspondingly ranked reliance on them. In addition, I maintain an explicit record of the basis on which each coding interpretation is made. In this way unambiguous cases are coded on the basis of rigid and reproducible rules, while more complicated cases can be coded using a more flexible (but less reproducible) range of data sources.

One necessary result of the attempt to define simple and replicable coding procedures is that some arbitrary rules are necessary. The combination of these rules with the flexibility of the hierarchical approach makes the best use of the data while maintaining control over the criteria used in coding each case. In analysis, I draw on subsets of the data based on the level of reproducibility required (see chapter 6). The specific discussion that follows should make this strategy clearer.

An additional point regarding my coding strategy is the degree to which it intentionally masks variability. This applies particularly at the level of site components, where I classify components according to a specific function and season(s) of use. This ignores ethnographically known variability in the pattern of site use (cf. Roberts 1990). The intention is to classify sites normatively in a way that permits identification of broad patterns of behavior. These data would not be well suited for analysis of variation around these behavioral central tendencies, and such an analysis is not my goal.

My basic unit of analysis is the component, defined as a discrete occupational episode at a site. Use of components as analytic units requires three steps. First, each site's boundaries must be specified to delineate discrete spatial units. Second, the site's settlement history must be analyzed to distinguish separate occupational episodes (components) on the site. Finally, the date, function, and seasonality of each of the components must be identified.

As outlined in appendix A, the BMAP identified site boundaries based on "common sense" spatial criteria that were visible in the field and fairly unambiguous in most cases. To subdivide these spatially discrete sites into temporal components I rely primarily on combination of dendrochronological and ethnographic data, although I also use less reliable criteria when necessary. In general, temporal components are fifteen years or less in length, and are ranked in a hierarchical fashion according to the reliability of the dates assigned to them. This hierarchy ranges from sites with multiple tree-ring dates (permitting reliable dating) to pure guess-dates. The hierarchy of dating criteria permits the analyses in chapter 6 to be restricted to varying degrees of dating certainty.

In addition to the chronological analysis, I also classify site components into functional categories such as habitation sites (defined as a component with at least one permanent dwelling and one sheep or goat corral; these are the sites on which most of my analysis in subsequent chapters concentrates) or any of a range of special activity sites. In addition, I identify season(s) of occupation for each component. Again, the criteria used in identifying site-component function and seasonality form a hierarchy, ranging from most reliable (based on site structures and features and information supplied by informants with direct personal knowledge of a site) to least reliable (guesses based on site location). Within the sites, I classify individual structures and features according to function and date and assign them to site components.

Figure 5.2 illustrates this procedure for a typical habitation site. Site D:11:4239 (SIU) includes the remains of three hogans, a large sheep/goat corral, a lamb pen, and a probable ramada (shade) as well as associated hearths and ash piles. The site lies on a slight south-southeast-trending slope in a setting moderately protected from winter storms. The corral walls contain abundant brush—an indication of cold weather use—and the lamb pen suggests early spring occupation. This was confirmed by an elderly woman (a granddaughter of Left Handed's clan nephew, Who Has Mules or Many Mules) who lived at the site. She recalled fall, winter, and spring occupation of the area. She lived there with her mother, her husband, and her three oldest children, the youngest of whom was born around 1930. A younger daughter, born around 1940 (who also served as an informant), recalled subsequently living at the site in the fall and spring, probably in the early 1960s. The surface of the site is scattered with about 135 artifacts, including a large number of bones, some metal cans, nails, sawn wood, glass, and other miscellaneous objects. Most of the datable artifacts (such as the steel cans) suggest a mid-twentieth-century date.

Tree-ring dating and structure-by-structure analysis refines this information. Structure 1 (probably originally a forked-stick style hogan according to one of the former occupants) yielded one isolated nineteenth-century date (1897+rLB), two dates in the late 1920s (1928G and 1929G), a 1948+ rLGB, and a 1957cLGB date. All of the dates are from wood samples with bark or other indications that the dates are very close to the actual year of tree-death (this is what the symbols r, L, G, and B indicate).[1] These dates suggest possible construction around 1929, with rebuilding around 1957, which matches the informant accounts of site use in the 1930s and 1960s. Structure 1 is the hogan Many Mules' granddaughter lived in with her three children. According to her, the structure had been used in a wedding ceremony prior to her occupation. This is also the structure her daughter lived in

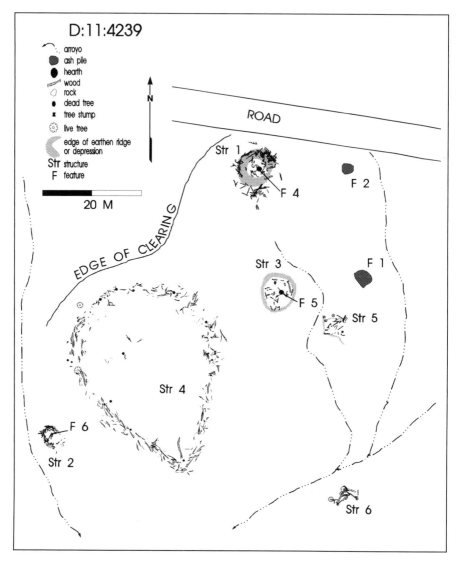

Figure 5.2. Example of Site Layout

several decades later in the early 1960s. The multiple occupations and rebuilding of the hogan are supported by evidence of remodeling of the hogan's interior hearth.

The two other hogans (Structures 2 and 3) lack evidence of reuse. Structure 2 yielded three dates (1922 + G, 1930 + + LGB, 1932G), suggesting construction within a few years of Structure 1 (perhaps 1932). Structure 3 had four dates that clustered tightly in the late 1920s (1926 + rLB, 1927vv, 1928vv, and 1928 + rLGB), strengthening the evidence for a late 1920s occupation (construction in 1928 in this case). This is the hogan occupied by the elderly informant's mother, one of Many Mules' daughters. The corral, Structure 4, yielded a scatter of dates (1920G, 1924vv, 1925vv, 1927LGB, 1936 + LGB) that again confirm a late 1920s (perhaps 1927?) occupation as well as later repair. The structure's good condition suggests considerably more recent use as well. The evidence of recent use matches the late 1950s date from Structure 1, the mid-twentieth-century artifacts and the informant reference to a 1960s occupation. The probable shade, Structure 5, yielded one date of 1929G. Finally, the lamb pen lacks tree-ring dates, but its condition and the suggestion by the informants indicate an association with the early period of site use.

Based on this information, the site is divided into two components, both of which are habitation sites. The first was occupied initially about 1927 as a fall-winter-spring settlement. This component includes all of the structures and features on the site (all three hogans with associated hearths and ash piles, the corral, the shade, and the lamb pen). Subsequently, one of the hogans (Structure 1 with its associated hearth and ash pile) and the corral were re-used, starting around 1957. This defines a second, smaller, spring-fall habitation component.

This breakdown of the site is not perfect. For instance, I ignored Many Mules' granddaughter's recollection of additional lamb pens around the corral, because she gave no specific information about them and no evidence of them was preserved. My use of a 1927 starting date (based on the dates from the corral) may also represent a minor distortion, because far stronger evidence of site use begins with clustered tree-ring dates in 1928. The precise dating of the later period of site use is also uncertain, as the 1957 date is based on a single tree-ring sample. On the whole, however, this breakdown fairly closely approximates the use history of the settlement.

Appendix A details these coding procedures for site components, structures, and features. By following the rules listed there, I assign all structures and features to one or (less often) several site components. The combination of these structure-feature data and the site component codes provides considerable detail regarding the settlement history on northern Black Mesa. Barring errors in coding, site components approximate ethnographic residence groups and dwellings represent households. In principle these data are amenable to the sorts of spatial analyses of ethnographic settlement patterns described in chapter 4.

The analysis of those ethnographic patterns highlights several important methodological implications. Most notable is the necessity of considering patterning at different scales within a single settlement system. That is, the degree of clustering or dispersion can only be meaningfully interpreted with reference to the scale at which the pattern is being considered. In fact, clustering and dispersion can co-occur in the same settlement system.

The cluster analytic approach I described for the ethnographic analysis in chapter 4 cannot be used in the Black Mesa case, however, due to two related limitations of the archaeological data. First, as noted previously, the settlement data do not form a contiguous block. Despite the large size of the study area as a whole, none of the six subregions patched together around the data gaps (fig. 5.1) exceeds 35 km^2 (see table 5.1). These areas are arbitrary in shape and location, the product of the history of archaeological research in the BMAP area, which in turn was shaped by the course of strip mining. A cluster analytic method such as that used for the ethnographic data (Rocek 1985) would produce nonsensical results, because the overwhelming patterns would be the clusters of sites formed by the subregions. The cluster analytic method also will not work within the individual subregions. This is because of the second major problem of the archaeological sample, the small sample size within subregions. Despite the large total number of sites, the subregions yielded far too few site components for meaningful analysis when the sites are subdivided by subregion and time period.

For these reasons, I rely heavily on nearest neighbor analysis in the succeeding chapters. As noted in the discussion of ethnographic patterns, nearest neighbor analysis is not sensitive to variation in the scale of patterning, and is a poor way to interpret spatial patterns of mixed scale such as "dispersed clusters." However, a comparison of the cluster analytic and nearest neighbor approaches (Rocek 1985, 1994) indicates that, except where interresidence group distances are markedly bimodal, the nearest neighbor approach generally provides a fair approximation of the microscale of patterning. Because any identifiable multiresidence group units are likely to be relatively small, a nearest neighbor approach is acceptable. In addition, I employ a complementary quadrat analysis (see later in this chapter), to partly circumvent the nearest neighbor technique's lack of sensitivity to scale.[2]

Despite its limitations, nearest neighbor analysis offers benefits that make it useful for the BMAP data. Because it is based on mean intersite distances, values from noncontiguous subregions can be combined into a single grand mean. So long as the subregions may be assumed to form part of a single settlement pattern, the grand mean should reflect this spatial pattern, while providing a larger sample size than found in any single subregion. In addition, the quantification of the spatial pattern into a single statistic by the nearest neighbor method permits comparisons among subregions or among different time periods. This is more straightforward than the subjective comparisons of graphical representations of clustering procedures I used for the ethnographic samples (Rocek 1985, 1994). Although the simplification to a single number may mask actual variability, it also provides a useful form of data reduction.

The nearest neighbor technique works by comparing the observed average distance between sites with a calculated "expected" average distance. The resulting statistic is a ratio of the observed over the expected mean distance between nearest neighbors. A value less than one indicates that sites lie closer together (are more clustered) than random, while a value exceeding one indicates dispersion. This statistic must be adjusted to correct for interactions between the number of sites and the size and shape of the study area, because a site's true nearest neighbor may actually lie outside of the study sample. Such a case inflates the observed nearest neighbor distance (this problem is collectively known as the "boundary effect"; see e.g., McNutt 1981; Pinder et al. 1979; Whallon 1974). I use a modified form of the nearest neighbor statistic, adjusting it specifically to the size and shape of the subregions.[3]

Given the limitations of the nearest neighbor technique and the goal of my analysis (the comparison of settlement patterns among each other, *not* against probabilistic models), the exact value of the statistic is not of great interest. What is important is to remove the effect of varying sample sizes when comparing settlement patterns from different time periods in the same study areas. The boundary effect is sensitive to sample size. The fewer the sites in a sample, the more likely that a given site's true nearest neighbor lies outside the sample. Given a constant settlement patterning but decreasing site density (hence smaller sample sizes), an uncorrected nearest neighbor statistic is shifted towards increased values. The correction factor is intended to remove this sample size bias. Elsewhere I have evaluated the modified nearest neighbor statistic by simulating reduced sample sizes, and the results indicate that it does adequately correct for the shifting boundary effect problem (see extended discussion in Rocek 1985).

Because nearest neighbor analysis is insensitive to multiple scales of patterning in a single distribution, another technique is needed to explore the scale at which sites cluster or disperse. To attack this problem, I use a form of quadrat analysis using the subregions as the quadrats. Quadrat analysis compares the distribution of sites among a series of spatial blocks (quadrats) with the distribution expected under a random pattern. The resulting statistic, a ratio of the variance to the mean of quadrat site frequencies, is higher than one if sites concentrate in only a few quadrats and lower than one if sites are evenly dispersed among quadrats. This technique evaluates clustering or dispersion at a single scale—the size of the quadrats. Because the subregions are my quadrats, I can judge the degree to which clustering or dispersion occurs at the scale of the subregions, which are spatial blocks that average a bit over 20 km^2.

Unlike conventional quadrat analysis, in which quadrats are of uniform area, the subregions vary in size. This requires some modifications in the technique, and I use a "corrected variance/mean ratio" to evaluate the spatial pattern. The interpretation of this ratio in terms of interquadrat clustering or dispersion remains the same as in the usual form of the technique.[4] The ratio may be used to compare the degree to which sites cluster into subregions from time period to time period. As described in chapter 6, the quadrat analysis serves primarily as negative evidence, to show that the spatial patterns identified by the nearest neighbor technique operate at below the subregional scale.

This method does not give the same continuous information on the scale of patterning as that provided by the cluster analytic method used for the ethnographic data. It does, however, provide a check on the scale of the patterns that cause variations in the nearest neighbor statistic. The combination of the nearest neighbor and quadrat analyses gives an indication of the scale of clustering, despite the limitations imposed by the archaeological spatial data. With this suite of spatial analytic techniques, we can monitor changes in settlement patterns alongside the simultaneous changes in population, economy, and social group composition. The Black Mesa archaeological data provide a record, however imperfect, of how these variables have covaried over more than a century.

6

Measuring Change
on Northern Black Mesa

Black Mesa's archaeological record offers the chance to follow long-term changes in Navajo life, but it raises methodological challenges as well. Describing changes in population, economics, and small-scale (residence-group) units is relatively straightforward. Discerning multiresidence group cooperative units is more complicated.

The Population

Shifts over time in the number of tree-ring dates, site components, or structures all track the changing population of northern Black Mesa. The level of resolution of these data can be adjusted by varying time intervals, site types, seasons, or geographic areas, but by and large the results are internally consistent.

The simplest approach is to count the number of individual tree-ring dates by period. Traditional Navajo wooden structures require frequent repair and replacement (see appendix A), so a continuous stream of architectural wood cutting accompanies life on the mesa. Figure 6.1 shows *all* tree-ring samples, including dead wood samples and noncutting dates (lacking the B, G, L, c, r, or v symbols; see chapter 5, note 1). Although dates extend to before the nineteenth century (the oldest sample falls in the twelfth century), most of these earliest specimens are isolated noncutting dates and dead wood. Small groups of dates cluster around 1775 and 1805 to 1810. These clusters, again mostly noncutting dates, may represent poorly preserved wood from sparse early occupations, but there are not enough samples to adequately demon-

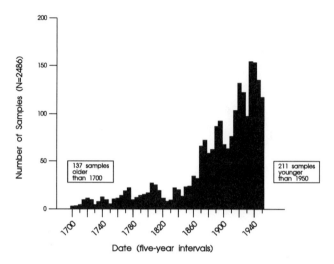

Figure 6.1. All Tree-Ring Sample Outer Dates, Including Dead Wood and Noncutting Dates.

strate this. The next group of dates falls in the 1830s and contains the earliest cutting dates clustered on individual sites. Marked growth begins after the end of Navajo captivity at Fort Sumner in the late 1860s and extends up to recent times. This large group of post-1860s dates indicates a clear increase in use of the area starting around 1870, although it may also reflect wider availability of axes for wood-cutting (Brugge, personal communication 1985). The growth trend breaks several times, around 1880, 1900, after 1920, and again after about 1940. This last decrease is due to a lack of dates from occupied sites, rather than to a population drop. Because the BMAP did not map occupied sites, very few recent tree-ring samples are available.

Counts of site components or individual structures show similar patterns (see also Rocek 1985). Figure 6.2 shows all reliably dated components (that is, it excludes components guess-dated solely on the basis of their condition; see appendix A). The pattern is similar to figure 6.1, although survey data on occupied sites (which lack tree-ring dates) add another spike around 1980. The oldest well-dated sites (based on clustered tree-ring cutting samples) are in the late 1830s. Although early sites may be underrepresented due to attrition, the figure suggests that Navajo settlement in the area was light through the mid-nineteenth century. As suggested by figure 6.1, increased construction began in the late 1860s and 1870s. The number of components dipped slightly around 1880, fell again sharply during the first decade of the twentieth

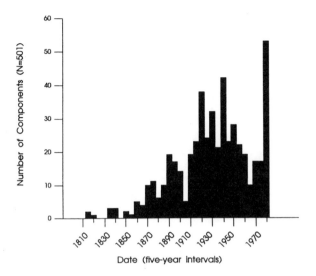

Figure 6.2. Site Component Dates by Five-year Intervals for All Site Types, Reliably Dated Components Only.

century, and leveled off and dropped again slightly after 1920. Construction rebounded in the 1940s, after which the curve falls off. Again, the gap in post-1940s components is an artifact of the lack of data on sites occupied at the time of the BMAP surveys. Occupied sites are arbitrarily dated to the year they were surveyed (primarily in the 1970s and early 1980s), and information regarding their actual construction date and use history is unavailable.

Although the tree-ring and component counts give a general indication of population trends, further refinement is possible. Breaking component counts down by subregions (fig. 5.1) gives additional details of settlement history (fig. 6.3). All subareas show increased occupation shortly after the 1860s, although subregion 3 also exhibits the greatest concentration of late pre-Fort Sumner components (late 1850s and early 1860s). Subregion 6 has the most sites from the Fort Sumner period, perhaps because of its rugged terrain and relatively high elevation, which made it an attractive refuge area. Subregion 1 is notable for its fairly steady site density in the 1880s and around 1905, in contrast to the decrease in the study area as a whole. The mid-1930s dip also varies between subregions.

A step beyond component counts, numbers of habitation site components (as defined in chapter 5 and appendix A, these are sites with both a corral and a permanent dwelling) provide still clearer population measures. Restricting

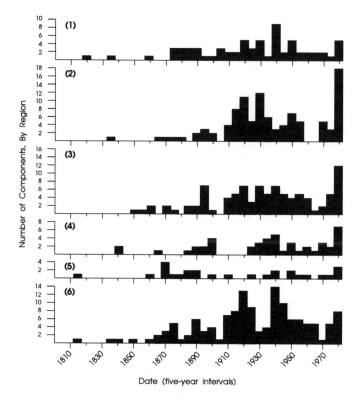

Figure 6.3. Site Component Dates by Five-year Intervals by Subregion, All Site Types, Reliably Dated Components Only.

analysis to habitation sites eliminates the variability of special activity sites such as piñon camps, travelers' camps, and isolated corrals. This makes the counts easier to interpret in terms of local population. In contrast to many special activity sites, habitation site seasonality is also relevant to residence group settlement choices and to interresidence group cooperation.

As noted in chapter 2, historical and ethnographic records suggest a shift from initial winter settlement on Black Mesa to a year-round pattern in the early twentieth century, although with considerable variation from year to year and among different areas. Archaeological and informant data are similarly mixed, but habitation site counts by season show this change. Counts by five-year intervals of winter and summer habitation components show a seasonality shift around 1920.[1] Although all seasons are represented throughout the sequence, the proportion of summer relative to winter sites increases over time.

Summer sites exceed winter in only three time intervals prior to 1920 while winter sites exceed summer sites in ten. Subsequently, summer sites dominate in nine intervals, and winter sites in only one (see also Rocek 1985, 1988). The variability of this pattern is highlighted when examining these trends by subregion. Table 6.1 shows that different areas reflect the seasonal shift to variable degrees. Subregions 4 and 6, the two highest elevation areas nearest the mesa rim, show the increase in summer habitation sites. The pattern is less clear, or even contradicted in other areas, for example subregion 2).

The seasonality data are significantly affected by differential preservation. Summer sites are in part recognized archaeologically on the basis of evidence for impermanent summer structures such as shades and tents. This evidence is more likely to be preserved on recent sites. In addition, the rugged terrain chosen for defensive purposes on early sites (Kemrer 1974) often provides sheltered locations resembling those used in later periods for winter sites. Thus, identification of early site seasonality may be biased in favor of winter, because sheltered site location is one of the bases used to identify seasonality.

Still, the subregion differences probably do reflect different seasonal settlement patterns. Winter occupation on the mesa and summer movement to the adjacent lowlands may have been more characteristic of the families living near the rim. In the mesa interior, seasonal moves were perhaps confined to the mesa itself at an earlier date (cf. Hoover 1931:327–28).

The habitation site data show that a reconstruction of population trends must take seasonality into account. Furthermore, instead of merely counting components, the number of permanent dwellings (houses and hogans) on habitation site components provides the most direct measure of relative population. Before dwelling counts can be interpreted in terms of population, however, we must control for two additional variables: the number of occupants per dwelling and the duration of component occupation.

Many archaeological studies use formulas based on site or roofed surface area rather than dwelling counts to estimate population, but I take a simpler approach based specifically on Navajo settlement practice. I assume that the average size of the smallest social unit, the household, remains constant. Outside of urbanized regions, reservation-wide data indicate a relatively steady household composition ranging from about five to seven people (mean 5.9, standard deviation .6; data from Kelley 1982b:91). Russell's investigations in the BMAP area yield similar figures: 328 people in 55 households, or 5.96 people per household (data for Eastern Lease area from Russell 1981a; data for Western Lease area derive from Russell n.d.).

Table 6.1. Habitation Site Component Seasons by Subregion; Percentages of Reliably Dated Components, All Bases of Seasonality Assessment.[a]

Decade	Subregion 1				Subregion 2				Subregion 3			
	Total Count	Summer %	Winter %	Other/ Unk.	Total Count	Summer %	Winter %	Other/ Unk.	Total Count	Summer %	Winter %	Other/ Unk.
Pre-1840	2	..	100	..	1	100	..	..	..	..	..	..
1840–1849	..	..	..	..	..	..	..	..	..	..	..	..
1850–1859	..	..	..	..	..	..	..	..	1	100	..	..
1860–1869	..	..	..	..	..	..	..	..	..	..	..	..
1870–1879	..	..	..	..	1	100	..	..	2	..	..	100
1880–1889	2	100	..	..	..	..	..	..	..	..	..	..
1890–1899	2	..	..	100	..	..	..	..	3	..	..	100
1900–1909	1	..	100	..	..	..	..	..	..	..	..	..
1910–1919	3	..	..	100	3	33	67	..	5	60	..	40
1920–1929	3	..	67	33	5	80	20	..	2	..	50	50
1930–1939	2	100	..	..	6	..	50	50	7	43	..	57
1940–1949	5	..	20	80	4	50	25	25	9	56	..	44
1950–1959	4	50	..	50	4	50	25	25	3	..	..	100
1960–1969	..	..	..	..	..	..	..	..	..	..	..	..
Post-1969	5	60	..	40	10	30	10	60	2	50	..	50
Total	29	31	21	48	34	41	27	32	34	38	3	59

	Subregion 4				Subregion 5				Subregion 6			
Decade	Total Count	Summer %	Winter %	Other/ Unk.	Total Count	Summer %	Winter %	Other/ Unk.	Total Count	Summer %	Winter %	Other/ Unk.
Pre-1840	...	...	...	...	1	...	...	100	1	...	100	...
1840–1849	1	...	100	...	...	...	...	...	...	...	...	...
1850–1859	...	...	...	...	...	...	...	...	1	...	100	...
1860–1869	...	...	...	...	...	...	...	...	1	...	...	100
1870–1879	1	...	100	...	2	...	100	...	4	25	75	...
1880–1889	...	...	...	...	2	50	50	...	4	25	50	25
1890–1899	1	...	...	100	1	100	...	...	2	...	50	50
1900–1909	...	...	...	...	...	...	...	...	4	...	50	50
1910–1919	...	...	...	...	...	...	...	...	6	17	67	17
1920–1929	1	...	100	...	1	...	100	...	9	56	36	11
1930–1939	4	25	50	25	1	100	...	100	3	...	100	...
1940–1949	2	50	...	50	1	100	...	...	14	21	21	57
1950–1959	2	50	...	50	2	...	100	...	4	25	50	25
1960–1969	...	...	...	...	...	...	...	...	...	...	...	...
Post-1969	4	50	...	50	2	...	50	50	5	40	40	20
Total	16	31	31	38	13	23	54	23	58	24	47	29

a. Reliably dated habitation site components only. Summer category includes summer, spring-summer, summer-fall; winter includes winter, fall-winter, winter-spring, fall-winter-spring; other/unknown includes: year-round, spring, fall, and unknown. These seasonal categories differ from those used in later analyses below, where seasonal overlap of occupation is the primary concern. There, for instance, *both* summer and winter counts include year-round sites, rather than treating them as a separate category.

Ethnoarchaeological data from the McKinley Mine area on the eastern reservation documents the number of dwellings per household on sites of various ages (Kelley 1982b: 360). Kelley uses a similar definition of the household as followed here (chapter 5), but includes dependents (usually elderly relatives) living in adjacent structures. She finds a steady mean of 1.2 to 1.3 dwellings per household. Kelley (1982a: 51–55) also examines the number of occupants per square meter of dwelling (hogans in particular). She finds that hogan floor area is a function of factors including the range of indoor activities carried out over the course of occupation, but dwelling size is not a good indicator of the number of occupants. This point is even clearer in a sample including Anglo-style multiroom houses along with hogans, because the use of floor space in these structures is very different.

So, a household (by Kelley's definition) occupies an average of 1.2 to 1.3 dwellings and consists of around six individuals. This suggests that each permanent dwelling on a Navajo habitation site averages slightly under five occupants. One minor correction suggested by Kelley's analysis is that hogan-like structures smaller than 3.5 meters diameter (about 9.5 m^2 floor area) typically do not serve as dwellings, but function instead as shelters for herders or for storage. Therefore, I excluded structures smaller than 9.5 m^2 in floor area from my population calculations.

Aside from variation in the number of dwelling occupants, changes in the duration of site component use would affect estimates of relative population over time. Different sites clearly vary in the number of years that they were used; the critical issue is changes over time in the average number of years families reused sites. To control for this possibility, I examine duration of occupation in several ways. Most directly, if the duration changes, then structure and feature dates of different ages should show differences in their temporal spread within components.[2] That is, changes in the difference between the latest and the earliest structure or feature dates within components should reflect changes in occupation span. But in fact there is no significant correlation between habitation site component age and the span of dates per component (Rocek 1985).

Kelley (1982b: 359, 363; 1986: 38, 188) offers another approach, using ethnographic estimates of occupation duration, to investigate site-use span in the McKinley Mine area. She finds a relatively constant mean length of homesite use (ten years) from 1880 up to 1950. Subsequently, average duration rises sharply to sixteen years. The most common reason for site abandonment (over 50 percent of known cases) is a death on-site. Kelley relates the 1950s

increased use span to improved roads and easier hospital access, which reduced the occurrence of deaths at the sites. Shrinking land availability and
increased investment in permanent facilities may also have contributed to a
reluctance to abandon sites. In any case, her data suggest that changes in
occupation duration of habitation sites should not be an important factor until
the most recent periods.

Finally, Blomberg (1983) uses archaeological measures of habitation sites
to suggest an increase in site occupation intensity in the BMAP area through
time. She shows an increase in the number of several categories of features
and animal enclosures and in the distance of ash piles from hogans. These
changes match her model of a shift to longer site occupations during the early
twentieth century. She suggests that extended settlement should lead to increased site complexity and separation of waste disposal from dwellings.

Blomberg's findings regarding changes in site characteristics are clearly
valid. For instance, the number of animal enclosures (of all types) per habitation site correlates significantly with time ($r = .16$, $n = 166$, $p < .04$), as
does ash pile distance from hogans ($r = .46$, $n = 77$, $p < .01$) (though compare Kelley 1982b:307, 311 for an alternative interpretation of ash pile placement). Other measures of increased use intensity that only marginally correlate with time in Blomberg's study are more clearly significant in the present
(larger) sample; for example, estimated ash pile volume correlates with time
($r = .24$, $n = 203$, $p < .01$) (cf. Kelley 1982a:66–67). Blomberg (1983:20)
postulates an increase in the length of individual use events at sites (how many
months a site is occupied in a particular year), as well as an increase in the
overall duration of reuse (how many years a site is visited and reused). The
site characteristics she investigates do not distinguish between these two aspects of site-use. In addition, some of the variables are clearly subject to
taphonomic effects, such as erosion of old ash piles. Given the structure-
feature date distributions on site components and Kelley's ethnographic observations described previously, at least a substantial part of the change demonstrated by Blomberg most likely relates to increasing length of annual site-use
events rather than to a shift in the interannual duration of site-use.

Therefore, in my population estimates I assumed that average component
occupation duration did not change markedly until after the mid-1940s. To
the extent that I neglected changes that did occur in occupation span, I *over-*
estimated early population levels, because all lines of evidence suggest increased span. Despite this, the early site frequencies are low, indicating sparse
populations in any case.

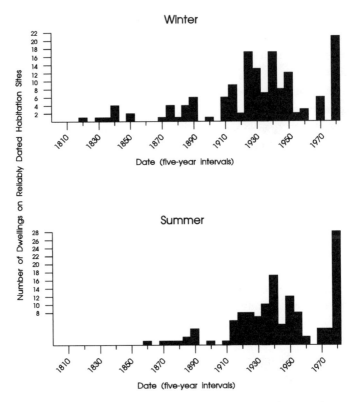

Figure 6.4. Counts of Permanent Dwellings (Hogans and Houses) on Reliably Dated Habitation Site Components, by Five-year Intervals and by Season.

With these considerations in mind, figure 6.4 shows dwelling counts by five-year intervals on reliably dated habitation components. I included only structures with an area not less than 9.5 m² (because small structures are rare, I assumed that unmeasured dwellings are larger than 9.5 m² and included them in the analysis). Components were divided into winter and summer categories on the basis of whether they were occupied in that season, regardless of whether they were also used at other times of year. For instance, the summer count includes multiseason components such as spring-summer and even year-round occupations. Some components are included in both counts, because they were used during both times of year. Due to differential preservation, the summer counts are probably somewhat less reliable than the winter, possibly underrepresenting relative population during the early periods. In addition, the data undoubtedly miss some of the people living in temporary warm-weather structures (tents and shades). Despite these limitations, however, I used both figures, because the summer data should reflect summer population more directly than the winter counts.

The trends suggested for the two seasons are comparable, although with several specific differences. Most notably, the summer pattern lacks substantial occupation until around 1890; this may reflect the predominantly winter use of the mesa in early years. It also lacks the sharp fluctuations in dwelling counts that the winter pattern shows around 1920. Overall the dwelling data mirror the tree-ring and component counts described in figures 6.1 and 6.2. The first major growth in permanent habitation occurred around 1870, after the Fort Sumner period. A notable characteristic of both seasons is evidence of depopulation around the turn of the century (an earlier possible population drop occurs around 1880, but this is only reflected in the winter counts). This fluctuation is certainly a relatively local phenomenon, not reflected in tribal-wide population figures. That is, this was a period during which the families that normally used this area of Black Mesa used it less often; these families did not die out. Russell's (1983b:59) study of Navajo settlement just south of the BMAP area also suggests a hiatus around the turn of the century, indicating that this temporary population shift covered a substantial area of northern Black Mesa.

Climatic data suggest a possible explanation of this apparent decline. Tree-rings show declining local conditions starting from moist conditions (high tree-ring indices) around 1840 and culminating in a low about 1900 (Dean 1982:fig. 1). That low is worse than all negative tree-ring index values because the late 1700s and this late-nineteenth-century drought cycle constitutes "one of the most severe droughts of the 1600-year [Black Mesa area tree-ring index] record" (Dean 1982:6). This period corresponds to a cycle of drought years described by Left Handed, when he and his family abandoned their regular seasonal pattern in favor of long ranging migrations in search of forage (see chapter 2; Dyk 1967). Left Handed's account refers to an earlier part of this cycle in the 1870s. This drought interval also marks the beginning of the recent cycle of erosion in the study area and elsewhere in the Southwest. The tree-ring record shows that the late-nineteenth-century decline is marked by two distinct peaks of low index values—one around 1875 to 1880 and one sharper spike at 1900. These peaks may explain the two-cycle fluctuation in dwelling counts noted earlier, one around 1880 and the other more drastic one around 1900.

Three other fluctuations in the winter population data may reflect larger-scale changes in resident population. The dip around 1920 (not shown in the summer counts) may mark the 1918 to 1919 flu epidemic. This period (1920 and 1921 in particular) also shows a peak in windbreak construction, reflecting the temporary jump in mobility and short-term occupations immediately following the epidemic. The sharp rise in permanent dwelling construction in the succeeding period probably represents the establishment of new habitation sites by survivors who abandoned death sites.

This dip and subsequent peak in dwelling construction thus represent not only demographic fluctuations but also short-term changes in construction activity. This observation is relevant to two other dips, one in the mid-1930s and again in the 1940s. There is no reason to believe that either of these represent actual drops in Navajo population. These were, however, both periods when major national and world-scale turmoil affected the Navajo reservation (the Depression and stock reduction in the former case and World War II in the latter). In both cases an immediate impact was a major economic shift toward increased wage-labor involvement. In the 1930s, the brief boom in federally sponsored jobs (Civilian Conservation Corps and Soil Conservation Service) probably diverted the male labor force from domestic construction activities. In the 1940s, the boom in off-reservation wage jobs created by the war (as well as actual military service) physically removed a part of the labor force from the reservation for substantial periods of the year, again discouraging major construction (see also Rocek 1988). Although these interpretations cannot be demonstrated, they serve as cautionary tales regarding the interpretation of the archaeologically derived population data. Although the broad trends probably do accurately reflect patterns of population change, the short-term fluctuations are much more sensitive to the specific factors influencing the timing of activities on the local level.

For these reasons, I use a form of moving average on the dwelling counts in my subsequent consideration of local population (table 6.2). My approach is to compute the total number of dwellings by overlapping decades, for example, 1840 to 1850, 1845 to 1855, 1850 to 1860, and so on. I also perform similar analyses using fifteen-year intervals overlapping by ten years. These counts mask some of the sorts of fluctuations outlined previously and perhaps lose some detail on short-term population fluctuations. They should, however, be more representative of the overall trends in locally resident population than the immediate pattern of house construction.[3] The dwelling counts derived from these longer, overlapping intervals are of course higher in their absolute values, but closely follow the trends of the five-year counts.

Table 6.2. Permanent Dwelling Counts on Habitation Sites, by Overlapping Decades and Fifteen-year Intervals.[a]

	Decade			Fifteen-year		
	Dwelling Counts				Dwelling Counts	
Interval Midpoint	Winter	Summer		Interval Midpoint	Winter	Summer
pre-1835	1	0				
pre-1840	1	0		pre-1830	1	0
1830	1	0		pre-1835	2	0
1835	4	0		pre-1840	6	0
1840	5	0		1838	6	0
1845	2	0		1843	7	0
1850	2	0		1848	2	0
1855	2	1		1853	2	1
1860	0	1		1858	0	1
1865	0	0		1863	1	1
1870	1	2		1868	2	2
1875	6	2		1873	6	3
1880	5	1		1878	6	5
1885	7	3		1883	14	6
1890	10	6		1888	10	6
1895	4	5		1893	10	5
1900	1	1		1898	1	2
1905	1	0		1903	3	1
1910	11	3		1908	11	4
1915	15	10		1913	16	13
1920	10	16		1918	21	21
1925	23	16		1923	31	23
1930	27	12		1928	34	20
1935	16	16		1933	37	29
1940	25	27		1938	34	35
1945	33	25		1943	41	39
post-1969[b]	50	41		post-1965[b]	62	59

a. Only dwellings larger than 9.5 m^2 included. See text for discussion of seasonal categories and for the recent time period data.

b. Surrogate dwelling counts (see text).

In addition, to compensate for the incomplete data on occupied sites, I adjust estimates of recent populations in two ways. First, I simply omitted the dwelling counts after the mid-1940s (when the decadal and fifteen-year interval counts began to fall off). To provide a basis for analysis of the final period (1975 for the decade analysis, 1973 for the fifteen-year intervals), however, I use a value of 1.5 times the highest previous permanent dwelling count (which occurred in the 1940s) as a surrogate estimate of relative population. This is an arbitrary value, but is intended to take into account three critical factors. First, dwelling counts on occupied sites are almost certainly underestimated, because these sites were only surveyed and not mapped. BMAP survey estimates of structure counts are almost invariably lower than the number identified during actual mapping. Second, population estimates based on dwelling counts for the final period are poorly comparable to counts from previous periods due to the proliferation of non-hogan housing. To compound the problem, the number of rooms in unmapped non-hogan dwellings is unknown. Finally, population in the study area undoubtedly continued to increase substantially from the mid-1940s onward, but permanent and temporary outmigration also increased greatly. Therefore, the factor of 1.5 times the 1940s levels is considerably lower than the known overall growth rate of the Navajo population, which more than doubled during this period (Goodman 1982:61).

The value of 1.5 times the maximum permanent dwelling count serves as a general indicator of what dwelling counts might be if housing technology had not changed and occupied sites had been investigated fully. This value permits direct comparison with dwelling counts from previous periods. Clearly this is an approximate solution to the problem, but it should roughly indicate the direction of recent trends. The values of these final period "surrogate dwelling counts" are 50 and 41 respectively for the winter and summer decadal counts. The corresponding values estimating dwelling counts over fifteen-year intervals are 62 and 59 respectively (table 6.2). Encouragingly, multiplying these figures by the roughly five- to six-person average per dwelling yields numbers fairly close to the low 300s level of recent population in the study area. Still, the intent is to use these figures for relative, not absolute population estimates.

The Economy

Like human population, the core of the domestic Navajo economy—livestock population—is open to fairly direct archaeological scrutiny. Corrals provide

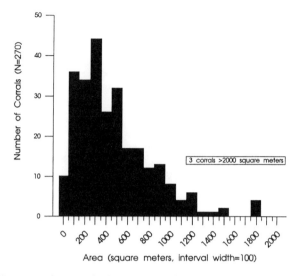

Area (square meters, interval width=100)

Figure 6.5. Corral Areas (m²) on Mapped Sites, Measured Corrals Only.

the most direct measure of the pastoral economy. I use estimates of corral area derived from length and width measurements of corrals on mapped sites (see Rocek 1985 for details). The distribution of corral sizes (fig. 6.5) has several large outliers, including entire canyons fenced off at their mouths as well as several large diffuse soil disturbances marking possibly corral boundaries. Both of these kinds of enclosures (or possible enclosures) reflect a different use of corral space than the majority of normal corrals and I excluded these outliers, larger than 1700 square meters, from further analyses (cf. Kelley 1982b:317–18). The remaining mapped corrals average 450 m². I substituted this value for the area of corrals that were not measured. These corral area data are the basis for two indices of livestock for each mapped site: total corral area per site, and the ratio of corral area to number of permanent dwellings (hogans and houses).[4] The former could serve as a general estimate of per-site livestock population, while the latter should more accurately reflect live-stock per site inhabitant. I calculated these indices on well-dated habitation sites that have been mapped (survey estimates of corral area and dwelling counts are unreliable), and then derived medians by time intervals. The two indices produce similar results but the latter index (corral area per dwelling per site) appears to best track livestock population (see discussion that fol-lows, and Rocek 1985). Therefore, I focused on this measure.

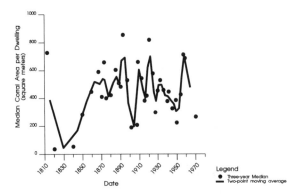

Figure 6.6. Corral Area (m²) per Permanent Dwelling on Habitation Sites

Figure 6.6 shows corral area per permanent dwelling on each site, plotted against time. To minimize extraneous sources of variation the figure includes only mapped, reliably dated, habitation site components. Medians cover three-year intervals (represented by the dots), and are smoothed using a two-point moving average over each pair of points (the line). I use medians to minimize the effects of outlier data, and to better represent the central tendency of the skewed underlying distribution (fig. 6.5). The high value around 1810 represents a single poorly dated site. Ignoring this one point, the graph shows low initial levels followed by a rise up to around 1860. Subsequently, the index increases less steeply to a peak in the early 1890s. The most notable drop during this period of increase falls in the mid-1870s, although there are also dips in the mid-1860s and 1880s. A sharp drop began in the late 1890s, culminating in a low around 1905. The index increases up to about 1920 (with one sharp drop in the mid-1910s), and then fluctuates in a slowly decreasing trend until the mid-1930s. A more consistent drop occurred from 1936 until 1950, followed by a rapid rise in the mid- to late 1950s. Finally, the single point from around 1970 suggests a new drop in the index. Because corral area and the enclosed sheep population correlate strongly in ethnographically studied Navajo corrals (Russell and Dean 1985), this figure should track livestock holdings. Correlation of the index with livestock census data suggests that this is indeed the case.

The most detailed livestock data available for the period covered by the archaeological sample derive from the stock reduction period and later, in the mid-1930s through the late 1950s. Young (1961:171) tabulates stock censuses from 1936 through 1959 for each reservation grazing district, as well as for the reservation as a whole (fig. 6.7). As noted in chapter 2, the study area lies primarily in District 8, although it also covers a small part of Districts 4 and 2. Because stock reduction regulations were administered by district, the census values from District 8 are most relevant.

Census data between 1936 and 1959 can be sampled at the same three-year intervals as the corral area index (and interpolated for missing years). This yields 9 data points, which show that the index correlates significantly with the District 8 stock censuses (r = .63, n = 9, one-sided p < .04). This corresponds to the pattern in figures 6.6 and 6.7 where the corral index (fig. 6.6) from the mid-1930s to late 1950s neatly tracks the reduction era decrease and subsequent rebound in stock levels (fig. 6.7). Corral-based livestock measures could be refined further. Navajo settlement strategy suggests that cold-weather sites should more accurately reflect stock numbers. Winter sites are more elaborately constructed and maintained than other sites in the seasonal round, and the spacing of livestock in muddy winter corrals is most critical (Kelley 1982b:319–22). Furthermore, the correspondence of human population and permanent dwellings (as opposed to shades and other seasonal structures) is more reliable on cold-weather sites. Therefore, indices based on cold-weather sites should even more accurately reflect livestock population and per-capita stock. Restricting analysis by excluding sites used in the summer in fact *does* strengthen the stock census-corral area index correlation despite a drop in the number of years with available data (r = .71, n = 7,

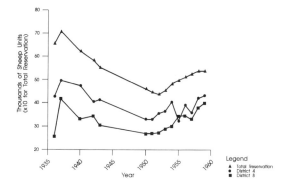

Figure 6.7. Tribal Stock Census Data, Grazing District 4, District 8, and Entire Reservation, 1936 to 1959.

one-sided p < .04). In this seasonally restricted sample, even raw corral area per site approaches a significant correlation with the livestock census (r = .62, n = 7, one-sided p < .04).[5]

Although these correlations justify using the corral area index to measure changes in relative stock populations, two further questions remain: What is the nature of the livestock population actually being measured, and what are potential limitations of the corral measurements as indicators of herd sizes in periods long before stock reduction?

The first question is raised because of several factors. First, the close fit between crude livestock census data and the index of corral area per permanent dwelling is not intuitive, because actually a per-dwelling index should relate to per-capita livestock ownership. The rapid increase in Navajo population makes per-capita stock census figures differ substantially from the raw livestock counts, however, and using per-capita census data would destroy the correlation with the corral per dwelling index. This factor relates to a second characteristic, which is the anomalously high levels of stocking suggested by the index. For instance, during the worst of stock reduction, the lowest that the index fell is 225 square meters of corral space per dwelling, or 125 square meters if only cold weather sites are considered. Given an approximate 1 to 2 square meters per sheep (Kelley 1982a:59; Van Valkenburgh 1956, cited in Kelley 1982b:45, 317), this suggests a value of 63 to 215 sheep per household, or perhaps a median 13 to 45 sheep per-capita (the value depending on whether 1 or 2 m^2 per sheep is used and whether analysis is restricted by season). These values are more comparable to census data from early in the stock reduction period, for example, twenty-two sheep per-capita in District 8 in 1936 (Kunitz 1977:188), than to values at the peak of reduction.

Both of these discrepancies between actual per-capita stock levels and the index of corral area per dwelling suggest that the index is a measure of per-capita livestock values for a *subset* of the population, specifically people living in the traditional residence group settlements and maintaining livestock herds. In contrast, Navajo population as a whole includes settlement concentrations around agricultural projects and towns, in which livestock holdings are very low. This is consistent with the discrepancy between census per-capita stock estimates and the index, because one effect of stock reduction was to drive a substantial number of Navajo households entirely out of the stock economy and out of traditional residence patterns. For example, in 1960, an estimated 50 percent of families lacked grazing permits, and presumably significant livestock holdings (Young 1961:164). The effective population with regard to which the index is calculated is a shrinking proportion of the total Navajo population, and increases much more slowly than the total population. Thus, the index is a reasonably accurate reflection of the pattern of change within the traditional rural settlement system up until the recent period of modified settlement introduced by the coal mine economy and associated with the growth of trailer courts and settlement aggregates around utilities (see chapter 2).

The reliability of the index further back in time is more difficult to evaluate. Kelley (1982b:315–25) outlines a range of potential factors that disrupt the correspondence of corral area and livestock populations. Most notably, changes in animal husbandry practices may modify the relation of stock enclosures to herd sizes. In the past, some Navajo herds were bedded down without corrals (Brugge 1980:156; Kelley 1982b:45), and Navajo informants interviewed by the BMAP indicated that sheep and goat breeds (presumably those used before the intensified stock improvement efforts that accompanied stock reduction) were more easily left overnight without corrals. Kelley (1982b:320) also gives evidence of changes in corral area per sheep in different time periods. These observations suggest that corral area may underestimate livestock population at some earlier sites.[6] Similar factors are introduced by changes in seasonal use of the study area and in the degree of residence group mobility. This latter factor may particularly affect estimates prior to Fort Sumner, when the danger of warfare encouraged mobile settlement, although the distribution shown by figure 6.6 actually shows substantial corral areas during the early periods when these factors are most relevant. Therefore, even if these changes influence the exact levels of the index and underestimate early herds relative to later ones, it is reasonable to suppose that the pattern of change is correctly indicated. Overall, the index seems to measure livestock levels well.

Aside from the stock reduction era drop in stock holdings, figure 6.6 indicates one other major fluctuation on Black Mesa, around 1900. This corresponds to the culmination of the late nineteenth-century climatic deterioration and to the evidence of depopulation of the study area (see earlier discussion). The drop in the corral area indices may reflect decreasing herd sizes as well as movement of herds away from the mesa during this period. The rapid jump in the index in the early twentieth century probably reflects the return of herds, as well as some degree of recovery of the herds that remained. This matches the historical evidence of a temporary collapse in the livestock economy in this period (Bailey and Bailey 1986:104). The index suggests that livestock levels reached a high in the study area just before the turn of the century, after which they leveled off and fluctuated, but never exceeded the late nineteenth-century peak. This also matches the historic data. Although historic records of Navajo livestock holdings prior to the 1930s must be viewed with caution, the period around the turn of the century appears to have marked a turning point in the growth of Navajo stock holdings (Aberle 1966: 30–32; Bailey and Bailey 1986:104), a point confirmed by the corral data.

Table 6.3 shows the median corral area index by overlapping decadal and fifteen-year intervals for comparison with the data on population and residence group size (tables 6.2 and 6.4). I used these data in the analyses that follow.

Aside from livestock production, the most important Navajo domestic economic activity has traditionally been agriculture. Unfortunately, the BMAP's agricultural field data are limited. In particular, because many fields remain in use, they were usually not mapped. Furthermore, it is not always possible to tell whether a particular field was included in the site surveys as part of an adjacent habitation site, as a separate site, or was not surveyed at all. As a result, not only the data collected during site mapping but even the survey data on fields are difficult to use. Russell (1981a; n.d.) collected informant data regarding agricultural fields in the lease areas that partially fill in the missing information. Figure 6.8 shows the dates of new fields, that is, the dates when informants indicated that particular fields in the lease area were first used. The exclusive use of informant data limits the temporal span and probably limits the precision of the dates, but they do give an indication of general trends. In particular, as noted in chapter 2, they suggest a peak in new field construction in the mid-1940s, perhaps in response to the economic hardships of stock reduction and the loss of livestock (cf. Kelley 1982b:102; 1986:136). A jump in local labor supply as men returned from war-related activities may also have encouraged agriculture.

This figure also suggests a break in field starts in the early twentieth century, and a renewed rise in field construction in the 1970s. The former drop may be a slightly misdated reflection of the period of turmoil suggested by the loss of human and livestock populations around the turn of the century (see earlier discussion). Alternatively, the gap in dates may simply be a product of the gap between twentieth-century fields dated on the basis of childhood recollections of older informants, and late nineteenth- to early twentieth-century fields dated on the basis of recollections of their parents. The rise

Table 6.3. Median Corral Area per Permanent Dwelling per Habitation Site, Overlapping Decades and Fifteen-Year Interval Medians.

Decades		Fifteen-year	
Interval Midpoint	Area per Dwelling (m²)	Interval Midpoint	Area per Dwelling (m²)
		pre-1830	384.16
pre-1835	384.16	pre-1835	384.16
pre-1840	61.36	pre-1840	61.36
1840	52.33	1838	52.33
1845	43.29	1843	52.33
1850	286.28	1848	164.79
1855	368.02	1853	368.02
1860	449.76	1858	368.02
1865	591.81	1863	520.79
1870	591.81	1868	591.81
1875	420.02	1873	424.56
1880	413.34	1878	420.02
1885	558.35	1883	468.23
1890	504.77	1888	504.77
1895	514.29	1893	521.41
1900	530.93	1898	497.64
1905	209.95	1903	530.93
1910	224.88	1908	217.42
1915	389.28	1913	389.28
1920	519.25	1918	486.95
1925	544.64	1923	516.73
1930	508.94	1928	512.83
1935	486.95	1933	488.33
1940	449.25	1938	449.76
1945	335.72	1943	383.60
1950	335.72	1948	335.72
1955	639.10	1953	428.22
1960	697.27	1958	639.10
post-1965	266.49	1963	697.27
post-1969	266.49	post-1960	266.49
		post-1965	266.49
		post-1969	266.49

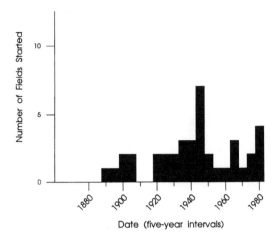

Figure 6.8. New Field Starts in the Lease Area, Based on Informant Data.

in new fields in the 1970s and 1980s may result from clearer memories of recently started fields, though it may also reflect an effort to increase land value prior to its annexation (and payment) by the coal-mining operation (Richard I. Ford, personal communication 1984).

Although stock raising and agriculture leave distinct archaeological traces, the magnitude of production specifically for market is harder to observe (many Navajo market *purchases* are, of course, visible as artifacts discarded on the sites). Until the period after stock reduction and World War II, Navajo involvement in the market was based primarily on returns from pastoral production, particularly the sale of wool, as well as blankets, rugs, hides and pelts, and in later periods, lambs. Neither wages nor public assistance superseded livestock income until after reduction (Kelley 1982b:66). Although a significant subsistence activity, agricultural production was also not important in the market economy, at least in the Black Mesa area (Downs 1964:16; Russell 1983a:63, 302).

The availability of trading posts grew along with the livestock populations of the late nineteenth century, and the rate at which new trading posts were established peaked in the 1880s (Kelley 1977:35). Therefore, the growing herds both increased Navajo economic potential and paralleled the development of a marketing network to accommodate this potential. So, the stock levels documented in the archaeological record should approximately correspond to changes in Navajo market involvement. Ideally, the more stock available, the more livestock products sold to the trading posts, and the more the Navajos could purchase from the posts. This generalization is of course a simplification, because it ignores other factors affecting purchasing power, particularly fluctuations in livestock and trading-post prices. Still, during this period market involvement included both sides of market transactions: Navajo sales to the trading posts were dependent on pastoral production, and Navajo purchases were in turn funded by the returns from these sales. As noted in chapter 2, the peak in livestock holdings in the late nineteenth century appears to correspond to a temporary minor peak in artifacts on sites, and further growth in purchased goods is evident in the early decades of the twentieth century. After the 1930s and 1940s, this reciprocal relationship broke down as Navajo purchasing ability became tied to wages and public assistance, and livestock income assumed a secondary role.

Therefore, for the purposes of this study I assume that involvement in the market parallels livestock levels in the period up to the 1930s or 1940s. During the most recent period, after stock reduction and World War II, the importance of the market grew dramatically as wages and public assistance replaced livestock as the primary bases of the economy.

The Social Units

Social units at two scales concern us here, residence groups and middle-level units. The measure of residence group social unit size follows directly from the reasoning behind the population estimates: I count the number of permanent dwellings per habitation site component. Again, I exclude structures with an area of less than 9.5 m². As with population counts, the major complicating factor is the data on recent sites, because occupied sites were only surveyed rather than mapped, and survey reports tended to consistently undercount structures. Further confusing the issue, occupied site data generally lack chronological detail that would permit breaking sites down into temporal components. So, abandoned structures may be included in counts of recent dwellings. There is no way to evade these problems with the available data. For the purposes of this analysis, I assumed that the two factors affecting surveyed but unmapped sites (undercounting of structures and failure to subdivide structures among temporal components) roughly balance out and I have included unmapped sites in the analysis that follows. This permits observations regarding recent trends in site size, although possible inaccuracies in these data must be kept in mind.

The number of dwellings on habitation site components from all periods range between 1 and 6, with a mean of 1.63, and a median of 1. As with

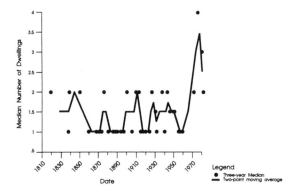

Figure 6.9. Median Counts of Permanent Dwellings per Habitation Site, Three-year Medians.

corral areas, the distribution of dwelling counts is highly skewed. Many sites have one or two dwellings and only a few have larger numbers. Therefore, the mean (which is commonly reported as a summary statistic for describing site composition) does not adequately represent the central tendencies in site size, and the median is a better indicator of trends in dwelling counts.

Figure 6.9 shows three-year-median counts of permanent dwellings per reliably dated habitation site component, analogous to the corral data in figure 6.6. Sites of all seasons are included. The solid line shows a 2 point moving average over the three-year medians. Prior to Fort Sumner, residence groups were relatively large, with a median of two dwellings per site in three of the five time intervals from this period.[7] Habitation components from about 1860 until 1900 were predominantly small, with a median dwelling count of one in all but one time interval. This corresponds to the period of peak herd levels (fig. 6.6). Residence group size rose in the early twentieth century. This rise was broken by an interval of smaller sites around 1920, the final period of prereduction high stock levels. Larger sites were again common through the stock reduction era of the 1930s up to the late 1950s, when they shrank once more. Finally, the most recent sites are the largest in the occupation history of the area, although the biases introduced by unmapped sites may be responsible for this apparent recent jump in size.

Because the analyses that follow are based on overlapping decadal (as well as fifteen-year) time intervals, table 6.4 shows the residence group size data by decadal intervals, with adjacent intervals overlapping by five years (cf. tables 6.2 and 6.3).

Table 6.4. Median Number of Permanent Dwellings on Habitation Sites, by Overlapping Decades.[a]

Interval Midpoint	Number of Sites	Median
pre-1835	2	1.5
pre-1840	4	1.5
1840	3	2.0
1845	1	2.0
1850	1	2.0
1855	2	1.5
1860	1	1.0
1865	1	1.0
1870	7	1.0
1875	9	1.0
1880	4	1.5
1885	7	1.0
1890	12	1.0
1895	8	1.0
1900	3	1.0
1905	3	2.0
1910	9	2.0
1915	15	1.0
1920	17	1.0
1925	22	1.0
1930	22	1.0
1935	19	1.0
1940	27	2.0
1945	29	2.0
1950	21	1.0
1955	17	1.0
1960	8	1.0
1970	3	2.0
post-1969	25	2.0
post-1975	22	2.0

a. Includes all permanent dwellings (houses and hogans) larger than 9.5 m², on reliably dated habitation site components, both mapped and unmapped. (Structures without measurements are assumed to be larger than 9.5 m².) Sites of all seasons are included.

Although population, livestock, and residence group size estimates follow directly from the composition of individual sites, middle-level units span multiple residence groups. In chapter 4 (and Rocek 1994) I explored the correspondence of intersite spatial patterns and middle-level social units, with mixed results. I showed that spatial proximity correlates with social relationship—spatial clusters *do* map onto middle-level social groups. In the available (post-stock reduction) ethnographic data, however, I found no clear correspondence between the existence of supraresidence group units and the formation of site clusters. Changes in spatial clustering may, nevertheless, reflect changes in social relations among residence groups under the stronger pressures toward cooperation operating *before* stock reduction. Here, I examine the Black Mesa sites under this working hypothesis. Lacking detailed ethnographic information, we cannot directly test the correspondence of spatial and social units in the archaeological data. By showing predictable correlations between changes in the spatial patterns and in population, economics, and residence group size, however, I argue that middle-level units *did* in fact develop during periods when livestock levels were high, population was low, and families (nuclear or extended) lived in small residence groups. The picture fits Left Handed's description of late nineteenth-century life on Black Mesa, and the evidence that residence groups became increasingly independent as the livestock economy collapsed in the twentieth century.

As outlined in chapter 5, I relied on two spatial-analytic techniques, nearest neighbor analysis and (to a lesser extent) quadrat analysis. The analysis includes only reliably dated habitation site components broken down into two seasonal categories, summer and winter-spring, analyzed separately. These two categories are not exclusive, because all that is required for inclusion in a category is evidence of use during certain seasons. For instance, the summer category includes not only summer sites, but sites used during spring-summer, summer-fall, spring-summer-fall, summer-winter and year-round. The subdivision is intended to identify a subset of habitation components likely to have been used contemporaneously some time during the summer months.

The second seasonal category combines winter-occupied *and* spring-occupied components. As in the summer category, this includes habitation components used during either of these times of year, regardless of occupation at other times as well. Combining spring- and winter-used sites increases the risk of including in the same analysis sites that were not actually occupied simultaneously, but rather formed sequential steps in a seasonal settlement round. However, several points favor pooling spring and winter sites. Lamb pens (the most characteristic indicator of spring use)[8] are associated with sites showing winter rather than summer use. Fischer exact probabilities for a positive association of lamb pens with winter-occupied components are .0002 if all site types are considered, and .0874 if only habitation sites are counted (Rocek 1985). This suggests that the inhabitants of winter sites often stayed on into the late winter and early spring lambing season. Therefore, winter sites may be occupied contemporaneously with spring sites. In addition, this suggests that some sites classified as spring occupations because they had lamb pens may actually be winter-spring sites.

Furthermore, because the goal is to examine interresidence group cooperation, sites from periods of maximum seasonal labor requirements should be examined. Lambing, which straddles the late winter–early spring, is one such period. Herders often stay up night and day to care for the ewes and newborn lambs, while other workers are needed to care for the rest of the herd. Finally and more pragmatically, the combination of seasonal categories increases the sample size.

As a measure of intersite spatial patterning, the nearest neighbor statistic (D) of reliably dated spring and winter habitation site components displays a complicated sequence of changes. Table 6.5 lists values of D, corrected for boundary effect (see chapter 5), computed by overlapping decadal intervals. The boundary effect correction can only be performed for intervals with more than three sites (otherwise, the formula yields the square root of a negative quantity), so only those intervals have D values.

Two factors suggest that the number of intervals used in analysis should be further reduced. First, as discussed previously, data from the 1950s and 1960s are unreliable due to occupied sites that were surveyed but not mapped. Similarly, the final period (the decade from 1975–1984, represented by "post-1975" in the table) lacks occupied sites that were surveyed in the early 1970s and thus "dated" to before 1975. The bias introduced by these factors is particularly serious for spatial data, because the number of unmapped sites varies depending on the year when a particular area was investigated by the BMAP. For these reasons, I delete the decadal intervals with midpoints 1950, 1955, 1960, 1965, 1970, and post-1975 from further analysis.

The second factor is the impact of sample size on random fluctuations in nearest neighbor analysis. Table 6.5 shows that the extreme values of D (for instance the 1880 and 1920 decades in the winter-spring data) correspond to intervals with low sample sizes. Although this may reflect a genuine tendency

Table 6.5. Nearest Neighbor Statistic Applied to the Study[a]

	Decades					Fifteen-year			
	Winter/Spring		Summer			Winter/Spring		Summer	
Interval Midpoint	N	D	N	D	Interval Midpoint	N	D	N	D
pre-1840	5	.65	..	.....	1833	5	.65	..	.....
1870	7	.68	..	.....	1868	7	.68	..	.....
1875	9	.77	..	.....	1873	10	.96	..	.....
1880	5	.38	..	.....	1878	11	.83	..	.....
1885	7	.67	..	.....	1883	10	.61	..	.....
1890	7	.98	..	.....	1888	9	.70	6	.375
1895	..	....	..	.....	1893	8	1.19	..	.....
1900	..	....	..	.....	1898	..	....	..	.....
1905	..	....	..	.....	1903	5	.64	..	.....
1910	9	.91	..	.....	1908	10	1.02	..	.....
1915	9	.86	8	.854	1913	12	.94	8	1.510
1920	6	.27	13	.703	1918	12	.86	14	1.010
1925	14	.85	11	.586	1923	17	.71	18	.870
1930	18	.94	9	1.042	1928	21	.83	15	1.370
1935	18	.81	11	.953	1933	29	1.10	16	1.300
1940	23	.99	20	.918	1938	30	.93	24	.980
1945	23	.96	23	.740	1943	34	.90	30	.829
1950	14	1.20	15	1.074	1948	26	.99	28	.718
1955	10	.99	9	1.203	1953	21	.95	19	1.004
1960	7	.72	..	.....	1958	10	.99	9	1.203
1965	..	....	..	.....	1963	7	.72	..	.....
1970	..	....	..	.....	1968	13	1.03	17	.767
post-1969	13	1.03	17	.767	1973	13	1.03	17	.767
post-1975	12	1.06	15	.730	1978	13	1.03	17	.767

a. Clark and Evans (1954) nearest neighbor statistic, corrected for boundary effect as described in chapter 5. Time intervals and seasonal categories as described in text.

of Black Mesa inhabitants to cluster close together when few neighbors were present, these extreme values are very sensitive to minor changes in the placement of individual residence groups and to any errors introduced by missing, misdated, or misidentified sites. The intervals with smallest sample sizes are also most sensitive to inaccuracies in the correction for the boundary effect. Restricting the nearest neighbor analysis to cases with larger sample sizes should reduce the random variation ("noise").

In fact, deleting the intervals with the fewest sites does reduce the fluctuations. For the winter-spring decadal data, restricting analysis to time intervals with seven or more sites reduces the variance of D dramatically (from .049 to .007) with the loss of three of the fifteen intervals from the sample. Therefore, I restricted analysis of the winter-spring decadal nearest neighbor statistic to intervals with seven or more sites (see Rocek 1985 for details of the calculation of this sample size restriction).

To further increase sample size per time period, I also calculated the corrected D value over fifteen-year intervals, with each span overlapping adjacent intervals by ten years (table 6.5). Lengthening the intervals increases the risk of including noncontemporaneous sites within a single analysis and masks short-term patterns of change. In addition, the potential for autocorrelation in the nearest neighbor data (the correlation between D for adjacent time periods; see further discussion in chapter 7) increases due to the ten-year overlap. As with the decadal data, I excluded the periods in which occupied sites are undercounted (the intervals with midpoints from 1948 through 1968, as well as 1978) and reduced fluctuations in D by deleting time intervals with the fewest sites. In the winter-spring case, using a minimum of nine sites per fifteen-year interval causes the optimal decrease in the variance of D, still leaving thirteen intervals for analysis (Rocek 1985).

Figure 6.10 shows the winter-spring nearest neighbor statistics, restricted

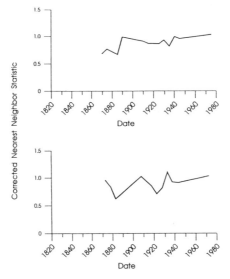

Figure 6.10. Nearest Neighbor Statistic, Spring and Winter Sites. Data points above are at ten-year intervals, below are fifteen-year intervals.

to the time intervals described previously. Despite some notable differences between the ten- and fifteen-year data, the two approaches suggest similar trends. The earliest sites from periods with sample sizes big enough to be included in the analyses (from around 1870 up to 1890) are, on average, somewhat clustered. Around 1890 the statistic jumps sharply up to suggest random or even slightly dispersed spacing. Although the fifteen-year data lack sufficient sample size in the period immediately after 1890 to be included in the analysis, they do show an increase in the next available data point (1908). Following this jump, a trend toward increasing interresidence group clustering starts again, culminating in maximum clustering (minimum nearest neighbor statistic) in the 1920s. After the early 1920s, D again begins a jagged climb. The final period, which includes the occupied sites, has a D value comparable to or slightly higher than the late 1930s to 1940s level, indicating continued lack of clustering among residence groups.

A comparison of the pattern of change in D and settlement maps (appendix B) indicates that even with the restriction to larger sample sizes of sites per time interval, the nearest neighbor statistic remains sensitive to outlying isolated sites. For instance, the contrast between the decades 1880 to 1889 and 1885 to 1895 is due to a relatively small change in site distribution involving a single isolated site in the southwestern part of the study area (subregion 1) in the latter time interval.

Still, the overall pattern of change indicated by the nearest neighbor analysis is visible in the maps. The relatively clustered pattern in the earliest time intervals with adequate sample sizes (the 1870s) corresponds to the formation of a loose east-to-west or northwest band of sites across the north-central portion of the study area. This region includes portions of the Yellow Water or Coal Mine Wash territory described by Left Handed as his family's winter area in the 1870s (Dyk 1967; location identified by Russell 1981a:49–50; n.d. interview: 6/15/76, p.3). In the early twentieth century, settlement began to fall into two major concentrations, one in the east (subregion 6), and a looser pattern in the southwest and west (particularly subregions 1–3). This is the second period (around 1920) of slightly more clustered settlement (low D).

The periods of relatively greater clustering (as measured by D) correspond to loose aggregations of sites rather than tight clumps of residence groups. The settlement fluctuations documented by changes in D, however, do not operate at the subregion scale. That is, the different degrees of clustering reflect primarily the spacing of sites within subregion-sized areas rather

Table 6.6. Subregion Quadrat Analysis[a]

Interval Midpoint	Variance/Mean (Spring and Winter)	Variance/Mean (Summer)
pre-1835	.507	.636
pre-1840	.866	.636
1840	.751	.....
1845	1.392	.....
1850	.480	.....
1855	.480	.816
1860	.....	.816
1865	.480	.....
1870	.657	.459
1875	.750	.459
1880	1.061	2.017
1885	.555	1.166
1890	.707	.724
1895	.535	.712
1900	.571	.....
1905	1.024	.....
1910	.878	.816
1915	.794	1.602
1920	2.124	.931
1925	.638	1.112
1930	.545	.395
1935	1.494	1.260
1940	.667	.887
1945	1.075	1.009
1950	.668	1.251
1955	.482	1.829
1960	.499	1.332
1970	.480	.459
post-1969	.456	1.579
post-1975	.533	1.657

a. Intervals are overlapping decades, variance/mean is the "corrected variance/mean ratio" as defined in chapter 5.

than the concentration of sites into particular subregions. This is shown by comparing the nearest neighbor results to a quadrat analysis by subregion. Table 6.6 shows the "corrected variance/mean ratio" modified to correct for unequal quadrat sizes as described in chapter 5. I limited analysis to the same time intervals as the decadal nearest neighbor analysis.

The quadrat data do not correlate with D ($r = -.071$, $N = 12$, $p > .82$). Therefore, the scale of patterning measured by the nearest neighbor most likely lies below the level of the subregion. That is, although the low values of D do not always correspond to the formation of tight clusters of sites, they also cannot be explained in terms of broad subregion-scale collections of residence groups. With the available sample size the scale cannot be pinned down precisely, but the settlement maps (appendix B) suggest that neighboring sites lie within a few kilometers of each other. Given the descriptions of middle-level groups, such a spacing between cooperating settlements seems likely.

In contrast to the winter-spring patterns, the spatial arrangement of summer sites is quite different. The analytical methods for the summer sites directly parallel the winter-spring case. Table 6.5 summarizes the nearest neighbor results. As in the winter-spring case, I deleted all but one of the recent time intervals (the deleted decadal interval center points range from 1950 to 1970 and after 1975; corresponding fifteen-year intervals are 1948 to 1968 and 1978). Also, I reduced fluctuations in the nearest neighbor statistic by deleting cases with small sample sizes; the minimum is ten sites per time interval (decreasing the number of usable intervals from eight to six) for the decadal analysis, and seven sites per interval (reducing sample size from nine to eight) for the fifteen-year case (see Rocek 1985 for details).

Figure 6.11 shows the D values for summer plotted against time, using only the time intervals satisfying these sample size minima. The short period over which summer site distributions can be examined in this sample seriously limits the analysis. Several characteristics do stand out. The summer decadal and fifteen-year patterns are comparable to each other, although there is some offset in their exact timing. Both graphs show low D values (high clustering) in the early to mid-1920s, followed by a peak in dispersion around 1930 to 1935; both also show a subsequent fall in D. The fifteen-year interval data suggest a somewhat earlier date for this drop—around 1938—than is indicated by the decade data (in which D falls after 1940). The major feature indicated by both the decade and fifteen-year patterns is the peak in interresidence group dispersion in the early to mid-1930s.

The decadal and fifteen-year data suggest greater clustering (lower value of D) in the summer than in the winter-spring settlements in corresponding time intervals, although the sample sizes limit the statistical significance of the comparison (pairwise t tests: decadal, $t = 1.746$, $N = 5$, $p < .16$; fifteen-year intervals, $t = 2.190$, $N = 8$, $p < .07$). The summer pattern has some

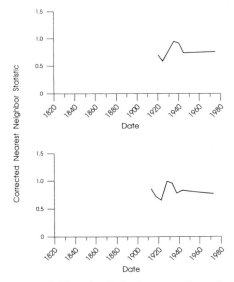

Figure 6.11. Nearest Neighbor Statistic, Summer Sites. Data points above are at ten-year intervals, below are at fifteen-year intervals.

resemblance to the winter-spring results (compare figs. 6.10 and 6.11). The sample size constraints limit the number of years that summer data are reliable, and this small sample does not yield a significant correlation between the two seasonal patterns (decadal data: $r = .015$, $N = 5$, one-sided $p > .49$; fifteen-year data: $r = .463$, $N = 8$, one-sided $p > .12$).

Like the winter-spring settlement data, the summer nearest neighbor results show no correlation with the summer quadrat analysis ($r = .038$, $N = 6$, one-sided $p > .53$). This suggests that the nearest neighbor clustering is at a smaller scale than the subregion. In fact, the settlement maps (for instance figure B.6, appendix B) show groups of sites within a kilometer or less of each other rather than loose groups of settlements scattered within subregions. This clustering, like that observed ethnographically at Shonto (see chapter 4; Rocek 1994), tends to follow major valley systems and probably corresponds to families settling around good farm land.

Population, Economy, and Society: Correlations

If cooperation among Navajo residence groups is structured as I argue in chapter 1, the changes in population and economy outlined previously should correlate with fluctuations in residence group size and with the prominence of middle-level social units (shown by clustering). Of course correlation between

Table 6.7. Correlations among Selected Variables

Var. 1[a]	Var. 2[a]	Exp.[b]	Winter-Spring						Summer					
			Decade Intervals			15-Year Intervals			Decade Intervals			15-Year Intervals		
			r	N	p<[c]	r	N	p<[c]	r	N	p<[c]	r	N	p<[c]
NN	POP	+	.739	12	.01	.364	13	.12	.137	6	.40	−.171	8	.66
NN	LS	−	−.580	12	.03	−.554	13	.03	−.141	6	.40	.112	8	.60
NN	RGS	+	.629	12	.02	.....	:	....	.243	6	.33	.....	:	....
NN	QD	−	−.071	12	.42	.....	:	....	.038	6	.53	.....	:	....
QD	POP	+	−.144	12	.33	.....	:	....	.586	6	.89	.....	:	....
QD	LS	+	−.123	12	.65	.....	:	....	−.559	6	.88	.....	:	....
QD	RGS	−	.003	12	.50	.....	:	....	.121	6	.59	.....	:	....

a. Variable abbreviations:
NN—Corrected nearest neighbor statistic (D).
POP—Population estimate (by season, number of permanent dwellings, on habitation sites).
LS—Livestock estimate (median corral area per dwelling per habitation site).
RGS—Residence group size (median number of dwellings per habitation site).
QD—Quadrat Analysis: corrected variance-mean ratio.

b. Direction of correlation expected according to hypotheses in chapter 1.

c. Significance levels are one-sided.

two variables does not demonstrate a causal relation, but causality should, under most circumstances, result in correlation (see chapter 7 for further discussion).[9]

As shown in figure 6.9 residence group size shows several shifts through time, although not a single consistent trend. Sites shrank from the pre-Fort Sumner period to a low throughout the late nineteenth century. This prolonged low was followed by a rise that began around 1900. The rise was broken in the 1920s and late 1950s. Residence group size was highest in the most recent period.

The drop in site size following the Fort Sumner period could have been a response to decreasing fear of warfare, although two factors render this interpretation unlikely. First, none of the pre-Fort Sumner habitation sites has more than two dwellings. Although median size was higher than in subsequent periods, the sites were not large aggregations useful for defense, unlike those such as the early eighteenth-century Big Bead Mesa defensive communities in the eastern Navajo country (Keur 1941). Second, the drop in size occurred around 1860, slightly before Fort Sumner. Because the threat of Ute raids persisted after 1868, declining warfare can not explain size decrease. Admittedly, the very limited samples in these early periods make all interpretations tentative.

Overall, however, shifting livestock levels suggest a better explanation for the changes in size. Residence group size (table 6.4) has a strong negative correlation with livestock levels as measured by the corral area-per-dwelling index (table 6.3) ($r = -.757$, $N = 29$, $p < .001$). This correlation is of dubious significance, because the corral area index contains counts of dwellings (which are also used to measure residence group size) in its denominator. The negative correlation persists, however, if just median corral area per habitation site (without dividing by number of dwellings) is used in the comparison ($r = -.522$, $N = 29$, $p < .01$). So, as livestock levels increased, the size of residence group (number of dwellings, and hence households) decreased.

Several additional variables relating specifically to winter-spring settlement patterns are correlated. Table 6.7 shows the correlations of the nearest neighbor statistic and quadrat analysis with residence group size, livestock levels, and human population. The most consistent correlation is between the winter-spring nearest neighbor statistic and livestock. Both the decadal and fifteen-year data show this correlation and (ignoring for the time being the question of the independence of data from overlapping time periods) even suggest that the correlations are significant at the .05 level or better. The relationship is a negative one; as livestock levels increased the value of D fell, indicating that families moved their residence groups closer together.

A second relationship in the decadal data, although less clear in the fifteen-year intervals, is a positive correlation between population and D. As population increased, so did dispersion. With low population, residence groups lived nearer each other. As noted previously, winter-spring clusters generally took the form of loose scatters with nearest neighbor distances of one or two miles (1.6–3.2 km). The loose nature of this clustering does not correspond to larger spatial units such as the subregions. The quadrat analysis does not correlate with either population or livestock (table 6.7), suggesting that the spatial shifts associated with changing human and animal populations were on a smaller scale than the subregion.

Residence group size also correlates strongly with the nearest neighbor statistic. When residence groups were relatively widely dispersed, they tended to be large. When they clustered, the individual residence groups were smaller. This correlation also conforms to the relationship between herd size and residence group spacing. As noted previously, residence group size correlates negatively with livestock levels. So, periods with large herds tended to be times with small but clustered winter-spring residence groups.[10]

Although the winter-spring sites show these intriguing correlations, *none* of the summer site patterns correlate in any meaningful way (see table 6.7; in fact, the only notable correlations involve the quadrat analysis and are in the opposite direction from those predicted). Unlike the winter-spring sample, the summer data derive almost entirely from the twentieth century. No periods earlier than 1910 have enough sites for reliable spatial analysis, so the summer data cover few time intervals and a small range of economic and demographic conditions. Therefore, the lack of correlations is not strong evidence of differences in the factors determining summer and winter settlement. In addition, the poor preservation of summer structures may bias against archaeological recognition of summer sites and obscure patterning.

Alternatively, the lack of patterning may indicate that summer locations were set by factors independent of those considered here. This may have been true particularly when summer sheep camps were widely used, freeing summer habitation site locations from many livestock-related constraints. Choices of summer settlement were probably more closely tied to the permanent field locations than to changing social or economic factors. As noted previously, the summer patterns are in general more clustered than are the winter-spring. Environmental parameters such as elevation, local topographic relief, distance to nearest drainage, and percentage of open (unwooded) land within 500 m (see Rocek 1988) all show less variation (as measured by standard deviation) on summer than on winter habitation sites. The total range in all of these variables except percentage of unwooded land is also lower among summer sites. This suggests greater concern specifically with such environmental characteristics in summer than in winter locations.

Summer settlement patterns do not change in any obvious way during the 1940s peak in agricultural field starts (fig. 6.11). If summer sites were located relative to agricultural concerns, these concerns did not shift in response to short-term changes in the intensity of agricultural production. In short, summer settlement patterns show no correlation with any of the major economic or demographic variables I examine. This may simply represent limitations of the sample, but it may also reflect genuine differences in the factors guiding the selection of summer site locations.

The combination of winter-spring and summer patterns raises two sets of issues, methodological and substantive. The limitations of, and possible improvements on, analytical techniques are important both for this study and for other attempts to use archaeological data to investigate questions such as those I have raised. The substantive issues return to the questions raised in chapter 1: Have Navajo residence group and middle-level units fluctuated in response to the economy and population, and do these groups compare to similar units in other societies?

7

Culture Change on Black Mesa:
Issues and Conclusions

The Black Mesa archaeological data offer tentative support for the changes in Navajo life hypothesized in chapter 1. Briefly, I argued that (1) as population increased, so did interresidence group competition; (2) increased pastoral production encouraged interresidence group cooperation; and (3) increased market involvement took two forms. When based on local pastoral production, market involvement simply strengthened interresidence group cooperation. When based on income *not* dependent on local production, however, it decreased interresidence cooperation, while encouraging intraresidence group aggregation and cooperation.

The first of these hypotheses, that families in adjacent residence groups competed when under pressure from crowding, fits the correlation of winter-spring dispersion and increased population. When there were too many people, they spread out. The second hypothesis, that high livestock levels fostered increased cooperation, also finds support. Winter-spring residence group clustering, which I argue reflects the formation of middle-level cooperative groups, correlates with high livestock levels.

Market involvement in the Black Mesa data cannot be separated from rising livestock levels until the stock reduction era. Both historic and archaeological evidence suggest that the large herds of the late nineteenth and early twentieth century also corresponded with stronger links to the market economy. Therefore, increased market involvement correlated with large herds and growing middle-level cooperation (indicated by increased clustering). This supports the first part of the third hypothesis. In addition, the large herds correlate with small residence group sizes. This suggests, perhaps, the transfer of some residence group-level labor organization (tasks such as shearing, for instance) to the supraresidence group level.

During the final period, after the collapse of the livestock economy, clustering decreased and residence groups were large. Despite data limitations of this period (see chapter 6 and following discussion), these changes support the second part of the third hypothesis: Increased market dependence under conditions of decreased local (livestock) production seems to break up the winter-spring residence group clusters and encourage aggregation into larger residence groups.

So, the data are compatible with all of the hypotheses, but these conclusions require qualifications and extensions. They must be seen in light of limitations of the methods of data collection and analysis, and they also should be viewed in the context of pancultural patterns of social organization beyond the Navajo case.

Critique of Methods

The way the data were collected (see chapter 5, appendix A, and Haley et al. 1983) limit and bias them in several ways. These factors are important both for evaluating the results of the Black Mesa study and for designing future archaeological efforts at social analysis.

Selection of the sample primarily using sites mapped during the BMAP 1980–82 field seasons should not introduce major biases, because the sample covers a cross-section of the topographic and environmental range in the area. The most significant bias is the limited data on recently occupied sites, many of which continue in use and were not mapped. By incorporating survey information, however, I was able to include the most recent period of use on occupied sites. As described in chapter 6, I did not analyze spatial distributions and population changes for the late 1940s through early 1970s, when the data are most affected by the missing information about earlier periods of use on occupied sites.

Current occupation patterns are not the only constraint on the archaeological data. The patchwork history of mining and associated archaeological work in the early days of the BMAP restricts spatial analysis to the subregions discussed in chapter 5. The division of the study into subregions, combined with the subdivision of components by date, function, and season, limits sample sizes. This division also constrains the analysis, because many analytical methods can only be applied to contiguous spatial blocks. These problems might in part be solved in future work simply by using larger data sets.

Restricting analysis to relatively well-studied blocks of contiguous land also limits data on portions of settlement systems beyond the boundaries of the study area (see chapter 5; cf. Kelley 1982b:202–3; Roberts 1990). The variation among subregions in seasonal data noted in chapter 6 implies that parts of multiple settlement systems are included. Although some families lived year-round on the mesa, others moved off on a seasonal basis. Even most of those living full-time on the mesa probably moved outside of the BMAP study area during part of the year. The scale of nineteenth-century mobility and variability in mobility among families and over time makes analysis at the level of the full settlement systems impossible. The goal here is less ambitious; it is simply to examine the behavior of the occupants of a series of sites who shared a region in certain decades and at certain seasons. Patterns of cooperation should be visible at this scale.

The definition and dating of site components is another limiting factor in the data. My coding strategy emphasized dating of construction episodes, and then assumed an approximately uniform occupation duration for all habitation sites. Emphasis on construction as a basis for dating site components is well grounded in many cases, because the BMAP tree-ring record provides an extremely precise way of dating many of the sites. Assuming constant occupation duration is not accurate, however, because informants make it clear that some habitation sites may be used only briefly, while others may be occupied for an extended period. The detailed data necessary to identify duration of occupation for each component are not available for the majority of sites, so an approximation such as the one I use is necessary. As a result, even with the tight tree-ring chronological control, contemporaneity of component-use is known only approximately. In the spatial analyses described in chapter 6, some of the sites within a decadal or fifteen-year interval may in fact be occupied at slightly different times, or even represent consecutive occupations by the members of a single residence group. As discussed later, there is evidence that this kind of error does occur in some cases. Furthermore, if changes in occupation duration covary with other factors, then spurious spatial patterns may result. For example, if habitation sites were moved short distances more frequently when livestock levels were high, this could produce the appearance of clustering correlated with livestock levels. Because I find a correlation of clustering and livestock, the risk of such spurious relations is significant. If, however, the arguments for an approximately constant *average* occupation duration up until the recent period is correct (chapter 6), this problem should be roughly constant through time and should not seriously affect the results of the analyses.

The lack of systematic reliable ethnographic information on site function and ownership compounds the problem. It is clearly possible that groups of sites classified as a cluster here would actually represent specialized sites of a single residence group.

Additional data limitations relate to the coding of component season. Although seasonality was coded on the majority (186 out of a total of 217 or 85 percent) of habitation site components, the procedure for specifying seasonal categories is only approximate and does not accurately determine which sites were actually in concurrent use. This is due to the imprecise seasonal categories (spring, summer, fall, and winter) and to the unreliable criteria available for identifying season. This latter problem is particularly severe on sites lacking informant data. Structure types, site layout, and location are the only bases of seasonality assessment on these sites (see Rocek 1988). Even where informant data are available, the seasonal categories are too vague to identify precisely what sites were lived in simultaneously. For instance, a site identified as a summer habitation by an informant could have been occupied anywhere within a range of several months and over a period ranging from days to more than half the year.

These weaknesses in precise seasonality identification are the reason for lumping spring and winter sites in the spatial analyses in chapter 6. That is, many of the sites identified as having winter use were probably also used in part concurrently with sites identified as spring occupations. This lumping of seasonal categories undoubtedly also results in the inclusion in a single spatial analysis of some sites that were not actually used concurrently. Some of this error could be eliminated by more detailed informant interviews and a more detailed investigation of the timing of seasonal activities. To some extent this must be recognized as a potential source of error in any archaeological analyses such as the one attempted here, which is intended to investigate interactions among concurrently used sites (cf. Roberts 1990).

Paradoxically, seasonality uncertainty is greatest on occupied sites. Due to the limited study of these settlements they have very little informant data. Of sites within subregions 1 to 6, 22 percent of occupied sites lack seasonality data, while it is unknown for only 11 percent of reliably dated habitation site components overall. Furthermore, 66 percent of season determinations for all habitation components include some informant input, but only 29 percent of the occupied sites' seasonal determinations included informant data. The missing data on recent sites are particularly unfortunate because they limit the possibility for separating certain correlated variables. In particular, the recent period is the only time when there is a clear divergence between livestock levels and market involvement. Whereas in earlier times increases in livestock were associated with growing participation in the market economy, after stock reduction, the drop in livestock caused an accelerated dependence on the market rather than a return to nonmarket subsistence. Increased data on the recent period as well as analyses of artifacts and of trading post records could help unravel the interconnections among the economic variables.

Aside from the data collection, the analytical methods impose constraints on the interpretation of the archaeological patterns. Chapters 4 and 5 outline many of these limitations, including the inability when using nearest neighbor analysis to distinguish multiple scales of patterning, its sensitivity to outliers in small samples, and the boundary effect problem (exacerbated by the multiple small subregions). Each of these has been corrected for to some degree.

To control for scale, quadrat analysis helps show the small size of clusters identified by the nearest neighbor analyses. Additional methods could be used, such as multiple quadrat analyses, for example, the dimensional analysis of variance used by Whallon (1973), nth-order nearest neighbor analysis, or a cluster analytic approach such as that used with the ethnographic patterns discussed in chapter 4 (see also Rocek 1994). All of these would be appropriate to a larger, single-block study area.

To minimize the effect of outliers and the "noise" introduced by small sample sizes, I deleted the time intervals with the smallest sample sizes from the spatial analyses. The variability of the nearest neighbor statistic (D) decreases with progressive restriction in sample size (Rocek 1985: tables 6.9, 6.11, 6.17, 6.18), because small samples are the most likely to produce "noisy" extreme values. This approach also creates a potential risk, however, because it could mask patterns in periods with very few residence groups (families living under very low population densities might actually form tight clusters with their sparse neighbors). Deleting the small samples would ignore this pattern. For instance, the winter-spring site nearest neighbor statistic correlates with both livestock levels and population. If periods with small sample sizes are included in the analysis, the strength of the livestock correlation falls drastically, although the correlation of D with human population remains strong. This is because periods that were deleted due to low sample size also have low populations. So, elimination of small samples may be underestimating the strength of the relation of clustering with population compared to livestock. Clearly, a larger overall sample, rather than the selective elimination of small samples, would be a preferable solution.

The solution to the nearest neighbor "boundary effect" is also not ideal, because it is an approximation of a complicated geometric problem (Rocek 1985). Because the values of D are simply compared among each other rather than used as probabilistic estimates, the error introduced by this approximation should not be severe. In addition, elimination of the smallest sample sizes reduces the sensitivity of the results to inaccuracies in the approximation.

The problem of small sample sizes, however, also exacerbates the dangers inherent in numerous analytical decisions involved in using archaeological data. For the spatial analysis, restriction to cases with a fairly large number of sites limits the impact of both random fluctuations from small samples or changes in the selection criteria of sites for inclusion in particular analyses. This renders the correlations between the spatial analysis and other variables fairly robust.

Other measures include cases with few sites, and so are more sensitive to small changes in which sites are included. For instance, median residence group size yields several interesting correlations discussed in chapter 6 and later in this chapter. This analysis includes sites of all seasons (and of unknown season), creating the danger that it confounds changes in the seasonal use of the mesa with changes in residence group size. If residence group size is recalculated using only sites with winter occupations (based on the assumption that winter-occupied sites have a tighter relationship between number of permanent dwellings and population), the sample size of components drops by more than 50 percent and the index changes in many decades (and three decadal intervals drop from analysis because they have no winter-use components). Not surprisingly, this can affect the correlations outlined in chapter 6. The correlation of residence group size with the nearest neighbor statistic is only trivially affected (increased from $r = .629$ to $r = .670$), because it is already restricted to time intervals with large sample sizes. The correlation of the corral area per dwelling index with residence group size is weakened (from $r = -.757$, $n = 29$, one-sided p<.001 to $r = -.329$, $N = 26$, one-sided $p < .06$), and the correlation with corral area itself is nearly eliminated, dropping from $r = -.522$ ($N = 29$, one-sided $p < .005$) to $r = -.199$ ($N = 26$, one-sided $p < .17$).[1] Clearly, the data used to demonstrate the latter correlation are less robust and are sensitive to particular analytical decisions. Independent methods of evaluating the relationships suggested by the archaeological data are needed.

The use of correlations to test the hypothesized patterns of cause and effect raise similar problems. Many of the variables correlate with each other, and many of them also correlate with time. Partial correlation analysis lends support to the interpretation presented here. The occurrence of the predicted correlations at least fails to falsify the hypotheses. But the ultimate evaluation of the results cannot rest on correlations alone; external (particularly ethnographic) examination of the suggested patterns is essential, a point I will return to later.

Two final issues bear on the reliability of the results: the problem of missing data and the question of an appropriate measure of intersite distance. The first of these is a universal problem in archaeological spatial analyses. As described in chapters 5 and 6, the site sample was designed to provide data that were as complete as possible on the areas included in the analysis. When the analysis is restricted to "reliably dated" habitation site components that also are identified to season, the sample is reduced to 168 out of 217 components (77 percent). Although not ideal, the percentage (23 percent) of missing cases (components not included in the analysis because of unknown date or season) is not extreme.

Assuming that missing data are distributed randomly across the study area, the effects of missing cases on the spatial analyses can be estimated by randomly deleting sites and recalculating D. A series of nine simulations of this sort (Rocek 1985: table 5.6) using a slightly higher average percentage of missing data show that D from the full samples and simulated partial samples (with 29 percent missing cases) have a strong correlation ($r = .82$, $N = 9$, $p < .01$). So, even with 29 percent missing cases, the nearest neighbor analysis from the partial samples account for roughly 67 percent (r^2) of the variability in the full sample.

The other problematic aspect of the nearest neighbor analyses is the use of linear-distance-based measures of spatial relations. As indicated in chapter 1, the reasoning behind the predicted spatial correlates of social units is the expectation that travel time and effort between residence groups will be minimized when they are members of the same cooperating middle-level unit. Ideally, then, it would be more appropriate to use a measure of travel time rather than simple distance. Such an approach might use estimates based on differences between speed of travel along valleys versus travel between them, or the effect of topographic variability along travel routes. Although the present study uses simple linear distance as a first approximation, such refinements could be developed using geographical information systems (GIS) techniques in future work.

A related issue is the effect of changes in transportation technology on settlement patterns. In the earliest time periods, foot and horseback travel were the primary means of transportation. It is possible that as horse herds grew in the Black Mesa area in the 1880s and 1890s (Dyk and Dyk 1980:52, 266–267), reliance on horses increased at the expense of foot travel. Wagons probably did not become widespread in the area until the last decade of the nineteenth century or so (Dyk 1967:333; Dyk and Dyk 1980:385, 387), but by the early 1910s, they were widely distributed across the reservation (Brugge 1980:291).

The wagon constrained choices of residence location by making areas too rough for wagons undesirable. This restriction was probably relatively slight, however, because wagons are capable of traveling over very rough terrain. At the same time, wagons permit greater freedom from other settlement constraints. For example, hauling water to a residence from a distant source is more practical with a wagon than with a horse. Perhaps then, the decrease in clustering around the turn of the century (fig. 6.10), is in part a consequence of the availability of improved transportation. This possibility can be tested using data on changes in site placement relative to resources such as water, agricultural land, and hidden or easily defensible terrain. Changes in transportation should also be included in computations of intersite travel time. Finally, shifts in transportation, first the wagon and then motor vehicles, may also have affected settlement duration (Brugge, personal communication 1985; Kelley 1982b, 1986).

After the early twentieth century, travel technology probably did not undergo major changes until the late 1950s and early 1960s (Russell n.d.), with the construction of new roads and the purchases of motor vehicles. These changes should only affect the most recent time interval in the spatial analyses. Reliance on motor transport is likely to encourage families to settle along improved roadways. As noted in the analysis of settlement at Copper Canyon (chapter 4), this results in the formation of linear site clusters along roads. A shift to increasing clustering of this kind is not shown by the Black Mesa settlement patterns of either the winter-spring or summer sites (figs. 6.10 and 6.11). As in all of the ethnographic patterns except Copper Canyon (see chapter 4; Rocek 1994), a shift to roadside locations does not seem to be a major factor in settlement in the study area, though some informants did indicate that access to roads influenced their seasonal movements (Russell n.d.:1980 interviews, p. 50).

In addition, given the uncertainty regarding seasonal identification for the final time period, it is possible that the analyses miss some changes. For instance, despite the historically known shift toward year-round occupation, only 29 percent of occupied habitations could be coded as year-round based on the available data. This is because, lacking informant data, sites are only classified as year-round if they show clear indications of multiseason use: for instance shades, lamb pens, and sheltered (winter) corrals all on one site. Lacking such clear evidence, sites are usually classified according to the most distinctive characteristics: summer shades, spring lamb pens, or winter corrals in sheltered locations. These interpretations based on prominent season-specific structures may reflect the former function of a site, before it came to be regularly used year round. In any case, it is likely that seasonal identifications on sites lacking informant data are biased to miss evidence of multiseason use.

If we assume that *all* currently occupied habitation sites in the sample are now occupied year-round, the resulting corrected D statistic is .89 (N = 27), suggesting an increase in clustering in winter-spring locations (but a slight drop in summer sites, see table 6.5). Clearly, additional seasonality data on these recent sites would be of considerable value.

The Lessons of Black Mesa

Despite the methodological limitations, the results of the Black Mesa analyses suggest several conclusions, as well as avenues for future research. Although the specifics must be tailored to the available data, the type of period-by-period analysis employed here could be applied to other well-dated archaeological sequences. The data in chapter 6 suggest that archaeological measurement of population and economic change on Black Mesa is relatively straightforward. As noted in chapter 4 (and Rocek 1994), the correspondence of spatial proximity and shared membership in social units is encouraging, because it suggests that spatial association may reflect aspects of social relations. The test for a correspondence between the existence of middle-level units and the occurrence of spatial clusters (chapter 4) fails. Given the limited ethnographic cases available, however, this failure is insufficient to reject the possibility of such patterns among the stronger cooperative units that existed prior to stock reduction.

The ethnographic analyses (chapter 4; see also Rocek 1994) also suggest substantive results regarding variation in Navajo settlement. Residence groups tend toward dispersion at the finest scale of analysis; they maintain greater than random spacing among themselves. Furthermore, this dispersion does not correlate simply with population or residence group density, but appears to relate to other factors such as economics or the distribution of resources.

The analyses of residence group size and interresidence group spacing discussed in the second half of chapter 6 directly address the issues of social organization raised in chapters 1 and 3. Residence group size correlates negatively with livestock levels: as livestock population increases, residence group size falls. This contradicts a common-sense expectation that residence groups of rich individuals will be large (cf. Netting 1982).[2] Furthermore, it suggests that as herds increased in size, the intraresidence group labor pool actually decreased, rather than increasing to compensate for the growing number of livestock.

As discussed in chapter 1, I suggest that, during periods with high livestock levels, labor cooperation expands beyond the residence group to a middle-level unit. The social group filling occasional labor requirements need not be very large, except in the case of extremely big herd owners. The sort of unit is more likely comparable to Kluckhohn's (1966) group or Collier's (1966) cooperating-groups than to the larger types of outfit level units (cf. Kelley and Whiteley 1989).[3]

If the decrease in residence group size is accompanied by the formation of supraresidence group cooperating units, I argue that these should be recognizable as spatial clusters of sites. The results of the winter-spring spatial analysis fit this expectation: There is a correlation of clustering with increases in livestock levels and with decreases in residence group size. This clustering is on a relatively small spatial scale, compatible with small middle-level groups of several families.

Given the results of the ethnographic spatial analysis, the increase in archaeological site clustering cannot be proven to represent the formation of middle-level cooperating units. But increased clustering associated with high livestock levels is not what would be predicted based on competition for grazing land; increased dispersion would seem a more likely response. So, the combination of decreasing residence group size and increasing interresidence group aggregation is compatible with the formation of supraresidence group cooperation, most likely among closely related families (see chapter 3). The combination of small intraresidence group social units with supraresidence group cooperation would limit aggregation of livestock within a single residence group's grazing range, but facilitate access to extra labor from other residence groups when needed. If this interpretation is correct, this case suggests an interesting variation on Sahlins' (1972:224–27) argument that interhousehold cooperation decreases with specialization for market production. In the Black Mesa case, the unit of close interhousehold cooperation, the residence group, may be decreasing in size. However, the formation of less tightly organized supraresidence group units provides access to assistance lost by the shrinkage in residence group size.

Human population levels also correlate with dispersion among winter-spring habitation sites, at least in the decadal-interval calculations (table 6.7). Because both population and livestock correlate with the nearest neighbor statistic, the relative importance of the two variables in predicting settlement changes is important. That is, does one of the variables by itself explain the variation in D while the other merely covaries with the trends in this first variable? Partial correlation analysis offers an answer by measuring the degree of correlation between a pair of variables after the effects of another variable have been accounted for. In this case, I measured the correlation of D with population after accounting for the correlation of D with livestock levels, and the correlation of D with livestock levels after accounting for its correlation with population. These partial correlations retain the same patterns suggested by the variables considered separately: Growing population is associated with greater dispersion regardless of changes in livestock levels (decadal partial $r_{PD.L} = .64$, $n = 12$, one-sided $p < .02$; fifteen-year interval partial $r_{PD.L} = .34$, $n = 13$, one-sided $p < .14$), and higher livestock levels go with more clustering (decadal partial $r_{LD.P} = -.38$, $n = 12$, one-sided $p < .13$; fifteen-year interval partial $r_{LD.P} = -.54$, $n = 13$, one-sided $p < .04$; where P, D, and L represent population, the nearest neighbor statistic, and livestock levels respectively). The implication of these comparisons is that neither population nor livestock by themselves account for winter-spring settlement variability; each variable is important, even after the effects of the other are considered. The summer values show no such pattern (the strongest summer partial correlations yield one-sided probabilities exceeding .47).

This approximate equality in partial correlations depends strongly on the deletion of time intervals with small sample sizes. As noted in the critique of methods previously discussed, the inclusion of periods with very few sites would drastically shift the relative values of the correlations in favor of population and away from livestock. Based on time intervals with relatively large samples of sites, however, the correlations suggest that both decreases in livestock *and* increases in human population covary with increases in spacing among winter-spring habitation sites. Following the argument outlined in chapter 1, if rising livestock levels encourage residence groups to cluster near each other for mutual assistance, rising population increases competition for land and the tendency for residence groups to avoid settling too close to their neighbors.

The positive relationship between population and interresidence group dispersion differs from the ethnographic spatial analysis (chapter 4, Rocek 1994), where no such correlation was evident. The Black Mesa data confirm that population is not the only relevant factor, however, because livestock levels also correlate with settlement patterns. In addition, the correlations in the BMAP analyses relate to winter-spring settlement, whereas the ethnographic results were clearer in the summer patterns.

The Black Mesa summer settlement patterns do not show the same trends as the winter-spring sites. Although this may simply reflect the smaller sample of time periods and the greater taphonomic problems associated with summer sites, it may also reflect a genuine contrast between the factors guiding summer and winter-spring settlement. Much of the labor-intensive activity (lambing and shearing) associated with sheep occurs in the late winter to early spring. Agriculture is more closely tied to permanent, immobile fields, which might decrease flexibility in summer site placement. The stronger clustering of summer compared with winter-spring habitation sites may reflect concentration around agricultural land.

Overall, then, results of the Black Mesa analyses fit the ideas outlined in chapter 1. The interaction of archaeologically identified social units with changes in population, the livestock economy, and the market are all compatible with the hypotheses I outlined there. The BMAP archaeological data do not cover the most recent case of market involvement in which wages become dominant and reliable for some families. This further development of the wage economy and the resultant disparities in income may now (or soon) be disrupting the large residence groups suggested by the limited data on recent sites (cf. Aberle 1989:410; Goode 1963; Levy et al. 1989:356; Wilk and Netting 1984:10). This predicted change would take the form of outmigration of nuclear families to centers of wage labor and, perhaps, the development of more nuclear family residence groups within the study area.

The match of the archaeological results and the hypothesized changes in social units is not conclusive. Informant data suggest a few relatively clear cases where my analytical procedures resulted in the identification of spatial clusters of sites that actually represent sequential occupations of a single residence group, rather than a spatial aggregation of concurrently occupied, cooperating residence groups. The eastern cluster of spring-winter sites during the period 1915 to 1924 (see table 6.5 and appendix B) represents such a case. Because of the sample size of only six sites, this interval was not used in the decadal spatial analyses. It does, however, enter into the fifteen-year interval results. Here, informants identified at least the two closest neighboring sites as having been occupied by themselves and their families. The two sites were used within a few years of each other, probably by some or all of the same people. The third, more distant site in the eastern cluster probably also belonged to the same family, although the informant data regarding this site are somewhat sketchy.

In contrast, there are cases in which informant identifications of occupants at contemporary adjacent sites imply only partial or no overlap in residence group membership, and hence perhaps true contemporaneous supraresidence group clusters. Generally, informant data are simply too imprecise to identify exact residence group membership. Informants often simply refer to a "family" or some particular individuals who occupied a series of sites. Middle-level units have been described as developing through a cycle of fissioning from a parental residence group into multiple, related cooperating residence groups (Reynolds et al. 1967; see chapter 3). So, the identification of the same "family" or some particular individuals who occupied nearby sites is inadequate to distinguish sequential use by a single residence group unit from concurrent occupation by fissioning closely related residence groups. The Black Mesa informant data also make reference to cases where a daughter sometimes shared her mother's residence and sometimes lived separately, a pattern of fluctuating residence group composition that fits the period of fission and the operation of a nascent middle-level unit.

Resolution of these issues requires more extensive and detailed informant data on the occupants and duration of use of sites identified here as contemporary. Such an approach has its costs as well as benefits, however, because shifting to primary reliance on informant data increases the likelihood of bias introduced through selective or faulty memories. What is needed is an intensive *combination* of ethnographic and archaeological investigation (particularly one using separate interviews with multiple informants). Given the sensitivity of the archaeological measures used here to the various coding and site selection criteria, only such a combination of ethnographic and archaeological data can give confidence in the interpretations of site dates, functions, and in the composition of the social units.

Still, the available informant data also offer support for the interpretation of the settlement patterns proposed here. A case in point is an east-west division in site locations that developed in the early twentieth century among the winter-spring sites. Although parts of these eastern and western clusters probably represent sequential site occupations of the sort noted previously, the division between the two clusters fits well with the informant-based genealogical history in the study area. The two clusters appear to correspond to descendants of two different wives of one of the original Navajo settlers of the region, Many Mules or Who Has Mules (see chapters 2 and 5, and Dyk 1967; Dyk and Dyk 1980). The eastern sites were occupied by descendants of Many Mules' first wife (some informant data suggest a relationship through a sister of Many Mules in this genealogical line as well) and the affinal kin of these descendants. The western cluster is made up, at least in part, of descendants of Many Mules' second wife. The genealogical data further suggest a north-south division within the western cluster. The family of one of Many Mule's granddaughters along with her husband's siblings and their descendants occupied the south-central part of the western lease area, while her younger sister's family occupied the northern part. This division dates to the late 1920s or 1930s, because some sites from that period were occupied by both sisters (the granddaughters of Many Mules) together. So, the site sample documents the process of residence group fissioning. This represents an example of the developmental cycle of social units that is described ethnographically in the development of supraresidence group units (Goody 1958; Lamphere 1977; Reynolds et al. 1967).

The Black Mesa archaeological data may document the developmental cycle in another way, by a cyclical pattern of autocorrelation among adjacent time periods. Because several of the analyses use overlapping decadal and fifteen-year time intervals, adjacent intervals might be expected to produce highly correlated values. This would yield a high level of temporal autocorrelation; that is, a variable from time period t should correlate with the same variable measured at time period t-1, t-2, and so forth. This is methodologically important because it would render statistical tests for significance invalid in the strictly probabilistic sense (because observations from adjacent or close time periods are not independent).

Table 7.1. Autocorrelation of
Residence Group Size,
by Overlapping Decade Intervals.

Lag	r	N	<p
1	.54	28	.01
2	− .04	27	.86
3	− .32	26	.12
4	− .41	26	.04
5	− .12	25	.57
6	.25	24	.24
7	.34	23	.12
8	− .05	22	.82
9	− .55	21	.01
10	− .47	20	.04

See text and footnotes for details of the calculations.

The actual pattern of many of the variables do not match the expectation of autocorrelation. The population estimates for both summer and winter are the only variables that behave as expected. Both the decadal and fifteen-year interval population autocorrelations are strongly positive (most exceed values of .60) for lags ranging from one to ten intervals,[4] and in all cases the correlations are significant at better than the .05 level. This merely reflects the unsurprising fact that population in any time period is strongly dependent on population in previous periods.

Residence group size offers the most interesting contrast to the simple expectation of positive autocorrelation (table 7.1). Although the initial correlation (lag 1) is strongly positive, the correlations fall rapidly with increasing lag, reaching a strong negative value around a lag of three to four decadal intervals, about fifteen to twenty years. The correlations then rise again up to a lag of seven, about thirty-five years, and fall again at a lag of nine, or forty-five years. The pattern is not merely a simple positive correlation between adjacent time intervals, but rather a cyclical rise and fall with a period of around thirty-five years.[5]

The cyclicity in residence group size is suggestive of the family developmental cycle. For example, if a residence group begins as a single household consisting of parents and young children, it might occupy a single hogan. As daughters grow to adulthood, some of them would (following the Navajo ideal norm of uxorilocal residence) bring husbands and build hogans alongside their parents. This stage would produce a multi-hogan site. As the daughters' families get children of their own, the residence group eventually fissions and some daughters move off to found new independent sites, analogous to the original one-hogan residence group (Lamphere 1977:76–81). The predicted period of the cycle is difficult to estimate without specific demographic data, because the age at which fissioning occurs may vary from community to community (Lamphere 1977:28–29).

Because only a few ancestral residence groups made up the original Navajo settlement of the study area, generational cycles of the families may have remained roughly synchronous for some time, permitting recognition of this cyclicity in residence group sizes. The possibility of actually tracking this cycle archaeologically is intriguing, and warrants further study. Gilpin (1982) has also suggested evidence of the domestic cycle in Navajo archaeological data. Again, more detailed informant data would be valuable. For instance, analysis of residence group-size trends subdivided by family use areas might be productive.

Other variables yield similar though less clear results. Livestock levels, measured by the corral area index, suggest the same cyclicity, although with considerably weaker correlations. The period is around thirty to thirty-five years, but only the positive correlation for a lag of one (five-year offset) and negative correlation for a lag of ten (fifty-year offset) have strong significance levels (lag = 10: for decadal data $r = -.52$, $n = 19$, $p < .03$; for fifteen-year interval data $r = -.41$, $n = 22$, $p < .07$). Perhaps this cyclicity reflects the growth of family livestock holdings, associated with the social developmental cycle. This index may inherently follow patterns in residence group size, however, because it is computed by dividing corral area by residence group size (the number of permanent dwellings on each site). Median corral area per habitation site (not divided by dwellings) still suggests a possible cyclical pattern, but in this case the period is much longer and the pattern is less clear. The first peak in negative correlations does not occur until a lag of eight (forty years), and the period appears to be around seventy years (for lag 14, decadal data, $r = .69$, $n = 25$, $p < .01$).

The measures of interresidence group spatial relations cover too few time intervals to permit productive examination of autocorrelation. None of these variables even produce significant (at less than the .18 level) positive autocorrelations for a lag of one. Interestingly, all yield negative autocorrelations within the range of lag of one to four intervals, but none of these correlations are significant at better than the .16 level. Perhaps the same cyclicity shown by residence group size *is* present in the settlement data (representing the cycle of isolated residence groups fissioning into clusters of associated daughter groups, which eventually move off to reproduce the pattern of isolated residence groups and continue the cycle), but this cannot be distinguished from the general noise in the measures of settlement patterning.[6] It is clear that the simple model of strong *positive* autocorrelation that applies to population trends does not fit the settlement data.

So despite its limitations, the archaeological record of Navajo occupation on northern Black Mesa documents changes that conform to expectations derived from studies of both Navajo society and cross-cultural comparisons described in chapter 1. This is shown by the broad trends and inter-variable correlations discussed previously. A finer scale of developmental process underlying these trends may also be documented by the pattern of autocorrelations. The potential for further study is clear.

Some of the results contradict conclusions of previous studies. For example, the negative correlation of residence group size and livestock levels suggested here is unexpected in light of several ethnographic analyses that show higher rates of polygamy and extended family residence associated with high livestock dependence (Aberle 1961:120; Kluckhohn and Leighton 1946:55). Ethnographic data on residence group size (as opposed to family organization) is, however, comparable to the findings suggested by the Black Mesa data (cf. Henderson and Levy 1975:118). These results also match evidence of a recent trend toward increased residence group size (e.g., Kelley 1982b:115, 124). Again, a critical variable may be shifts in size and organization among different scales of social units. For instance, a higher rate of polygamy associated with high livestock levels need not lead to larger residence groups, if the wives live in separate residence groups or if the generational span of residence groups is reduced. Furthermore, synchronic data comparing several different communities or comparing families within a single community is not directly comparable to data on change within a community over time.

Many questions regarding the relationship of economic and demographic factors with changes in social organization remain to be investigated, and a wide range of variables are involved. This study has examined a few of these factors, under conditions not readily accessible to direct historic or ethnographic study. Future studies using ethnographic, historical, and archaeological data can contribute to an understanding of these issues, and clearly a heavier emphasis on *combining* detailed ethnographic data with archaeological data is warranted. These studies must also examine multiple levels of social organization simultaneously, rather than investigating a single level, such as the household or residence group, in isolation. The pattern of alternative levels of cooperation noted in Navajo society and investigated here may be a widespread social phenomenon, often neglected in studies that focus on just one scale of social analysis.

8

Middle-level Social Units:
Beyond the Navajo Case

Having presented a detailed case study of an archaeological approach to Navajo economic, population, and social unit change, the question remains what relevance this example has to social variability in general. In the introductory chapter, I presented arguments for the relation of social organization and underlying economic and demographic conditions. My perspective is best summarized by Eggan's (1960:49) remark that "social structures have jobs to do"; thus they may be expected to reorganize themselves as the "jobs" required of them change. In selectionist terms, when the conditions to which a particular social structure is adapted change, the current form of the structure is stressed and this stress is likely to select among alternative forms.

Multiple levels of social organization such as those described for the Navajos can be discerned in all societies. Variability in composition exists at all levels, ranging from the household to the largest subsets of a society, and change can occur at all levels. A substantial literature has developed in recent years regarding the household level of organization (e.g., Laslett and Wall 1972; Netting et al. 1984; Segalen 1986, with references). This interest complements a longstanding tradition of anthropological research on somewhat higher level social units (lineages, clans, communities and so forth; cf. Netting et al. 1984). This combination of research has given limited attention to middle-level units, however, and has neglected the interaction of changes at the different levels.

The major focus of the Navajo example was on change in outfit, cooperating group, or more generally middle-level social units, which have taken on significance during certain periods of Navajo history and in some parts of the

Navajo country. The middle-level is one that appears to offer great flexibility, as it brings together on a sporadic basis fairly independent and permanent units (residence groups). These groups come together under conditions requiring cooperation above the lowest levels. Rather than a restricted concern for whether a Navajo term or kinship category exists that corresponds to the middle-level units, my emphasis has been on the degree to which middle-level "action groups" (Freeman 1961) form with sufficient regularity to result in recognizable functional units.

It is instructive to examine the range of middle-level social units that have been described outside the Navajo context. Of particular interest are the kinds of situations in which middle-level units comparable to those among the Navajos occur and the circumstances under which they function. The following discussion is not exhaustive, but touches on several examples that occur under diverse circumstances.

Prior to examining middle-level groups in other cultures, however, it is useful to reiterate four of the basic characteristics most generally ascribed to these units as they occur among the Navajos.

First, although they have been characterized by some researchers as frequently containing a matrilineal core group, this does not define the unit. That is, although small matrilineage segments often make up part of an outfit or cooperating group, the groups are not in general coterminous with any lineage-based structures, nor are particular lineal ties essential for their formation. Not only can matrilateral or patrilateral ties link members, but affinal connections and perhaps even nonkinship criteria such as friendship may be involved. Thus, the groups typically contain the spouses as well as the children of component families. They are not unilineal structures; hence Adams' (1983) abandonment of his term the "resident lineage" and Aberle's (1981a, 1981b) abandonment of the "local clan element." So, unlike some of the examples of middle-level groups discussed in this chapter, the Navajo units exist largely independently of the lineage-based structures such as clans. Navajo clans, which *are* unilineally based, contrast to middle-level units in that they are geographically dispersed, and serve primarily only in the regulation of marriage. Although relatives who cooperate are of necessity often members of the same clan, the clan itself is not a basis for the establishment of cooperating units.

Second, although these units are not always characterized by direct residential contiguity, their composition nevertheless has a residential component. The member residential units must live in the same community, and as shown in chapter 5 (and Rocek 1994) some degree of spatial proximity is a correlate of membership.

Third, these units are in general said to either currently form action groups or to have functioned in some such way in the past. This does not mean that all of the members of the unit would actually come together on any occasion for a particular activity. Membership in the groups corresponds not merely to a social category, however, but to a web of cooperation that characterized some of the interactions among the member resident groups.

Finally, two different forms of integration appear to be included within the middle-level of Navajo social organization. "Cooperating groups" or "groups" as described by Kelley (1986), Collier (1966), and Kluckhohn (1966), and perhaps the "sibling groups" of Reynolds et al. (1967), contrast with the more diffuse outfits. The former are often spatially fairly closely aggregated, typically involve many close kin ties, and may be a basis for frequent cooperation in a variety of circumstances; the latter are larger, spatially more diffuse and have most often been cited in connection with the regulation of land. It is the former cooperating group level on which much of the analysis here has focused.

Are Comparable Middle-level Units Found in Other Societies?

Flexibility of kin-group composition and boundary definition comparable to that found in Navajo middle-level units has figured most prominently in three sorts of ethnographic cases. Lamphere (1977) has drawn attention to the relevance of two of these: nonunilineally organized (cognatic) groups and social networks. The first category of organization includes personal (bilateral) kindreds and nonunilineal descent groups (ramages). These occur most prominently in societies that have little or no development of unilineal corporate groups, many of which are found in portions of Southeast Asia and Oceania. The second type of organization, the network, is the form that Lamphere suggests is most relevant to the Navajo case. Although a network description has been applied to a variety of cases, it has most often been used to describe urban social groups.

A third case of flexible kin group composition is found in the literature of pastoral nomadic societies. Despite the range of particular kinship systems found in such societies, most appear to share this element of flexible middle-level group formation, which has economic significance similar to that proposed here for the Navajos.

Certain cognatic forms of organization found worldwide are clearly comparable to the Navajo case. The blend of kinship, local residence, and cooperation that characterizes the Navajo middle-level units do not fit neatly into the conventional pigeonholes of kinship analysis. As noted earlier, societies lacking in well developed unilineal corporate institutions display two broad classes of nonunilineal social units, nonunilineal descent groups (or ramages), and personal kindreds, which show similarities to the Navajo situation.

A ramage, which is defined as a group of kin who share a common ancestor (by either agnatic or uterine links) is in many ways analogous to lineages that are found in unilineally structured societies (Davenport 1959, 1963; Murdock 1949, 1960). Eggan (1960) has suggested that such units are in fact the bilaterally organized functional analogues of unilineal descent groups (cf. Fox 1967; Goodenough 1970). The larger forms of Navajo middle-level units (outfits), involving the fissioned descendants of an ancestral extended family, might well take on the form of a ramage.

Personal kindreds, in contrast to ramages, are not truly descent groups (based around an ancestor), but consist rather of an array of people cognatically related to a particular living individual. The kindred, or kindred-based group (Freeman 1961) is perhaps the most appropriate of the terms commonly employed in describing social units to apply to the Navajo cooperating group (cf. Lamphere 1977). In order for the term to apply to the Navajo case, the kindred must be taken in its broadest sense of a group containing "persons connected by genealogical (including marital) ties to [a] focal kinsman" (Goodenough 1970:47), but even beyond this definition the additional criteria of cooperation and local coresidence apply. Furthermore, although fairly close relatives usually make up Navajo middle-level units, the genealogical links may be defined very broadly so that, again using Goodenough's broad definition, the "open-ended extension of kin relationships makes it possible to develop extended kindreds in which membership is effectively bounded not by genealogical distance but by practical geographical and social constraints on social intercourse" (Goodenough 1970:49). This characterization of the kindred far exceeds some narrower definitions (e.g., Freeman 1961; Murdock 1964) but is sufficiently broad to include the range of middle-level units found in Navajo society. As indicated by Murdock (1960, 1964), kindreds may form "occasional kin groups"—social units that express their corporate functions on an occasional, rather than regular basis. At such times, they compose "action groups" (Freeman 1961), visible "on the ground" in terms of behavior.

Ramages and to an even greater degree personal kindreds are noted for their flexible composition and function (Davenport 1959, 1963; Goodenough 1955). There are probable historical factors that account for some of the patterns of distribution of cognatically organized societies and the prominence of ramages or kindred-based groups—for instance the distribution of these systems in Southeast Asia and Oceania. There is also evidence that the flexibility of these groups is critical and, as in the Navajo case, allows for change in social structure as different organizational needs develop.

Davenport (1959) has suggested a range in the degree of flexibility among contrasting forms of social organization. Unilineal systems tend to put the most constraints on group formation and change, ramage (nonunilineal descent) groups offer more options, and bilateral systems structured around personal kindreds are the most flexible. Based on this view, shifts in the principles of group formation should be one method of dealing with changing adaptive conditions. A few possible examples of such change illustrate this point.

Eggan (1960) describes how the Sagada Igorots, on the Island of Luzon in the Philippines, have apparently modified a system based around bilateral kindreds to a structure that includes more cohesive and stable geographically defined wards. This shift took place in the context of agricultural intensification and the growing threat of raids. He suggests that in other societies, including some Formosan groups, the development of lineage descent groups might have been another method of introducing stability into a system that was formerly purely cognatic in organization. The reverse process—loss of unilineal organization in favor of cognatic structure—has been suggested for certain reindeer pastoralists who have adopted extensive herding practices (Beach 1981; Pehrson 1957), and for some northern Athapaskan hunter-gatherers (e.g., VanStone 1974:53).

Aside from pointing out the comparability of cognatic structures, Lamphere (1977) has examined at length the applicability of the concepts of sets and networks to Navajo middle-level social cooperation. Network analysis has most often been applied in urban settings, usually to cognatically organized groups (e.g., references cited in Lamphere 1977; Lomnitz 1977; Segalen 1986). As Lamphere suggests, however, identification of the web of relations that form the network and analysis of the principles guiding network relations is a broadly applicable technique.

Although much of the discussion in preceding chapters has treated middle-level organization as a discrete (presence or absence) dichotomy, such organization actually forms a continuum from isolated households or residence groups to tightly linked collections of these groups. Lamphere (1970, 1977) has argued that the appropriate way to analyze Navajo interresidence group relations is through the use of the concept of the network and set. The former is defined as "an unbounded system of relationships between pairs of people making up a field of activity," while the latter is "a finite number of linkages initiated by an ego that forms part of such a network" (Mayer 1966, cited in Lamphere 1977:94). That is, the network is the web of relationships that define potential social units, although the latter is the "occasional group" or "action group" based on this web.

Although I have not used network analysis here, it is not at odds with my approach. In particular, the crystalization of relatively discrete middle-level social units that is the focus of this study represents one end of a range of degree and frequency of cooperative interaction and consistency along network channels (see discussion of Dyson-Hudson 1972 later in this chapter). The flexibility of middle-level organization derives from this characteristic of its units—they can range from tightly integrated clusters of cooperating domestic units to open networks of independent social units, without requiring reorganization of the smaller units or the creation of new categories of relationships. Two examples serve to illustrate the range of network integration and potential adaptability of systems that have been characterized as organized around networks.

Although not formally applying a network perspective, Yengoyan (1971) describes the Mandaya on the Island of Mindanao in the Philippines in terms of a very loosely integrated network of economically independent households. Relations between households in traditional Mandaya society are based around cognatically structured personal kindreds, and geographically derived neighborhood networks, neither of which possess significant corporate functions.

This pattern of loose interhousehold relations has been altered in part of Mandaya territory by a switch from extensive subsistence swidden farming to intensive, market-oriented cultivation. The result has been an increased need for capital in farm equipment, suitable land, and labor, and this in turn has encouraged changes in social structure. In particular, interhousehold cooperation has resulted in the consolidation of settlements into compounds (*sitios*) that, in turn, are clustered into *barrios*. Interfamily cooperation is most often structured around male sibling bonds. Yengoyan suggests that if the process of integration and stabilization of interfamily relations continues, a lineage structure may emerge.

Foster (1984) applies graph theory to a network-based analysis of flexible middle-level social relations in Thailand. He describes a loose association among households in the village of Tha Sung, where middle-level units are characterized by limited ties such as co-attendance at funerals, potential economic assistance, and kinship relations. Such units are comparable to recent forms of Navajo middle-level units as described by Lamphere and others. In contrast, Foster (1984) cites descriptions of more tightly integrated middle-level units in other Thai villages where labor, tools, work animals, and cooked food may be shared, kin ties are strong (the elder women of the constituent households are siblings), political cooperation is close, and the households may even occupy the same residential compound (Keyes 1975; Mizuno 1971).

Foster suggests that this contrast is due to the diverse economy of Tha Sung village, where most families have an independent source of income, as opposed to the more uniform agricultural focus of the other communities. Foster also suggests that the multiple independent sources of income within Tha Sung encourage economic pooling within households and that large, complex households form at the same time that middle-level interhousehold cooperation decreases (Foster 1984:94). Thus, much as in the Navajo case of decreasing local production and increasing wage income dependence, Foster's account suggests the co-occurrence of decreasing middle-level cooperation and increasing lower-level (household-residence unit) pooling and expansion.

The variability of middle-level relations indicated by the Thai data is comparable to that apparent in the Navajo case. Interestingly, as much as Navajo society has been characterized as flexible and "fuzzy" (Aberle 1963; Adams 1971), Thai social organization has been described as "loosely structured" (Embree 1950).

Pastoral Nomads

Given the pastoral focus of the Navajo economy until the 1950s and the livestock-related basis of many Navajo economic changes, pastoral nomad social organization is an obvious place to seek comparisons. As noted previously, groups practicing extensive forms of reindeer pastoralism have been cited as possible examples of the loss of rigid unilineal organizational principles in favor of flexible cognatic organization suited to their economies. Navajo social organization is not restricted to cognatically structured groups, but rather like most pastoralists (in contrast to those reindeer herders) *does* emphasize unilineal groups. The emphasis on flexibility in the reindeer herder's organization, however, may not be different in principle from the Navajo case. Overall, comparison of the Navajo case to the diverse literature of pastoral nomad social organization suggests numerous parallels, as well as some differences.

Nomadic societies are noted for their diversity and the analytical value of a general category of pastoral nomads has been questioned. Still, many nomadic pastoral societies do exhibit common characteristics in social organization. The organizational levels of most pastoral societies may be thought of in terms of primary herding units, camp or camp group, and local group levels. These levels roughly parallel the Navajo residence group, middle-level, and perhaps community levels, although the degree correspondence is variable. The discussion that follows draws heavily on Dyson-Hudson's (1972), Spooner's (1972, 1973) and particularly Tapper's (1979) summaries of the literature on pastoral nomadic social organization.

Most pastoral societies are established around some form of primary herding unit, consisting of one or several households (Spooner 1973). Among most cattle and some reindeer pastoralists, a single nuclear or extended family often fills this role; however, most other herders form larger groups (Spooner 1973:14–15). The primary units maintain a matched labor supply and pooled herd of manageable size. The pooling of labor and stock does not imply communal ownership (stock is owned individually, but cared for communally). The herding unit is most often formed along kinship (often unilineal) lines, but may be based on a variety of ties, including legal contractual agreements (e.g., W. Swidler 1972). This basic unit is of variable stability, but while in existence in a particular configuration, it is of fundamental importance for the organization of herding, as well as other forms of day-to-day cooperation. Among the Navajos, the residence group clearly corresponds to the primary herding unit level in both function and composition.

The primary herding unit may be an independent residential group, which forms a separate camp. In most nomadic societies, however, several such units combine at certain times of the year to form a larger camp or camp group. Tapper (1979) has termed this aggregation an "A-type community." Although involving less intense cooperation than the herding unit (e.g., herds are not generally pooled), these larger units are important bases of sharing, labor cooperation, joint defense, and reciprocal responsibilities. Like the primary herding unit, these larger camps are very often nominally organized around agnatic kin (typically lineage segments), but in practice may incorporate a broad range of kin and nonkin.

This large-scale residential unit shares similarities with the smaller of the

Navajo middle-level groups—the cooperating group of Collier (1966; cf. Kelley 1986) or the group of Kluckhohn (1966)—in its labor pooling functions, but differs most notably in its role as an actual residential unit, and also in that it typically contains several hundred people (Tapper 1979:58). It is possible that this larger-scale and seasonal cohesiveness at the cooperating group level in many nomadic societies, compared to the Navajos, relates to the requirements of true nomadic settlement, in contrast to the more limited mobility of the Navajos. In order for such a cooperating group to function among true nomads, its members must move as a unit.

Above the camp group level, many nomadic groups are organized into much less cohesive local groups, typically consisting of hundreds to several thousand individuals: Tapper's (1979) B-type communities. These units are almost always agnatically based, often corresponding to tribal sections or subsections. The degree of actual cohesion within such groups is variable. Some of these units (of widely varying size) hold land and in their smaller and more cohesive form may approximate the larger of the Navajo outfits (e.g., Barth 1961). In other cases, the units are of political significance, but lack land or other corporate estates.

A notable feature of the two lower levels of pastoral social units (herding groups and camp groups), though less true of the higher level ones, is a marked degree of population fluidity. Even when groups are formally defined in genealogical terms, a wide range of specific strategies creates de facto flexibility (see examples that follow). The result is a continuous reshuffling of population among social units. This movement permits changes in human labor force and livestock herd size to adjust to social and environmental constraints and fluctuations (e.g., Spooner 1972, 1973; N. Swidler 1972; Tapper 1979). Like the Navajos, nomads have been said to exhibit a pragmatic form of social organization that is better characterized by the analysis of networks rather than corporate groups (Dyson-Hudson 1972:9). In particular, Dyson-Hudson proposes the study of networks as an initial step in the isolation of functioning corporate groups where they are present. He concludes that "a prominent organizational feature of nomadic societies is the local exploitation group—a set of domestic and herding units periodically drawn together by a temporary mutual interest in the peaceful exploitation of local resources." This group corresponds to the camp group level described earlier. "Its composition and operation must be grasped to comprehend the functioning of any particular nomadic society" (Dyson-Hudson 1972:11). This characterization of flexibility in nomad social organization matches exactly the sort of units represented by the middle-level groups among the Navajos. Spooner (1973) has also noted a complementary relationship between the flexibility of the middle-level residential units versus the relative rigidity of higher level ties. The former permit frequent population movement and adjustment, while the latter are more directly linked to unchanging, distant genealogical relations (cf. Peters 1960), and lend stability and coherence to large-scale social relations.

Navajo social organization contrasts with that of other pastoral groups in a variety of ways—most notably in the matrilineal basis of Navajo kinship and the limited importance of lineage organization in general, as opposed to the near universality of agnatic principles and emphasis on patrilineal groups in other pastoral societies (Spooner 1973). Nevertheless, a few examples of the sorts of flexible social units found among various pastoral groups highlight the similarities in structure despite the contrasts in many specifics of social organization.

Peters (1960) describes how the Cyrenaican Bedouin maintain their agnatic idiom while manipulating group composition to adjust for fluctuations in ecology and demography. The Cyrenaican Bedouin are sheep, goat, and camel herders, with a well-defined system of patrilineages that are subdivided into progressively smaller lineage segments. At the highest level of integration, all of the Cyrenaican Bedouin view themselves as the patrilateral descendants of a common ancestor. Lower level lineage segments define tribal divisions as well as smaller-scale social units.

The unit of cooperation corresponding to the camp group level is the "tertiary segment," a group typically composed of 200 people (but see Tapper 1979:51) centered around a segment of a patrilineage. This unit generally combines into a single large summer (dry season) camp from six to eight months and disperses into four or five smaller camps at other times of the year. The tertiary segment is characterized by joint ownership of land and water supplies and shared responsibility for vengeance and blood money payment in cases of homicide. Thus, the unit resembles some of the larger but more integrated of the outfit groups described among the Navajos. In the Bedouin case the entire group forms a single camp for part of the year, a settlement pattern not found among Navajos at least in recent times (though see Keur 1941; it is possible that some larger Navajo units did form residential groups at certain times in the past).

Despite its patrilineal core, the Bedouin unit also resembles the outfit in its flexibility. The potential for adjusting group composition is provided by two major mechanisms. First, a portion of the tertiary segment camp is often composed of clients or Marabtin, people who are allowed to join the group *without* belonging to the lineage segment. Such additional population permits enlarging the group when necessary, and conversely, clients are the first required to leave the group when changing circumstances require a reduction in group size. There is a second class of people with ambiguous ties to the tertiary segment; these are the Laaf who are thought of as originating outside the lineage segment, but can be "grafted on" to the genealogy if their membership in the group becomes established over a long period. The Laff, then, demonstrate the second mechanism allowing flexibility within the unilineal tertiary group—this is the manipulation of genealogies to add and delete subgroups to the tertiary "lineage segment." This genealogical manipulation takes several forms, but is notable for its concentration at the tertiary segment level. That is, it is the tertiary segment that is expanded or contracted by the grafting and pruning of genealogies, while the higher order kinship links between segments and lower order lineal connections within tertiary segments are not typically modified.

The result of this manipulation is an appearance of agnatically based invariance masking actual constant change in size and composition of the tertiary segment. This flexibility and some of the functions attributed to the tertiary segment (particularly joint land ownership) are similar to the operation of nonunilineally organized large outfits among the Navajos as described here.

Bates (1972, 1973) describes another patrilineally based system that exhibits a different source of flexibility. Among the Yoruk of Turkey, camp groups averaging about five households (that in turn average eight occupants) are organized around patrilineages, but the details of group membership are based on a range of agnatic, uterine, and affinal, and even nonkin relations. An important element in group formation is the extension of credit by wealthy individuals. These men lease grazing land for the camp groups (this land is owned by sedentary agriculturalists) and then extend credit to others, often (but not always) poorer agnates who join the camp group. Thus, although the resulting group is organized around a patrilineage, its specific composition may vary, and is subject to continual renegotiation. Beyond its crucial role as the locus of economic cooperation for leasing of grazing land, the Yoruk camp group functions to provide protection to its members and their herds, seasonal herding assistance, and protection of the leased land from trespassers.

W. Swidler (1972) describes yet another approach to group formation. The Brahui of Baluchistan establish camps or *khalks* by written contract among agnatic, uterine, and affinal kin. The *khalk* is a more tightly integrated unit than those previously discussed, because its members pool their herds into a single communal flock. The composition of the *khalk* is negotiated every year and is adjusted so as to maintain stock numbers at optimal levels for herding (250 to 500 animals). Thus, the Brahui show again how cooperative units within a unilineal pastoral society may be manipulated to maintain a useful range of group size, although the group involved in this example falls more at the level of the Navajo residence group than that of the outfit.

A final example of a system with several marked similarities to the Navajos (despite a patrilineal basis) is that of the Yomut Turkemen of Iran (Irons 1972). The Yomut practice a restricted nomadic pattern of dry season aggregation and limited wet season dispersion into smaller camps. Yomut camp groups fall somewhere between the Navajo residence group and most tightly integrated cooperating group in scale and organization. The camp group typically consists of four or five households, and cooperates on a day-to-day basis, often (but not always) pooling the herd, sharing labor, beasts of burden, and tools. In keeping with Yomut patrilineal kinship organization, the camp group typically forms around a patrilineage or portions of one; however group composition changes frequently and may include nonagnatic kin or nonkin members.

Above the level of the camp group the Yomut are organized into *oba*, tribal divisions of 25 to 100 households. These divisions are considered by the Yomut to be residence units, although in practice a particular descent group typically is dominant. Like the large Navajo outfits, the *oba* is a unit concerned with exclusive access to grazing land, but it also controls water sources.

Finally, in addition to these social units, the Yomut use a range of (typically agnatic) kin-based reciprocal relations through which assistance and socializing is often organized; this resembles the more generalized network aspect of Navajo social organization.

The Navajo Case in Cross-cultural Perspective

The preceding examples highlight the degree to which middle-level relations are essential to the organization of certain types of societies, a point also made from an archeological perspective by Hayden and Cannon (1982). Hayden and Cannon also emphasize how certain kinds of middle-level social units (residential corporate groups) are important analytically.

My research focuses on a form of middle-level group at one end of the range considered by Hayden and Cannon. They discuss three types of corporate groups: those sharing a single dwelling, those sharing a residential compound, or those composing a neighborhood or barrio. The Navajos may fall in the latter class, but differ from Hayden's and Cannon's examples in being weakly integrated with minimal formal structure.

In contrast, several of the comparative examples considered here that share some of the functional characteristics of the Navajo middle-level units (the pastoral nomadic camp groups) do include a clearly defined residential and functional character analogous to groups considered by Hayden and Cannon. This brief survey of middle-level social units, and examination of their variability in the Navajo case, serves to emphasize the continuum of forms. They range from loosely integrated networks to tightly bound residential corporate units, and perhaps even entire villages integrated as corporate entities. Interplay between the economy, demography, ecology, and social ideology (descent concepts, residence and inheritance rules, and so on) structures the social units found at any place and time.

As emphasized by Lamphere (1977:94–95) from an ethnographic perspective and Hayden and Cannon (1982) from an ethnoarchaeological one, a crucial analytical need is the development of appropriate measures of intragroup links. Lamphere explicitly addresses the need to distinguish different kinds of intragroup ties. She mentions specifically the identification of distinct classes of bonds to kin and nonkin, and the use of measures of relationship based on content, value, and frequency of contact (cf. Foster 1984; Wood et al. 1982). From the archeological perspective, Hayden and Cannon discuss stylistic, architectural, and spatial indicators of group solidarity.

I have concentrated on only the latter of these three kinds of archeological data, and explicitly avoided the distinctions Lamphere suggested regarding different kinds of intragroup bonds. Given the weak bounding and limited coherence of the Navajo units, it is doubtful if architectural or stylistic attributes recognizable archaeologically would delimit different classes of bonds. Detailed ethnographic data on kinship and cooperative bonds among residence groups might serve as an independent line of evidence against which to compare Navajo or other societies' spatial, stylistic, and architectural indicators of middle-level group composition and integration. The combination of these approaches could permit evaluation of a substantially broader range of issues regarding such groups than are usually considered.

The research presented here highlights at least six essential aspects of middle-level social groups that warrant further exploration. First, the definition of alternative types of social units integrated by different kinds of bonds must be addressed. That is, precisely how are different forms of middle-level social units defined; how are they visible in behavioral or structural terms? Beyond the identification of the broad categories of ties previously noted, such as different classes of kinship relationships, non-kin ties, and varying levels and types of contact, lies the more basic question of how these different structures differ or resemble each other in origin and function.

Second, just as alternative types of integrative bonds must be identified and more precisely defined, different factors selecting for group formation or disintegration must be examined. The research described here emphasizes general economic, ecological, and demographic factors determining group composition. In order to allow rigorous comparisons among different conditions that the Navajos have faced, as well as comparisons with non-Navajo cases, however, these variables must be much more precisely specified. Specific parameters of the timing and scale of labor requirements, defensive needs, spatial layout of relevant resources, capital needs, and so forth are critical for determining the type of task groups that form. Additional factors such as past group composition and ideology must be considered (for instance, how do middle-level groups form in unilineally versus cognatically organized societies). These problems are relevant to ethnographic and archeological study.

Third, as emphasized throughout this work, task groups may be organized at different levels. That is, some functions are served by individuals, others by nuclear families or households, others by residence groups, and so forth.

Variation in social organization at multiple levels raises the question of the relationship among the levels. The neat, idealized classification of levels presented here does not manifest itself in many cases. As outlined in chapter 1, definitions for commonly used terms such as "household" vary. Even when a consistent definition is used, the classification of a particular social unit may be ambiguous. Several levels may coincide. For example, multiple family households (Laslett 1972:30) contain several conjugal families living together. In such units, the household level of organization may correspond with the residence group level, as those levels are conceived in the Navajo case.

It is possible to apply arbitrary rules to resolve the ambiguity. For instance, if the whole multiple family household habitually shares meals, it may be viewed as a single large household that also makes up a residence group, while if the conjugal units eat separately it may be considered a group of households that together make up a residence group, and also share a dwelling. More interesting than simple issues of terminology is the question of how and why variability occurs at different levels. Continuing with the preceding example, for instance, why do some societies have large multiple family households, while others have small households but group them together into larger residence units? Raising this question also serves to emphasize the crucial point often overlooked or de-emphasized in studies of social group composition, namely, the interrelation of factors governing groups at each level. For instance, the works that have demonstrated substantial stability in household size over time (e.g., Laslett and Wall 1972) are important, but should not be interpreted independent of data regarding interhousehold units (cf. Gaunt 1987; Segalen 1984).

Directly relating to the preceding point is a fourth aspect of middle level social groups: the question of the scale of particular social units. Most quantitative studies have focused on the size of the household; much less data are available regarding middle-level groups.

For the Navajo case, middle-level group size estimates range from Collier's (1966) data yielding an average of 19 individuals per cooperating group to Kluckhohn and Leighton's (1946:63) statement that outfits range from 50 to 200 people. Kluckhohn's own data from Ramah (Kluckhohn 1966) suggest outfits averaging less than 90 people (Henderson and Levy 1975 suggest a value close to 75). Other data (e.g., Adams 1963, 1983; Kelley 1982c:368–70, 1986:155; Kluckhohn and Leighton 1946:63) indicate average outfit sizes in the neighborhood of 40 to 70 people, if only residence groups that are members in multiresidence group outfits are counted. Estimates of average outfit size as low as around 30 people may be derived if independent residence groups are counted as individual outfit-level units alongside the residence groups that are members of multiresidence group outfits.

By way of comparison, Tapper's (1979) brief review of pastoral social units suggest herding groups that typically include two to five households or tents (perhaps 10 to 30 people), camp groups of 20 to 50 households (100 to 300 people), and local groups consisting of several hundred tents or households (typically 1000 or more people).

The spatial analysis undertaken here does not resolve the question of the scale of Navajo units. For the Black Mesa data, the nearest neighbor analysis gives no indication of cluster size. The cluster analytic technique applied to the ethnographic data in chapter 4 (see also Rocek 1994) does permit evaluation of cluster size, but as noted in that chapter, currently available data do not permit adequate evaluation of the nature of the correspondence of middle-level units and spatial clusters beyond the fact that comembership in a middle-level unit is associated with spatial proximity. Some of the ethnographic references to interresidence cooperation suggest spacing between adjacent residences on the order of a mile or so (sometimes even less) and total cooperating group territories of no more than a few miles (perhaps three to six) average diameter (e.g., Adams and Ruffing 1977; Collier 1966:53; Dyk 1966:136, 306–7; Kluckhohn 1966:367; Rocek 1994). This matches the results suggested for the Black Mesa archaeological data outlined in chapter 6, although there is abundant variation. If we examine territorial ranges used over the course of a whole year (rather than those used in a single season) and if we consider some of the larger forms of Navajo middle level units, then we find some territories ten or more miles average diameter (and fifty or more miles maximum distance) (e.g., Kimball and Provinse 1942; Levy et al. 1989).

Currently, criteria for counting middle-level unit membership, the relationship of unit size differences to the outfit versus cooperating group distinction, and most importantly the correspondence of social unit size with composition and function are unresolved. The need for quantification of group size goes hand in hand with the need for explicit identification of distinct kinds of intraunit bonds and measurements of the strength of these bonds.

A major emphasis of the comparative cases discussed in this chapter is the short term variability of many middle-level units, which is a fifth aspect of middle-level social groups. Middle-level organization, between the level of the household or residence group and the local community, appears to be an important source of flexibility in social organization that permits shuffling of personnel and relationships without requiring fundamental upheavals in the social fabric. Thus, an examination of the factors selecting for such flexibility in a particular context is of basic interest.

Ecologically oriented pastoralist studies offer one obvious example of such an approach, closely related to the research undertaken here. As I have tried to show in this chapter, however, middle-level flexibility comparable to that found in pastoral societies occurs in other kinds of economies. The economic and social factors necessitating group flexibility and the determinants of particular fluctuations in group makeup are of general interest beyond the pastoralist case.

Sixth and finally, the major focus of this volume is the longer-term variability in middle-level groups: the factors that strengthen them or weaken them and ultimately create or destroy them. The Navajo case, as well as some of the examples outlined in this chapter, indicate how middle-level organization can vary between virtually unbounded social networks to fairly rigidly defined corporate groups. In the Navajo case, I have examined a situation in which middle-level units appear to have varied within a fairly restricted range of integration, from situation-specific kin-based networks (or very loosely structured cooperating groups) to more clearly defined, but still quite informal, kindred based outfits.

It is intriguing to consider, however, that the sorts of fluctuations in complexity considered here may also form the basis of far more substantial changes in social organization. To cite just one example, Gall (1977) and Saxe and Gall (1977) describe a case in Melanesia where weakly integrated matrilaterally structured residential clusters referred to as "kin cores" are being strengthened under the impact of agricultural intensification (a shift from mixed crop swidden to intensive wet rice cultivation) and resultant increased scarcity of labor and suitable land. Saxe and Gall speculate that as this process continues, a well-defined lineage organization may develop— ultimately a nonegalitarian social order based around the differential access to land and labor offered by this new social structure. Thus the mechanisms involved in shifting forms of middle-level social organization integrate with the larger process of social evolution.

In short, the importance of middle-level social units in situations requiring flexibility, and the transformations that such units undergo, offer fruitful avenues for research at multiple levels. These range from the specifics of the operation of middle-level units in particular societies, to the broad question of the role these groups may play in major social transformations.

The social responses to economic or demographic shifts vary depending on the particulars of each example. Broad concepts such as intensification or increased market involvement are not adequate to evaluate social changes in each case unless they are linked with an analysis of specific constraints such as labor and capital requirements of particular subsistence activities, the amount, reliability, form and distribution of income, and so forth. It is perhaps for this reason that close similarities occur between the Navajo case and descriptions of flexibility in other pastoral societies. The types of social changes examined here are not unique to the Navajos, but represent examples of the more general issues of flexibility gained through the interaction of social unit changes at multiple scales.

The examination of flexibility in middle-range units among other societies adds plausibility to the argument for such flexibility in the Navajo case. The range of factors shaping such units and the variety of forms that they take add to the difficulty of resolving this variability in the archaeological record. The limitations of the archeological data and the numerous manipulations required to use it temper confidence in the Black Mesa case as direct documentation of the changes in social units that I have suggested. The archaeological pattern is compatible with these interpretations, however, and I find encouraging evidence that the archaeological measures track the variability that they are intended to assess.

It is clear that the time scale involved in the economic, demographic, and social changes that I address are at the limits of (or exceed) the temporal as well as spatial scale of most ethnographic data. A detailed ethnoarchaeological approach, taking archaeological data such as I have used but combining it with more thorough site-by-site documentation, is one of the best hopes for examining such changes. As the comparisons in this chapter suggest, middle-level social units and their flexibility are well worth such further study, not just in the Navajo case, but in others as well. In one form or another, the dilemmas facing Left Handed on Black Mesa in the late nineteenth century as he tried to maintain his family ties, respond to the shifting natural and social environment, and make a living are universal.

Appendix A: Data Coding

Definition of Site Boundaries

The emphasis of site definition is spatial—a site is a discrete cluster of structures and features. The settlement pattern on Black Mesa is sufficiently dispersed so that this definition is usually straightforward. Site boundaries were delineated during initial field survey, and subsequently refined by field crews mapping and surface collecting the sites. Occasionally field crews were uncertain whether to subdivide sites that appeared to contain temporally distinct concentrations of structures and features. Because I subdivided sites into temporal components for this study, this ambiguity in the field was not a significant problem.

Cases where field crews subdivided single residence group settlements into two or more sites raise a more serious difficulty. This happened most often with sweatlodges, which were classified as discrete sites separate from the residence groups that used them. This misclassification occurs frequently, because sweatlodges are usually away from other structures of a residence group to assure privacy. I have made no attempt to alter this subdivision of sweatlodges as separate sites, as it is often impossible to unambiguously assign an "isolated" sweatlodge to a particular residence group and because their distribution is not a topic of major concern in this research.

Other cases of subdivided sites could have more significant consequences for this analysis, because they can alter the data on residence group composition and on interresidence group spacing. My coding procedure uses functional criteria in establishing site definitions (e.g., an "isolated" corral immediately adjacent to a contemporaneous settlement lacking a corral would usually be coded as a "site fragment"—part of an adjacent site). I also use informant data to help resolve these kinds of uncertainty. Although I recognized some site fragments, my coding procedure does not allow recombining site fragments into adjacent sites if they were not recombined by the field crews (because I used the BMAP site numbers as unique identification codes for all sites). This leaves such fragments as a possible source of inaccuracy in the data. Of 772 site components, however, I found only 7 such fragments, consisting of 15 structures and features out of 3732 in all. Therefore, this should not be a serious source of error.

Definition of Site Components

After identifying sites as spatial units, the next step was to subdivide sites into discrete temporal components.[1] I initially assumed that each site represents a single component. I then used three criteria to define multicomponent sites. As indicated in the description later in this appendix, I followed a somewhat arbitrary set of rules to structure the interpretation of site use, based on a normative model of site use duration. The primary goal of these rules is to ensure that even sites occupied for long periods are subdivided into separate components such that within each component most of the structures and features were actually or nearly in contemporaneous use. At the same time, I tried to not subdivide sites into too many components, because much of my analysis uses ten- and fifteen-year time intervals, and sites must not be double counted.[2]

My most common basis for identifying multiple components is chronological evidence, typically, dendrochronological. To permit consistent coding of component subdivisions, I arbitrarily limit chronologically defined components to a maximum length of fifteen years. This period is intended to encompass the normal longest effective use-life (without major repairs) of traditional Navajo structures. Dean (1981:14), for instance, indicates that hogans are usually dismantled and rebuilt if they continue in use for more than a maximum of ten years (see also Ahlstrom 1985; Cameron 1990). Kelley (1982b:359) gives ethnographic data for the periods 1880 to 1950 suggesting that the mean duration of site use in her site sample from the eastern portion of the reservation is around ten years. Therefore, I consider structures or sites with evidence of construction or use over a period of more than fifteen years to be multicomponent, with each component lasting no more than fifteen years.

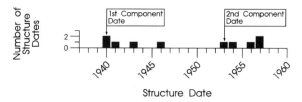

Figure A.1. Example of Site Component Division in Case of Date Clusters Less than Fifteen Years Apart

Conversely, in most cases I set the minimum intercomponent time span (the interval between the starting date of two sequential components) at fifteen years. That is, I usually coded two dates from a single site that are separated by less than fifteen years as parts of the same component. I make an exception to this fifteen-year minimum if a site has two date clusters that span more than fifteen years but for which some of the dates within the second cluster fall less than fifteen years after the start of the first cluster. Figure A.1 illustrates such a case: Although much of the construction in component 2 in this example dates more than fifteen years after the start of component 1, the earliest few dates for component 2 are less than fifteen years after the start of component 1.

Where multiple components involve reuse of the same structures or features in two consecutive components, I arbitrarily set the absolute minimum intercomponent interval at ten years, and I took shorter spans to represent repair and reuse episodes within the component. In cases where separate structures are involved, I permitted coding of even shorter component lengths. In such cases, there is no danger of double counting the same structures within a single analysis, because the structures included in each component are different. All of these exceptions to the fifteen-year minimum make up a small proportion of cases—usually multiple components on a site are separated by at least fifteen years.

Although reliable chronological data provided the major basis for subdividing sites into components, two additional sources of information can indicate multiple components: informant data and spatial or functional evidence. These criteria are somewhat subjective because they require an evaluation of the strength of evidence of multiple site use and they utilize prior knowledge of the range of typical site types on northern Black Mesa (Haley et al. 1983:290–92). For instance, I would subdivide a habitation site from a fence that happens to run near the habitation's structures, unless there was evidence of a functional association between the fence and the habitation. This is because there is no known pattern of fence lines functionally associated with habitation sites in the Navajo site data in the BMAP area (Haley et al. 1983). In general I used informant and spatial-functional evaluations of relative ages of portions of a site (such as structure and feature condition, artifact associations, and any available tree-ring data), as well as a functional interpretation of the site's structures and features in order to derive an internally consistent interpretation. Again, I did not divide site uses separated by less than fifteen years into separate components, except in cases of strong evidence of discrete occupations—use by separate families, complete change in site function, or clustering of construction dates such as discussed earlier.

Analysis of Site Components

The next (or concurrent) step is to evaluate the age, function, and season of each component. I consider four types of age indicators: (1) tree-ring dates, (2) informant data, (3) artifact associations, and (4) subjective field assessments of site condition and apparent age. Tree-ring dates under most conditions are the most reliable dating criteria in this study. In particular, cutting dates or other dates with evidence of proximity of the tree's outer surface (dates with a B, G, L, v, r, or c outer date code; see Dean 1969:19), combined with evidence of clustering among dates from different samples, provides the strongest basis for dating (e.g., Ahlstrom 1985; Dean 1981:6). I use an arbitrary rule for tree-ring dating: A site is coded as having been dated based on tree-ring data if it has a cluster of three or more dates falling within five years of each other, *and* if at least one of these dates has an indication of proximity of the tree's outer surface. The only exceptions to this rule are cases where a date cluster is followed by chronologically later dates from the same structure or feature, implying that the earlier date cluster may be the result of reuse of construction material rather than multicomponent use of the site (see the discussion of structure and feature dating that follows). Field observation of wood condition indicative of wood reuse aids in evaluating such cases.

This approach is patterned after the dating strategy described by Dean (1981), but differs in several respects. My examination of field assessments of wood condition (intended to distinguish freshly cut from dead wood; Dean 1981:5) indicates that the BMAP field interpretations of wood condition are of limited reliability. Numerous samples judged to be dead wood by field crews dated to the same year as fresh wood in a construction date cluster. Thus, I use field assessments of wood condition only to supplement dendrochronological evidence (particularly patterns of intrastructure and intrasite date clustering), and often ignore them. On the other hand, BMAP field crews attempted to gather dendrochronological samples likely to accurately date construction of each type of structure according to the criteria outlined by Dean (1981). For this reason, it is likely that the tree-ring samples contained a relatively low percentage of obviously dead or reused elements. Thus, the high error rate in identifying dead wood is not surprising in a population of samples already biased against easily identifiable dead wood.

Separating samples with ring-counts (outer date code + +; Dean 1969: 19) provided an additional basis for identifying less reliable dates. Using a subsample of the BMAP tree-ring data, I found that the "departure values" indicate a higher incidence of inaccurate (spuriously old) dates for + + cutting samples compared with other cutting dates. (See Dean 1981 for a description of departure values and their use in recognizing samples not accurately reflecting the construction date of a structure). Therefore, in cases of disagreement between + + and other dates, I gave the ring-count samples less weight than fully dated samples.

In cases where a cluster of three or more dates does not occur, I used less reliable criteria. I weighted internally consistent informant data provided by an individual with personal familiarity with a site (usually a former occupant or a close relative of one) more heavily than any data other than clustered tree-ring dates. I also heavily weighted unclustered tree-ring dates compatible with other factors (such as structure condition and reliable informant data). In cases with clear internal evidence of multiple dates based on alternative dating methods, I sometimes inferred multiple components. For instance, if a corral yields reliable, clustered early twentieth-century tree-ring dates from samples of brush, which is nearly always cut fresh and not reused (Russell 1981b:4; Russell and Dean 1985), but the corral also has intact walls and contains abundant recent animal manure, I would usually assign it to multiple components.

In general, I placed reliance on chronological data in the following order: (1) clustered tree-ring dates, (2) informant data provided by someone personally familiar with the site, (3) other informant data, nonclustered tree-ring dates, and/or artifact associations, and (4) structure and feature condition. Gross discrepancies in the latter factors (number 4), however, can override all other factors except numbers 1 and 2. For instance, I would assume that an intact hogan with an isolated 1830s "cutting" dendrochronological date represents a case of dead wood or wood reuse, regardless of field assessment of the sample, and ignore the 1830s date. Given that I used the dating criterion, "structure and feature condition" by itself without supporting tree-ring, informant, or artifact information as a last resort guess-date, I ranked this code lowest of all, and excluded it from most of the analyses described in the text. I referred to the better-dated components, those that exclude the guess-dated components (basis of date = structure and feature condition [site coding sheet variable 13 = 4]), as the "reliably dated" components throughout the text.

I define the site component date as the date of the *earliest* structure or feature in the component. The only exception is if an episode of structure use spans two components (see discussion that follows). In such (rare) cases, the component date is the age of the oldest structure in the component the use of which does not span the two components.

In addition to assigning each component a date, I assigned each to a functional and seasonal category. The functional typology follows that of Russell (1983b), as expanded by Haley et al. (1983). I have added additional descriptive categories to account for sites not matching any of the varieties included in Haley et al.

The primary criterion of the functional typology is the association of structures and features within the component. In addition, informant data and the environmental setting help classify component function. Informant statements reveal subtle aspects of site use (e.g., ceremonial functions), or functional characteristics obscured by missing structures (e.g., disassembled or destroyed corrals). I usually resolved discrepancies between site structure and feature composition and informant data by assuming multiple site functions. In cases of major inconsistency, I examined evidence of informant data reliability (e.g., the basis of the informant's knowledge of the site, the degree of agreement between the informant's assessment of site age and tree-ring dates, and evidence in the field notes regarding whether the site was actually visited with the informant). I resolved the disagreement based on the apparent relative reliability of the conflicting sources, with the archaeological remains receiving in general a somewhat heavier weighting. The environmental setting enters into only a limited number of site component function assessments. The major use is to identify piñon camps based on the presence of windbreaks in large stands of piñon trees.

The site functional categories emphasize the formal typological characteristics of sites at the expense of functional details. For instance, in contrast to
the typology employed by Kelley (1982b:287), I classified all sites with permanent dwelling structures (hogans or houses) and corrals as habitation sites.
Kelley classifies sites according to the duration of occupation per year, distinguishing sites used less than six months from sites used for longer periods
each year ("homestead sites"). Although I intended my classification of site
seasonality to encompass some of this variability of site use, the BMAP data
are not detailed enough to permit the kinds of distinctions Kelley makes in
her data. However, reliance on archaeologically observable site characteristics
does perhaps permit some greater freedom from the kinds of bias introduced
by selective informant memories (Kelley 1982b:207).

I based my interpretation of site seasonality on the same range of criteria
as site function, although with somewhat more even weighting placed on the
alternative sources of evidence (see Rocek 1988 for a discussion of these). I
assessed the environmental setting particularly with regard to the degree of
shelter afforded the site's corrals. On the basis of informant statements concerning important site environmental characteristics, I took locations sheltered from northerly winds and exposed to the south to suggest winter use (cf.
Kelley 1982b:350–51). The structures and features present on a site form a
second basis for identifying season. In particular, brush shades, ramadas,
agricultural fields, and underground storage features usually indicate summer
use, windbreaks are typically spring or fall structures, and lamb pens and
wool bag racks are characteristic of spring. Wall construction in corrals can
also help indicate seasonality, because winter sheep and goat corrals are
typically reinforced with freshly cut brush to shelter the livestock (Russell
1981b). Finally, in addition to site location and composition, I used informant
data to identify component season. I evaluated the reliability of informant
assessments, ranging from statements by the actual former occupants of sites
(reliable) to guesses based on general knowledge of site seasonal requirements
or on typical use patterns in a particular portion of the study area (less reliable). The degree of agreement of informant date estimates with tree-ring
dates and other factors noted earlier also help indicate the reliability of informant data regarding the site.

As with functional assessments, interpretations of seasonality combine
as many of these sources of data as are available, and resolve compatible
discrepancies by assuming multiseasonal use. Unlike site functional assess-

ments, however, I placed the greatest weight in identifying seasonality on reliable informant data. Structures, features, and location are variable and difficult to interpret, so I judged them of more limited reliability. In cases with less reliable informant data, I balanced the information available regarding the site on a case-by-case subjective basis. As with the site functional interpretations, I coded the basis of site seasonal interpretations to permit separate analyses of sites with different degrees of certainty (see Rocek 1988 for further details).

Following delineation of site components and identification of their date, function and seasonality, I coded a series of additional variables. These include the number of structures and features, total number of components per site (and an identification number for each component), elevation, whether the site is currently occupied, location, and a number of environmental characteristics (see Rocek 1985 for details). I initially coded site location (in UTMs) based on the coordinates of the site datum recorded by the survey and mapping crews. Subsequently I calculated the mean coordinates relative to the site datum of all structures (excluding sweatlodges) on each site component, and estimated a location based on this mean structure (centroid) position. I used these component-specific locations in the spatial analysis.

Structures and Features

The structures and features making up each site component form a more detailed level of analysis below the level of the component itself. At this level, I examined the exact composition of the site on a structure-by-structure (and feature-by-feature) basis, making intrasite spatial and temporal patterns observable. I coded basic characteristics of each structure or feature, including location relative to the site datum, dimensions, shape, orientation, and association with other structures and features. In addition, I coded a descriptive-functional type for each structure and feature based on a visual identification in the field. This typology was based on that summarized in Haley et al. (1983:286–88), and expanded to include additional forms. In cases where the field identification of structure or feature function is not in agreement with informant data, I followed the informant identification unless it was clearly contradicted by the remains. Such contradictions only occurred in a few poorly preserved structures or features.

I assigned each structure and feature a construction date; this was the only major ambiguous step in coding at this level. As with site component dating, I evaluated the dates of structures and features using a hierarchy of criteria including (in approximate order of reliability) tree-ring dates, informant data, the date of the rest of the site component, and a subjective estimate of condition. Clustered tree-ring dates are the most reliable basis of dating. For structures and features, a cluster is a group of two or more[3] dates from that structure or feature. These dates must lie within a five-year span, and at least one of them must have an indication of proximity of the tree's outer surface (B, G, L, v, r, c outer date codes). Usually, these dates must fall at the end of the range of dates from the structure or feature. I made exceptions to this latter requirement in one of two cases: First, if indications of repair, rather than construction (as identified by the context or form of the dendrochronological samples), follow after a cluster, then I still used the cluster to identify the date of construction. Following the assumptions regarding component length outlined previously, such repair episodes must lie within fifteen years of construction. Second, if a cluster occurs in a structure that has evidence of reuse (e.g., a corral with a clearly old construction date combined with evidence of recent reuse), or if assessment of the site as a whole indicates multicomponent use that corresponds to multiple date clusters in the structure and feature date series, then I sometimes used a cluster of dates prior to the end of the date series to define an early component construction episode.

If a cluster of two or more dates did not occur among the samples from an individual structure or feature, I relied on alternative evidence of age. This may include tree-ring cutting dates that clustered with dates from other structures or features (I ranked this criterion's reliability just below intrastructure clustered dates). Additional evidence included informant data, date of the rest of the site or component, and the appearance and condition of the structure or feature. This latter factor, along with spatial proximity and functional association with structures or features (e.g., lamb pens associated with corrals) is one of the methods I used to assign structures and features to components on multicomponent sites, and thus date them on the basis of "date of the rest of the component." I assigned such undated structures or features the site component's date (normally the date of the earliest dated structure or feature in that component), unless they are associated with some dated structure or feature in that component, in which case they are assigned its date.

As noted in the discussion of component dating, the subdivision of sites into temporal components may include cases of multicomponent use of structures or features. This is clearest where discrete multiple clusters of tree-ring dates give evidence of rebuilding. Other criteria for identifying repeated use include informant data, structure or feature condition, artifact associations, or functional associations of structures or features. The identification of multi-component use requires evaluation of the pattern of dates from the entire site as outlined in the preceding discussion of the definition of site components.

I normally assigned reused structures two different dates for the two separate clusters. In cases where components were separated by less than fifteen years (the minimum normal intercomponent time) and structure use spanned the two components, the date of the structure in the second of the components depended on the criteria used in identifying multicomponent use. Where the second use period was indicated by some specific dating evidence such as tree-ring samples, I used these to assign the second component date to the structure. A structure's use may also have been judged to have spanned two components because it was built near the end of the first component. I defined this assumption of multicomponent use in cases were a second component date is less than ten years after the construction date assigned to a structure in the previous component (this is an arbitrary figure meant to approximate the typical maximum use life of a structure without major rebuilding), and where there is no indication of nonreuse of the structure, such as spatial separation of the components or disparities in structure condition.

In cases where use spanned two components, I used an alternate set of rules to classify the structure construction dates. Specifically, I assigned the same date as in the first component to the structure even during its continued use in the second component, although this predates the date assigned to the second component as a whole. (This is the special exception referred to in the section on site component definition and dating, and it only occurs in a limited number of cases where components are shorter than the normal fifteen-year limit.) In all other cases, where more than ten years separate the initial structure construction and the subsequent use in the second component or where structure reuse is indicated by specific evidence of rebuilding in the later component, I treated the structure as rebuilt, and assigned a separate construction date in the second component (based on the date assigned to the second component and other structures included in it).

In table A.1, I have listed portions of the forms I used for coding. I did not list variables not discussed here; this accounts for the unused variable numbers (see Rocek 1985: appendix A for a complete listing). See Rocek (1985: appendix B) for a listing of the basic data used in the analysis. A copy of these data, along with a few minor corrections, are available on request from the author.

Table A.1. Examples of Computer Codes Used for Study

Historic Site Component Codes

1) site #
2) a/b/c code (site component code assigned to extra sites in the field)
    1) a   3) c
    2) b   9) none
3) year surveyed (give last 2 digits) (99 = not surveyed)
5) year mapped (give last 2 digits) (99 = not mapped) *[or 00]
7) # of components (−0 = unk)
8) component #
12) best date estimate
13) basis of best date estimate (add 50 to # in case of "knowledgeable informant";
    for example, 55 = "dendro. and knowledgeable informant")
    00) missing
    01) dendro (3 + cluster dates, at least one ok)
    02) informant
    03) artifacts
    04) visual estimate of condition or/lack of artifacts
    05) 1&2
    06) 1&3
    07) 1&4 (1−2 cluster dates & reasonable appearance)
    08) 2&3
    09) 2&4
    10) 3&4
    11) 1&2&3
    12) 1&2&4
    13) 1&3&4
    14) 2&3&4
    15) 1&2&3&4
    16) other
    17) 4 and/or 2 plus info on other site
    18) 1 and 2 plus info on other site
    19) 3 & 18
14) UTM north
15) UTM east
18) occupied?
    1) yes (location of site is occupied, even if site struct. themselves need not be).
    Artifacts not collected
    2) no
    3) 'yes', but only in the sense of 'in use', not actually lived in. Not collected
    4) no, but field forms suggest that artifacts were not collected
    5) like #3, but artifacts were collected
    6) no, but I have not recorded artifacts

Table A.1. Examples of Computer Codes Used for Study (*continued*)

    7) no, but only artifacts associated with a structure or feature that is uniquely associated with a single component were coded by me

    8) like #5, but *associated* artifacts were coded by me

46) site type

    00) missing
    01) habitation
    02) sheep camp
    03) field house site
    04) piñon camp
    05) ceremonial
    06) campsite
    07) isolated agricultural field
    08) isolated sweatlodge(s) (or sweat lodge f/c rockpiles)
    09) isolated sheep/goat corral(s) (may include lamb pen(s))
    10) isolated horse corral (see also 31)
    11) isolated cattle corral
    12) isolated lamb pen (may have nearby hearth)
    13) isolated hogan or house (only one)
    14) isolated circular brush shade
    15) isolated ramada
    16) isolated tent
    17) isolated windbreak(s)
    18) isolated burial(s)
    19) isolateds water/soil control device(s)
    20) isolated underground storage(s)
    21) isolated roasting pit
    22) isolated cairn(s) or shrine(s)
    23) pictographs or petroglyphs
    24) isolated trash/dump
    25) isolated fence(s)
    26) isolated cache(s)
    27) other
    28) unknown
    29) isolated hearth
    30) like habitation site, but no corral (more than just hogan, more than 1 str.)
    31) isolated horse/cattle corral
    32) windbreak(s) & lamb pen(s) (like sheep camp, but no corral)
    33) summer camp (like summer sheep camp, but no corral . . . more than 1 struct.)
    34) isol. childrens' play stru./fea.
    35) windbreak & sweatlodge
    36) isolated sheep & horse corral
    37) unknown isolated structure
    38) isolated horse corral & fence

Table A.1. (*continued*)

39) stone quarry
40) isolated lean-to
41) isolated misc. feature(s)
42) water source
43) isolated hearth and sheep/goat corral
44) cattle corral and tent shade/location (cattle camp)
45) water source, cattle corral, and fence
46) trading post
47) hogan and horse corral
48) isolated canvas shade type structure
49) isolated windbreak-or-hogan
50) isolated corral (unk/unsp)
51) wood gathering/chopping site
52) part of adjacent site—camp
53) part of adjacent site—isolated windbreak
54) isolated horse corral/trap
55) isolated ram pen
56) isolated pen and sweatlodge
57) hogan and unknown pen
58) isolated ram pen and misc. pen
59) windbreak & fence
60) part of adjacent site—isolated corral (may have lamb pen(s))
61) part of adjacent site—habitation site (corral & hogan at least)
62) part of adjacent site—isolated hogan
63) lamb pen, trail & fence
64) trailer camp
65) windbreak and ram pen
66) part of adjacent site—sheep camp (corral and windbreak at least)
67) isolated windbreak or ram pen
68) church
47) basis of site type
    01) structures/features
    02) environmental setting
    03) informant who knows
    04) informant, knowledge unclear (either informant may not be certain about facts, or identification of site may be uncertain)
    05) 1&2
    06) 1&3
    07) 1&4
    08) 2&3
    09) 2&4
    10) 1&2&3
    11) 1&2&4
48) secondary site type (code same as #40, above)

Table A.1. Examples of Computer Codes Used for Study (*continued*)

49) primary season

00) missing	09) 2&4
01) spring	10) 3&4
02) summer	11) 1&2&3
03) fall	12) 1&2&4
04) winter	13) 1&3&4
05) 1&2	14) 2&3&4
06) 1&3 (see also 17)	15) 1&2&3&4
07) 1&4	16) other
08) 2&3	17) 1 and/or 3

50) basis of season (code same as #47, above)
51) secondary season (code same as #49, above)
52) # of structures
53) # of features

Historic Structure and Feature Codes

1) site #
2) a/b/c code (site component code assigned to extra sites in the field) (see sites component form, variable #1)
3) component #
4) structure or feature? (code according to current structure/feature definitions, not according to which form was used in the field)
   1) structure
   2) feature
5) structure/feature #
6) center point—east (-0 = missing)
7) center point—north (-0 = missing)
8) # of dendro samples that haves produced available dates (00 = none)
9) # of good dendro dates . . . that is, dates that are v, r, c, G, L, or *B*. (00 = none)
10) # of cutting dates . . . that is, dates with B, G, or L and *not* + + outer ring condition codes (00 = none)
11) contains at least one of two or more dendro dates on the site that agree within five years?
    1) yes
    2) no (code 2 if 2 dates are not available)
12) minimum dendro date (last date, regardless of wood condition) (missing = -000)
13) best initial construction date estimate (-0 if missing)
14) basis of best initial construction date estimate (add 50 to any category for knowledgeable informant).
    01) dendro (cluster of 2+ dates, min. 1 = ok)
    02) informant

Table A.1. (*continued*)

   03) date of rest of site or component
   04) visual estimate of condition
   05) 1&2
   06) 1&3
   07) 1&4
   08) 2&3
   09) 2&4
   10) 3&4
   11) 1&2&3
   12) 1&2&4
   13) 1&3&4
   14) 2&3&4
   15) 1&2&3&4
   16) other
   17) missing
15) best last rebuilding date estimate (-0 if missing)
16) season from outer ring if available. Analyze for each structure separately. Only coded for sites with a substantial number of cutting dates, with multiple dates from the same year.
   0) missing
   1) spring/summer (some incomp, last year's comp)
   2) summer (all incomp)
   3) summer/fall (some comp, some incomp)
   4) winter (all comp)
17) structure/feature type
   01) forked stick hogan
   02) corbelled hogan (see also 43)
   03) cribbed hogan
   04) leaning log hogan
   05) stone hogan
   06) frame hogan
   07) cinderblock/cement hogan
   08) frame house
   09) cinderblock house
   10) circular brush shade
   11) ramada
   12) windbreak
   13) sweatlodge
   14) sheep/goat corral, season unknown
   15) horse corral
   16) cattle corral
   17) lamb pen (see also 39)
   18) underground storage
   19) fence

Table A.1. Examples of Computer Codes Used for Study (*continued*)

20) other hogan
21) hogan ring
22) robbed corral (i.e., sparse material scatter remains, but not sufficiently intact to infer form/function.)
23) palisade hogan
24) palisade house
25) summer sheep/goat corral
26) winter sheep/goat corral (based on construction, not just position)
27) other house
28) horse/cattle corral
29) tent shade/location
30) outhouse
31) manylegs hogan
32) log cabin/house
33) unknown pen/stall
34) shade with incorporated basal wall elements
35) windbreak-style (with tree incorporated) hogan
36) log cabin hogan
37) stone house foundation
38) "corral ring," i.e., vegetation distinct, believed to be corral location, but no structural material remains
39) roofed lamb pen
40) hogan or lamb pen or windbreak
41) tipi style windbreak or conical lean-to windbreak (see also 45)
42) misc. lean-to
43) cribbed/corbelled hogan
44) stone puppy pen
45) "conical lean-to shade" (may be same as 41)
46) roofed windbreak
47) play house
48) hogan or windbreak
49) unknown/robbed
50) double windbreak ("W" shaped)
51) stone house/building
52) jacal house/building
53) dog house
54) shelter of posts and tree supporting canvas
55) pig pen
56) sheep shearing pen
57) windbreak-style (w/ tree incorporated) f. s. hogan (maybe same as 41)
58) ramada & tent area
59) horse trap/corral
60) ram pen
61) ram or lamb pen

Table A.1. (*continued*)

62) unknown pen or loading chute
63) ramada and/or rack
64) trailer space
65) windbreak or ram pen
66) ceremonial area
67) windbreak or horse corral
68) cinderblock/frame house

90) corral (type unknown/unspecified)
91) unknown semisubterranean structure
92) unknown-type hogan
93) unknown-type shade
94) shade with hogan style roof

51) hearth (internal, or unk. location) (see also #68 below)
52) shelf
53) ash pile
54) fire cracked rock pile
55) trash pile/dump
56) rack (= platform, free-standing, or in tree)
57) burial
58) weaving area
59) tree storage (= elements in tree, use code 66 (below) for stored items)
60) fire cracked rock/ash pile
61) wood chopping area
62) wood pile
63) cache
64) check dam
65) field
66) item in tree (= artifact stored in tree . . . unmodified pieces of wire are considered 'elements', and should be coded as code 59 above)
67) other
68) external hearth
69) stone dome oven
70) corn drying area
71) stored construction material (includes more than just wood)
72) juniper bark concentration
73) trough
74) unknown post(s)
75) rock cairn/pile
76) petroglyphs/pictographs
77) coal pile
78) storage niche
79) unk pit

Table A.1. Examples of Computer Codes Used for Study (*continued*)

80) trash dump/burning area
81) ash pile or hearth
82) beaming post
83) roasting pit
84) engine hoist
85) posts or trees with wire between them
86) quarry area
87) wool rack
88) rock ring
89) misc. external work area
95) children's play area
96) charcoal scatter
97) horse holding area
98) trash pit
99) unknown

 1) masonry fireplace
 2) misc. rock pile (use code 75 instead of this)
 3) posthole/mold
 4) coal and ash pile
 5) misc. wood leaned against tree
 6) roasting pit
 7) ash can/barrel(s)
 8) rope clothesline
 9) flattened ~horizontal tree branch
10) ash pile & wood pile
11) coal & wood pile
12) length of wire in tree
13) trail
14) ash pit
15) trash & ash can
16) misc surface storage feature (or small possible structure)
18) length (− 0 = missing)
19) orientation of length (if degrees not available, use *9 0 'site orientation code'* (from Historic Sites Component Form Coding, variable 28) (eg '901' = 'north'), if not even quad information is available, − 00 = missing
20) width (− 0 = missing)
21) orientation of width (code same as #19 above)
22) height or depth (height only for intact structures, depth for all features, − 0 = missing)
23) shape
   00) missing data
   01) round
   02) oval

Table A.1. (*continued*)

03) triangle (include doorway as a side, if it forms one)
04) rectangular (include doorway as a side, if it forms one)
05) pentagonal (include doorway as a side, if it forms one)
06) septagonal (include doorway as a side, if it forms one)
07) seven or more sided (include doorway as a side, if it forms one)
08) trapezoid
09) arcuate/semicircular
10) irregular rounded
11) irregular straight sided (if both rounded & straight sided, record by predominant type)
12) linear (e.g., wire, tree storage)
24) doorway orientation (code same as #19 above) (-0 = missing)
35) remaining height (only for structures, -0 = missing)
36)–39) associated internal features, feature numbers, (99 = none) (00 = missing/unk)**
40)–43) associated external features, feature numbers, (99 = none) (00 = missing/unk)**
44)–47) associated structures, structure numbers, (99 = none) (00 = missing/unk)**

**Do *not* extend "associated"—i.e., if feature A is assoc. with feature B, which is associated with feature C, A and C are not associated with each other unless they are within one meter of each other. Variables 36–39 are coded 00 for "not applicable" also, in the case of features that can have no internal features.

List "most significant" associations first—e.g., if an ash pile is functionally assoc. with a hogan but also happens to sit next to a corral, the hogan association is listed in var. 44, the corral in var. 45. Of internal features, hearths are the "most significant," of external features, ash piles are (where functionally vs. merely spatially associated).

Appendix B: Settlement Maps

Figures B.1 through B.7 show the settlement distributions used in this analysis. Figure B.1 shows all site components, in order to give a visual impression of the overall distribution of sites in the study area. All subsequent maps are restricted to "reliably dated" habitation site components, as defined in the text. Each of these maps shows the location of components dating to particular decadal time intervals, beginning with pre-1840 sites and extending up to post-1969. Figures B.2 through B.4 show spring and winter habitation components; figures B.5 through B.7 show summer components. Only sites whose datum is located within the six subregions are shown (although some of the individual components' center-points fall beyond the fringes of the subregion boundaries).

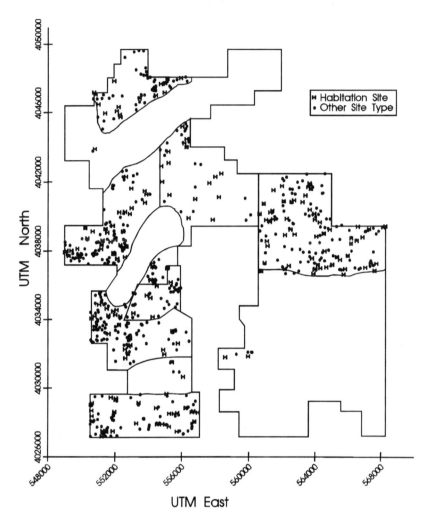

Figure B.1. All Site Components

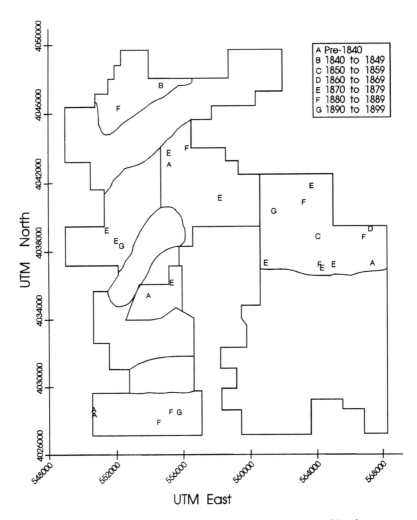

Figure B.2. Spring- and Winter-occupied Site Components Used in the Spatial Analyses; Pre-1840 to 1899, by Ten-year Intervals.

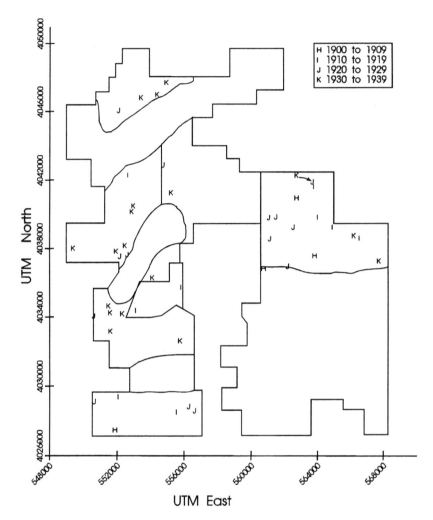

Figure B.3. Spring- and Winter-occupied Site Components Used in the Spatial Analysis; 1900 to 1939, by Ten-year Intervals.

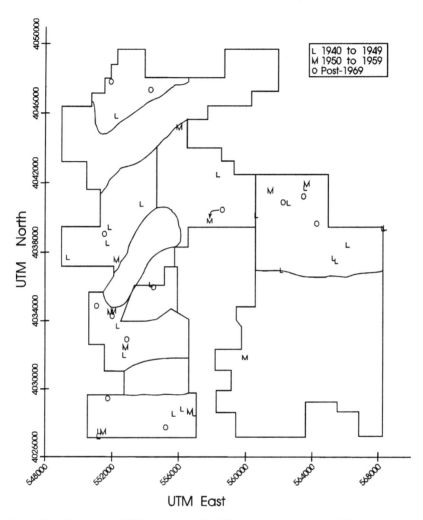

Figure B.4. Spring- and Winter-occupied Site Components Used in the Spatial Analysis; 1940 to Post-1969, by Ten-year Intervals.

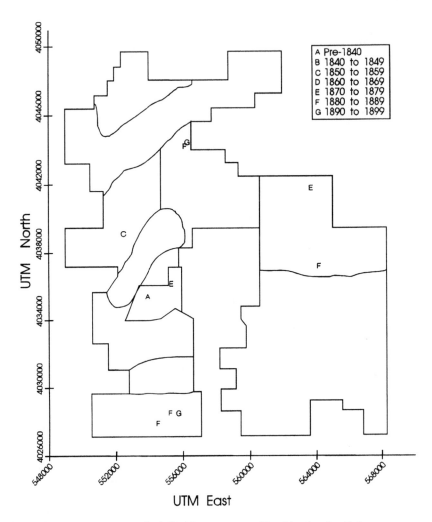

Figure B.5. Summer-occupied Site Components Used in the Spatial Analyses; Pre-1840 to 1899, by Ten-year Intervals.

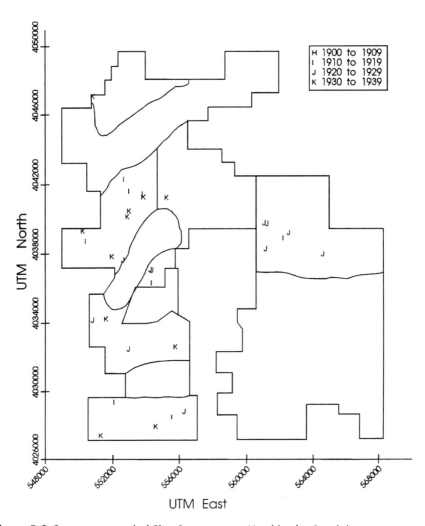

Figure B.6. Summer-occupied Site Components Used in the Spatial Analyses; 1900 to 1939, by Ten-year Intervals.

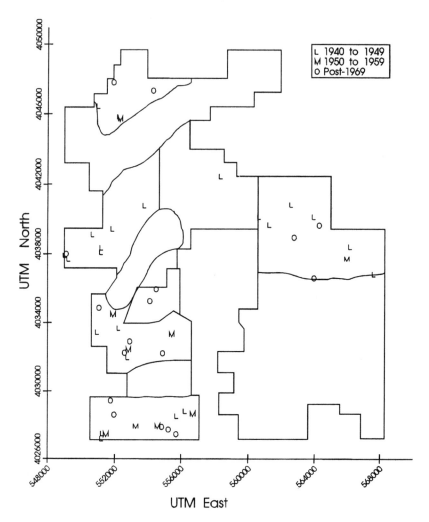

Figure B.7. Summer-occupied Site Components Used in the Spatial Analyses; 1940 to Post-1969, by Ten-year Intervals.

Notes

Chapter 2

1. An earlier version of part of this chapter appeared in Rocek (1984b), which was published and copyrighted by Southern Illinois University Press. The revised version is printed here with the permission of SIU Press. A major source used here to outline local history is Russell's work in the area immediately south of the Peabody Coal Company leasehold on Black Mesa (1983b), as well as his unpublished work dealing specifically with the study area (Russell 1981a, n.d.).

2. The wage figures for 1936 and 1940 include only jobs on the reservation (Bailey and Bailey 1980:1435, 1440–42), but these account for all or most of the jobs held by individuals from the BMAP area during this period.

3. Russell (1981a:30) suggests that even the 1940s job boom had little local impact, at least in the eastern coal-lease area, although in his field notes Russell (n.d.) includes several interviews with men who worked for wages during the 1940s.

Chapter 3

1. I follow Lamphere (1977) in this organization of social units. In using the terms "household level," "residence group level," and so on, I avoid specifying the particular definition used for the units at these levels. It seems best to use these terms, the general import of which is familiar to students of Navajo social organization, instead of introducing yet another set of terms to the already muddied lexical waters. When a more specific meaning is intended, rather than a general indication of the scale of Navajo social units, I use more explicitly defined terms.

2. Chapters are units of Navajo tribal political organization established with U.S. federal support in the 1920s, then cut off from support and allowed to lose political significance during the 1930s and 1940s. They were finally sanctioned by the tribe and expanded again in the 1950s. They form local units for the organization of tribal functions. Kluckhohn and Leighton's (1946) comparison of the "community" to the tribal chapter is based on data of the 1930s to early 1940s. Around 1960, chapters averaged 710 members (Williams 1970:47; see also Shepardson 1963; Young 1978).

3. Elsewhere (Henderson and Levy 1975:18), Levy suggests a total of seven residence groups, with 104 occupants.

Chapter 4

1. Rand's statistic compares the correspondence of two classifications based on the number of pairs of items (residence groups, in the present case) classified into the same cluster by the two classifications plus the number of residence group pairs classified into different clusters by both classifications, divided by the total number of pairs. That is, given N residence groups, the total number of pairs of residence groups is $N(N-1)/2$. In a particular classification, each of these pairs either lies within the same cluster, or the two residence groups lie in different clusters (the pair crosses cluster boundaries). Thus, the pairs may be divided into a 2-by-2 contingency table:

		Classification 2	
		Pair falls within a cluster	Pair crosses boundaries
C l a s s i f. 1	Pair falls within a cluster	A	B
	Pair crosses boundaries	C	D

Total $= A + B + C + D = N(N-1)/2$

Rand's statistic is $(A+D)/(A+B+C+D) = 2(A+D)/[N(N-1)]$. The statistic can range from 0 to 1, although its potential range may be more limited depending on the classifications being compared.

Because Rand's statistic has no known a priori distribution, this analysis compares the value of the statistic measured in the data against a set of fifty simulations in each case. A simulation consisted simply of randomly reassigning supraresidence group unit membership among the different residence groups, and calculating Rand's statistic to compare the resultant "middle-level units" against the spatial classification. Figure 4.4 shows the results of this simulation graphically; Rocek (1985, 1994) give the quantitative results. In each case, the observed Rand's statistic falls outside the range of the simulated random distributions, and exceeds the mean by well over four standard deviations.

Chapter 5

1. *B, G, L,* and *r* are symbols that indicate that the tree-ring sample probably includes the outermost annual ring that grew just prior to the death of the tree. *B* means that bark is still present on the sample; *G* means that galleries left by a variety of beetles that burrow just under the bark are visible; *L* stands for the occurrence of a characteristic sheen on the outermost layer of the sample, again indicating contact with the tree's bark; and *r* indicates that the outermost ring can be followed all the way around the sample's partial tree cross-section. The latter symbol is a less secure indication of proximity to the tree bark than are the other three. The + and + + symbols represent two alternative reasons for the possible failure of the sample to match all of its rings to the master tree-ring chart. This generally means that the date reported for the sample may be older than the actual date of the death of the tree; the former symbol represents a condition in which this discrepancy is likely to be zero to just a few years, while the latter may include more serious misdating. The vv symbol means that the sample shows no indication of the proximity of the bark, so that the reported date may be an unknown number of years older than the actual date of tree-death. See Dean (1969) for more details.

2. Along with these approaches, in previous work (Rocek 1985) I tried breaking the nearest neighbor analysis down by subregion. Because the sample sizes proved too small to produce meaningful results, however, I do not reproduce that analysis here.

3. The correction I use is a form of the statistic derived by modifying the work of McNutt (1981). The corrected nearest neighbor statistic is:

$$\frac{D_{obs}}{D_{rand}}$$

where D_{obs} is the observed mean nearest neighbor distance, D_{rand} = corrected expected mean nearest neighbor distance =

$$\frac{1}{2}\sqrt{\frac{A}{N-1-N_0}}, \quad N_0 = \frac{L}{6} \times \sqrt{\frac{(N-1)}{A}},$$

L is the total perimeter of the study region, A is its area, and N is the total number of points in the study region sample.

In order to apply this correction factor, I approximate the area and perimeter of each study subregion by subdividing it into smaller simple geometric shapes, and adding up areas and outside perimeters (see table 5.1 for the resulting values). See Rocek (1985) for a detailed discussion and derivation of these formulae.

4. The corrected variance/mean ratio is:

$$\frac{NS^2_{Y(i)}}{\Sigma 1/Z(i)\ \overline{Y}}$$

where N = number of quadrats, X(i) is number of sites in quadrat i, Z(i) = area of quadrat i,

$$Y(i) = \frac{X(i)}{Z(i)}, \quad \overline{Y} = \text{mean of } Y(i)\text{s, and}$$

$$S^2_{Y(i)} = \text{sample variance of } Y(i)\text{s} = \frac{\Sigma(Y(i)-\overline{Y})^2}{N-1}.$$

This formula corrects for the uneven frequency of sites among unequally sized quadrats and then uses a modified ratio to yield a quantity with an expected value of one under a random (poisson) distribution. I am greatly indebted to Professor W. Ericson of the University of Michigan Statistical Laboratory for deriving the expected values of alternative possible variance/mean ratios and suggesting the use of the one followed here. See Rocek (1985) for details of the derivation.

Chapter 6

1. These data are restricted to reliably dated sites but include seasonality assessments based on any criteria: the types of structures and features, site environmental setting, informant data, or the combinations of these. The categories "summer" and "winter" sites are grouped as defined in table 6.1(note).

2. Only small (intracomponent) changes in site-use duration are of concern, because the rules defining components break occupations exceeding fifteen years into multiple components (chapter 5 and appendix A). Thus any potential undercount of population due to duration increases exceeding a total of fifteen years would be compensated by an increased number of site components.

The measure of occupation span based directly on structure and feature dates has several limitations. First, I cannot examine occupation duration in the most recent periods, because data on currently occupied sites are lacking. Second, this measure assumes that occupation span will be directly reflected in datable construction episodes. In addition, restricting analysis to habitation sites may mask variability in the form of shifts from the use of short-term camps to habitation sites.

3. These intervals are a compromise between the ideal of year-by-year analysis, and the reality of limited dating precision in the archaeological record. The range of ten to fifteen years approximates the average duration of site use (see chapter 5, appendix A and discussion in this chapter). The assumption is that a site built at the start of a ten- (or possibly fifteen-) year interval will still be in use concurrently with sites built near the end of the interval. Thus, analysis by these intervals will primarily include sites used simultaneously for at least part of their existence.

The combination of ten- and fifteen-year intervals serves two purposes. First, the two different intervals provide a way of evaluating the consistency of the analyses. This is particularly valuable given the small sample sizes and the resulting potential for spurious patterning due to random "noise." Second, the two interval lengths emphasize two conflicting goals of the analysis: the desire to avoid including noncontemporary sites in a single analysis (facilitated by the use of decade intervals) and the desire to avoid *not* including sites that *were* occupied concurrently (less likely in the fifteen-year interval case).

4. In these calculations, the category of permanent dwellings is the same as that used in the population estimates in the previous section, except that I applied no size restriction here. The minimum structure size of 9.5 m² used in the population estimates (see earlier discussion) eliminates only ten structures on reliably dated habitation sites. Thus, the effect of this size restriction is limited and I ignored it here. The dwelling count data in appendix B of Rocek (1985) do include the 9.5 square meter size criterion for dwelling counts.

5. The "noisier" District 4 data (fig. 6.7) do not produce as clear a result as described earlier, but do support the use of the index; see Rocek (1985).

6. Kelley's (1982a:49) study area is one of the most economically stratified parts of the Navajo country. This may have skewed the distribution of livestock holdings and complicated the distribution of stock-related structures and features. This should be less of a factor in the BMAP study area.

7. Structures of uncertain function are not included in the calculation of median dwellings per site. As a result, one early site (D:11:4269 [SIU]), dating to 1833, is excluded from the tabulation of permanent dwellings per site, because its single dwelling structure may actually be a lamb pen or windbreak rather than a hogan. If this site were included, it would lower the median structure count for this period. D:11:4269 *is* counted as a habitation site and is included in the spatial analysis in the later parts of this chapter.

8. The correspondence of lamb pens and spring may be weaker on older sites when rams were not systematically separated from the ewes during the summer (see chapter 2), but the natural breeding cycle should still favor a spring bias in lamb births. Unlike some other studies that suggest that the use of lamb pens is relatively recent (Kelley 1982b:72), the BMAP data include lamb pens throughout the entire sequence. It is possible that some ephemeral early structures are misidentified as lamb pens. Lamb pens make up 10 percent or more of structures on reliably dated components in the BMAP sample from the earliest period up through the 1930s. Their percentage frequency is lower in three of the four subsequent decades (the exception is 1960 to 1970).

9. I restrict the spatial and population data to the time intervals identified in the preceding discussion as appropriate for analysis (see also note 10). This excludes population estimates and spatial data from the late 1940s through 1970 and the period after 1975 (because of the lack of data on occupied sites), and also excludes nearest neighbor or quadrat spatial statistics from time intervals with few sites (the particular periods depending on season and interval length; see earlier nearest neighbor discussion).

10. Although the correlation of winter-spring D (residence group clustering) with livestock levels is insensitive to the length of time interval over which the variables are measured, it is very sensitive to the effects of outliers introduced by time periods with few sites. If *all* time intervals with available data are included, the correlation of D with livestock disappears (decadal: $r = -.150$, $N = 15$, one-sided $p > .29$; fifteen-year intervals: $r = -.087$, $N = 17$, one-sided $p > .37$). On the other hand, the correlation of D with population is much less affected (decadal: $r = .615$, $N = 15$, one-sided $P < .01$; 15

year intervals: r = .383, N = 17, one-sided P < .07). This is because the outliers (periods with few sites, and hence also low population) tend toward clustering (low values of D). So, when there are very few sites, they tend to lie near each other regardless of livestock levels. Finally, the correlation of D and residence group size is only moderately sensitive to the inclusion of the outlier periods (r = .350, N = 15, one-sided p = <.11). The *lack* of correlations among summer patterns persists regardless of whether the time periods with low sample sizes are included in the analysis or not.

Chapter 7

1. In this example I include *all* criteria of seasonality assessment; the sample could be further reduced if more restrictive criteria were employed. I include all sites with some winter use, including winter sites, spring-winter sites, year-round sites, and so on. The pattern of autocorrelation of median residence group size, discussed later, is moderately affected by including only winter-used sites; the autocorrelation shifts described in table 7.1 are clear in the seasonally restricted data for the first twenty-five or thirty years, but disappear for lags greater than this (see table 7.1).

2. Netting's (1982) discussion actually applies to households, not household clusters such as the Navajo residence group. It is possible that the decline in Black Mesa residence group size is compensated by an increase in household size within the residence group. This is unlikely, however, given the evidence of relatively constant household size (see chapter 6) and the limitations of hogan living space.

Component-by-component (rather than decadal median) correlations of residence group size and corral area give a fuzzier picture. Using individual components, size (number of permanent dwellings) still correlates negatively with the index of corral area per dwelling (using mapped habitation sites only: r = −.488, N = 129, p < .001). The correlation of component size with corral area (*not* divided by the number of dwellings) is negligible (r = .080, N = 129, p > .37). So, the negative correlation between residence group size and corral area is visible when different time periods are compared to each other, but within a particular period, residence groups that are richer in livestock appear to be about the same or perhaps even trivially larger than their poorer contemporaries.

3. I am grateful to Klara Kelley (personal communication 1985) for suggesting the importance of this distinction among different sized middle-level units.

4. I used the product-moment correlation between lagged variables as the measure of autocorrelation; that is, if X(t) is the value of variable X measured at time period t, I measured the product-moment r[X(t),X(t − 1)] if the lag is one, r[X(t),X(t − 2)] if the lag is two, and so on. I restricted analysis to the same time intervals used in the analyses in chapter 6, eliminating the late 1940s through early 1970s as well as intervals with small samples where appropriate.

"Lag" refers to the difference between the time intervals being correlated. A lag of zero is a correlation of X(t) with itself, which of course has a correlation of one. For overlapping decadal intervals, a lag of one is the correlation of adjacent decades that overlap by five years, a lag of two compares two nonoverlapping adjacent decades, a lag of three involves decades whose end points are separated by five years, and so forth. The analogous definition applies to the fifteen-year interval data where a lag of one involves adjacent fifteen-year intervals overlapping by ten years.

5. Because residence group size (median number of permanent dwellings per habitation site) actually only takes on values of 1, 2, and in a few cases 1.5, Pearson's r is not really a valid measure of correlation, a rank order statistic would be more appropriate. Using Kendell's tau-b, the significance levels fall to $p < .053$ for lag of 1, $p < .244$ for lag 4, $p < .405$ for lag 7, and $p < .042$ for lag 9; however, the same pattern of autocorrelation remains. In general, I used the significance levels as a heuristic device. Because they are not calculated simultaneously and the individual correlations are not independent, the probabilistic calculations are invalid (cf. Ord 1979:38). Even the test of the significance of Kendell's tau-b is not strictly correct, given the large number of ties. Despite all of these factors negating the validity of the probabilistic tests, the cyclical pattern suggested by the correlations is clear.

6. Like the nearest neighbor results, the quadrat analyses also yield negative autocorrelations. This would not be predicted by the interpretation of these correlations in terms of social cycles unless the spatial scale of fissioning residence groups corresponds with subregions. The small sample sizes available for autocorrelation analysis (a maximum of seven time intervals for a lag of one in the winter-spring data, and only three time intervals in the summer data) render all interpretations tenuous.

Appendix A

1. In practice, I moved back and forth between identifying sites, breaking them down into components, and assessing component seasonality and func-

tion. This was particularly true for some of the sites that had been split into separate entities in the field but which I lumped together as single sites. I did this after I examined each site or site fragment for evidence of chronology, function, and seasonality.

2. For example, if I regularly subdivided sites into two- or three-year intervals, then a spatial analysis by ten-year intervals would yield sites that were their own nearest neighbors (two different components); clearly a nonsensical procedure. So, although I seek as fine a time frame as possible, it cannot be much finer than the time scale I use in the analyses. Furthermore, a time scale much finer than about ten to fifteen years exceeds the accuracy of dating of most structures in the sample. See further discussion of the issue of contemporaneity in chapter 7.

3. I define a date cluster in a structure or feature as two or more dates, as opposed to a cluster for an entire site component, which requires three dates. Because on average a whole site has more samples than any individual structure, I intend this difference in cluster definition to restrict the category of site components dated by clustered tree-ring dates to a more rigorous criterion, requiring a larger number of clustered dates.

References

Aberle, David F.
  1961   The Navaho. In *Matrilineal kinship,* edited by David Schneider and Kathleen Gough, 96–201. Berkeley: University of California Press.
  1963   Some sources of flexibility in Navaho social organization. *Southwestern Journal of Anthropology* 19:1–8.
  1966   *The peyote religion among the Navaho.* Viking Fund Publications in Anthropology No. 42. New York: Wenner-Gren Foundation for Anthropological Research.
  1981a A century of Navajo kinship change. *Canadian Journal of Anthropology* 2:21–36.
  1981b Navajo coresidential kin groups and lineages. *Journal of Anthropological Research* 37:1–7.
  1989   Education, work, gender, and residence: Black Mesa Navajos in the 1960s. *Journal of Anthropological Research* 45(4):405–30.
Adams, William Y.
  1963   *Shonto: A study of the role of the trader in a modern Navaho community.* Bureau of American Ethnology Bulletin 188. Washington, D.C.: Smithsonian Institution, U.S. Government Printing Office.
  1971   Navajo social organization. *American Anthropologist* 73:273.
  1983   Once more to the fray: Further reflections on Navajo kinship and residence. *Journal of Anthropological Research* 39:393–414.
Adams, William Y., and Lorraine T. Ruffing
  1977   Shonto revisited: Measures of social and economic change in a Navajo community, 1955–1971. *American Anthropologist* 79:58–83.
Ahlstrom, Richard V. N.
  1985   *The interpretation of archaeological tree-ring dates.* Ph.D. Dissertation, Department of Anthropology, University of Arizona, Tucson.

Amsden, Charles Avery

  1934   *Navajo weaving.* Santa Ana, CA: Fine Arts Press. Reprinted, 1972, Glorieta, NM: Rio Grande Press.

Appell, G. N.

  1967   Observational procedures for identifying kindreds: Social isolates among the Rungus of Borneo. *Southwestern Journal of Anthropology* 23: 192–207.

Bailey, Garrick A., and Roberta Glenn Bailey

  1980   Ethnohistory. In *Prehistory and history of the Ojo Amarillo,* edited by David T. Kirkpatrick, Vol. 4, Report No. 276, 1389–1523. Las Cruces: New Mexico State University.

  1986   *A history of the Navajos, the reservation years.* Santa Fe: School of American Research Press.

Bailey, Lynn R.

  1966   *Indian slave trade in the Southwest.* Los Angeles: Westernlore Press.

  1980   *If you take my sheep.* Pasadena, CA: Westernlore Publications.

Barth, Fredrik

  1961   *Nomads of south Persia: The Basseri tribe of the Khamseh confederacy.* Boston: Little, Brown.

  1969   *Ethnic groups and boundaries: The social organization of culture difference.* Boston: Little, Brown.

Bates, Daniel G.

  1972   Differential access to pasture in nomadic society: The Yoruk of southeastern Turkey. In *Perspectives on nomadism,* edited by William Irons and Neville Dyson-Hudson, 48–59. Leiden: E. J. Brill.

  1973   *Nomads and farmers: A study of the Yoruk of southeastern Turkey.* Anthropology Paper No. 52. Ann Arbor: Museum of Anthropology, University of Michigan.

Beach, Hugh

  1981   *Reindeer-herd management in transition, the case of Tuorpon Saameby in northern Sweden.* Studies in Cultural Anthropology 3. Uppsala, Sweden: Uppsala University.

Bellah, Robert N.

  1952   *Apache kinship systems.* Cambridge, MA: Harvard University Press.

Benavides, Alonso de

  1952   *The memorial of Fray Alonso de Benavides, 1630,* translated by Mrs. Edward E. Ayer, edited by Fredrick W. Hodge and Charles Lummis. Albuquerque: University of New Mexico Press.

Binford, Lewis R.

  1965   Archeological systematics and the study of culture process. *American Antiquity* 31:203–10.

Blomberg, Belinda
1983   *Mobility and sedentism: The Navajo of Black Mesa, Arizona.* Research Paper No. 32. Carbondale: Center for Archaeological Investigations, Southern Illinois University.

Blomberg, Belinda, and F. E. Smiley
1982   Ethnoarchaeological research: The Black Mesa Navajo. In *Excavations on Black Mesa, 1980, a descriptive report,* edited by Peter P. Andrews, Robert Layhe, Deborah Nichols, and Shirley Powell, 197–200. Research Paper No. 24. Carbondale: Center for Archaeological Investigations, Southern Illinois University.

Boyce, George A.
1974   *When Navajos had too many sheep: The 1940s.* San Francisco: Indian Historian Press.

Brewer, Sallie Pierce
1937   The 'long walk' to Bosque Redondo. *Museum Notes* 9(11):55–62. Flagstaff: Museum of Northern Arizona.

Brown, Gary M., and Patricia M. Hancock
1992   The Dinetah phase in the La Plata Valley. In *Cultural diversity and interaction: Prehistory of the Upper San Juan Drainage, Northwestern New Mexico,* edited by Lori Stephens Reed and Paul F. Reed, 69–90. Cultural Resources Series No. 9. Santa Fe: New Mexico State Office, Bureau of Land Management.

Brugge, David M.
1964   Vizcarra's Navajo campaign of 1823. *Arizona and the West* 6(3): 223–44.
1980   *A history of the Chaco Navajos.* Reports of the Chaco Center No. 4. Albuquerque: National Park Service, Chaco Center.
1983   Navajo prehistory and history to 1850. In *Southwest,* edited by Alfonso Ortiz, 489–501. Handbook of North American Indians, Vol. 10, William C. Sturtevant, general editor. Washington, D.C.: Smithsonian Institution.

Callaway, D. G., J. E. Levy, and E. B. Henderson
1976   *The effects of power production and strip mining on local Navajo populations.* Lake Powell Research Bulletin No. 22. Los Angeles: University of California.

Cameron, Catherine M.
1990   The effect of varying estimates of pit structure use-life on prehistoric population estimates in the American Southwest. *Kiva* 57(2):155–66.

Carlson, Roy L.
1965   *Eighteenth century Navajo fortresses of the Governador District.* Series in Anthropology No. 10. Boulder: University of Colorado.

William Wood, 102–12. Southeast Asia Series No. 41, Athens, OH: Ohio University Center for International Studies.

Gaunt, David

1987 Rural household organization and inheritance in northern Europe. *Journal of Family History* 12:121–41.

Gilmor, Frances, and Louisa W. Wetherill

1953 *Traders to the Navajos*. Albuquerque: University of New Mexico Press.

Gilpin, Dennis

1982 Historic sites data: Summary and analysis. In *Gallegos Mesa settlement and subsistence: A set of explanatory models for cultural resources on Blocks VIII, IX, X and XI, Navajo Indian Irrigation Project,* by Lawrence E. Vogler, Dennis Gilpin, and Joseph K. Anderson, 591–944. Navajo Nation Papers in Anthropology No. 12, Vol. 2. Window Rock, AZ: Navajo Nation Cultural Resource Management Program.

1986 Historical archaeology on the Navajo Indian Irrigation Project. Paper Presented at the 1st annual Navajo Studies Conference, Albuquerque.

Goode, William J.

1963 *World revolution and family patterns*. New York: Free Press of Glencoe.

Goodenough, Ward H.

1955 A problem in Malayo-Polynesian social organization. *American Anthropologist* 57:71–83.

1970 *Description and comparison in cultural anthropology*. Cambridge: Cambridge University Press.

Goodman, James M.

1982 *The Navajo atlas: Environments, resources, people, and history of the Diné Bikeyah*. Norman: University of Oklahoma Press.

Goody, Jack (ed.)

1958 *The developmental cycle in domestic groups*. Papers in Social Anthropology No. 1. Cambridge: Cambridge University Press.

1976 *Production and reproduction: A comparative study of the domestic domain*. Cambridge University Press, New York.

Gregory, Herbert E.

1917 *Geology of the Navajo country*. Professional Paper 93. Washington, D.C.: United States Geological Survey, U.S. Government Printing Office.

Gumerman, George J.

1970 *Black Mesa, survey and excavation in northeastern Arizona 1968*. Prescott, AZ: Prescott College Press.

Haley, Brian D., Thomas R. Rocek, Belinda Blomberg, and Dana Anderson

1983 Ethnoarchaeological research and historical excavations on Black Mesa, 1981. In *Excavations on Black Mesa, 1981, a descriptive report,* edited by F. E. Smiley, Deborah L. Nichols, and Peter P. Andrews, 281–99.

Research Paper No. 36. Carbondale: Center for Archaeological Investigations, Southern Illinois University.

Hayden, Brian, and Aubrey Cannon

1982   The corporate group as an archaeological unit. *Journal of Anthropological Archaeology* 1:132–58.

Hegemann, Elizabeth C.

1963   *Navajo trading days.* Albuquerque: University of New Mexico Press.

Henderson, Eric B.

1982   Social stratification and livestock reduction: the Red Lake case. In *Sheep is life: An assessment of livestock reduction in the former Navajo-Hopi Joint Use Area,* by John J. Wood, Walter M. Vannette, and Michael J. Andrews, 115–22. Anthropological Papers No. 1. Flagstaff: Northern Arizona University.

1983   Social organization and seasonal migrations among the Navajo. *The Kiva* 48:279–306.

1989   Navajo livestock wealth and the effects of the stock reduction program of the 1930s. *Journal of Anthropological Research* 45(4):379–403.

Henderson, E. B., and J. E. Levy

1975   *Survey of Navajo community studies 1936–74.* Lake Powell Research Project Bulletin No. 6. Los Angeles: University of California.

Hester, James J.

1962   *Early Navajo migrations and acculturation in the Southwest.* Papers in Anthropology No. 6. Santa Fe: Museum of New Mexico.

Hill, W. W.

1938   *The agricultural and hunting methods of the Navajo Indians.* Publications in Anthropology No. 18. New Haven: Yale University.

1940a   Some aspects of Navajo political structure. *Plateau* 13:23–29.

1940b   Some Navaho culture changes during two centuries (with a translation of the early-eighteenth-century Rabal manuscript). *Smithsonian Miscellaneous Collections* 100:395–415. Washington, D.C.: Smithsonian Institution.

Holley, George R., Belinda Blomberg, and Scott C. Russell

1980   Navajo sites investigated during 1979. In *Excavations on Black Mesa, 1979, a descriptive report,* edited by Shirley Powell, Robert Layhe, and Anthony L. Klesert, pp. 285–333. Research Paper No. 18. Carbondale: Center for Archaeological Investigations, Southern Illinois University.

Hoover, J. W.

1931   Navajo nomadism. *Geographical Review* 21:429–45.

Hubbell Papers

n.d.   Unpublished collection, University of Arizona Library, Special Collections, Tucson.

Irons, William

    1972   Variation in economic organization: A comparison of the pastoral Yomut and the Basseri. In *Perspectives on nomadism,* edited by William Irons and Neville Dyson-Hudson, 88–104. Leiden: E. J. Brill.

Iverson, Peter

    1981   *The Navajo Nation.* Albuquerque: University of New Mexico Press.

James, H. L.

    1976   *Posts and rugs, the story of Navajo rugs and their homes.* Globe: Southwest Parks and Monuments Association.

Jett, Stephen C.

    1978   Navajo seasonal migration patterns. *The Kiva* 44(1):65–75.

    1980   The Navajo homestead: Situation and site. *Yearbook of the Association of Pacific Coast Geographers* 42:101–18.

Johnston, Dennis Foster

    1966   *An analysis of sources of information on the population of the Navaho.* Bureau of American Ethnology Bulletin 197. Washington, D.C.: U.S. Government Printing Office.

Jorgensen, Joseph G.

    1971   Indians and the metropolis. In *The American Indian in urban society,* edited by Jack O Waddell, 66–113. Boston: Little, Brown.

    1972   *The sun dance religion.* Chicago: University of Chicago Press.

Karlstrom, Erik T.

    1983   Soils and geomorphology of northern Black Mesa. In *Excavations on Black Mesa, 1981, a descriptive report,* edited by F. E. Smiley, Deborah L. Nichols, and Peter P. Andrews, 317–48. Research Paper No. 36. Carbondale: Center for Archaeological Investigations, Southern Illinois University.

Keesing, Roger

    1966   Kwaio kindreds. *Southwestern Journal of Anthropology* 22:346–53.

Kelley, Klara B.

    1977   *Commercial networks in the Navajo-Hopi-Zuni region.* Ph.D. Dissertation, Department of Anthropology, University of New Mexico, Albuquerque.

    1982a   Ethnoarchaeology of the Black Hat Navajos: Historical and ahistorical determinants of site features. *Journal of Anthropological Research* 38:45–74.

    1982b   Ethnohistory. In *Anasazi and Navajo land use in the McKinley Mine area near Gallup, New Mexico,* Vol. 2, edited by Christina G. Allen and Ben A. Nelson. Albuquerque: Office of Contract Archeology, University of New Mexico.

    1982c   Yet another reanalysis of the Navajo outfit: New evidence from historical documents. *Journal of Anthropological Research* 38:363–81.

1986   *Navajo land use.* Orlando, FL: Academic Press.

Kelley, Klara B., and Peter M. Whiteley

1989   *Navajoland: Family settlement and land use.* Tsaile, AZ: Navajo Community College Press.

Kelly, Lawrence C.

1970   *The Navajo Indians and federal Indian policy 1900–1935.* Tucson: University of Arizona Press.

Kemrer, Meade F.

1974   *The dynamics of western Navajo settlement, A.D. 1750–1900: An archaeological and dendrochronological analysis.* Ph.D. Dissertation, Department of Anthropology, University of Arizona, Tucson.

Keur, Dorothy L.

1941   Big Bead Mesa: An archaeological study of Navaho acculturation 1745–1812. *Memoir of the Society for American Archaeology* 1. Menasha, WI: Society for American Archaeology.

Keyes, Charles

1975   Kin groups in a Thai-Lao community. In *Change and persistence in Thai society,* edited by G. W. Skinner and A. T. Kirsch, 274–97. Ithaca, NY: Cornell University Press.

Kimball, Solon T., and John H. Provinse

1942   Navaho social organization in land use planning. *Applied Anthropology* 1:18–30.

Kluckhohn, Clyde

1966   *The Ramah Navaho.* Bureau of American Ethnology Bulletin 196. Washington, D.C.: U.S. Government Printing Office.

Kluckhohn, Clyde, and Dorothea Leighton

1946   *The Navaho.* Cambridge, MA: Harvard University Press.

Kozlowski, E.

1972   The economic condition of the Navajos of Black Mesa. Ms. on file, Museum of Northern Arizona library, Flagstaff.

Kunitz, Stephen J.

1977   Economic variation on the Navajo reservation. *Human Organization* 36: 186–93.

Lamphere, Louise

1970   Ceremonial cooperation and networks: A reanalysis of the Navajo outfit. *Man* 5:139–63.

1977   *To run after them: Cultural and social bases of cooperation in a Navajo community.* Tucson: University of Arizona Press.

Landreth, Gerald K., and Sabrina Hardenbergh

1985   Navajo sites in Area VI. In *Excavations on Black Mesa, 1983, a descriptive report,* edited by A. L. Christenson and W. L. Parry, 317–86.

Research Paper 46. Carbondale: Center for Archaeological Investigations, Southern Illinois University.

Laslett, Peter
1972 Introduction. In *Household and family in past time,* edited by Peter Laslett and Richard Wall, 1–89. Cambridge: Cambridge University Press.

Laslett, Peter, and Richard Wall (eds.)
1972 *Household and family in past time.* Cambridge: Cambridge University Press.

Levy, Jerrold E.
1962 Community organization of the Western Navajo. *American Anthropologist* 64:781–801.

Levy, Jerrold E., Eric B. Henderson, and Tracy J. Andrews
1989 The effects of regional variation and temporal change on matrilineal elements of Navajo social organization. *Journal of Anthropological Research* 45(4):351–77.

Lomnitz, Larissa Adler
1977 *Networks and marginality: Life in a Mexican shantytown.* New York: Academic Press.

McNitt, Frank
1962 *The Indian traders.* Norman: University of Oklahoma Press.

McNutt, Charles H.
1981 Nearest neighbors, boundary effect, and the old flag trick: A general solution. *American Antiquity* 46:571–92.

McPherson, Robert S.
1988 *The northern Navajo frontier 1860–1900: Expansion through adversity.* Albuquerque: University of New Mexico Press.

Marshall, Michael P.
1991 The Pueblito as a site complex: Archeological investigations in the Dinetah District; The 1989–1990 BLM pueblito survey. In *Rethinking Navajo pueblitos,* by Michael P. Marshall and Patrick Hogan, i–ix, 1–282. Cultural Resources Series No. 8. Farmington, NM: Bureau of Land Management, Albuquerque District, Farmington Resource Area.

Marx, Emanuel
1977 The tribe as a unit of subsistence: Nomadic pastoralism in the Middle East. *American Anthropologist* 79:343–63.

Mayer, Adrian C.
1966 The significance of quasi-groups in the study of complex societies. In *The Social Anthropology of Complex Societies,* edited by M. Banton, 97–122. London: Tavistock.

Mitchell, Frank
1978 *Navajo Blessingway singer: The autobiography of Frank Mitchell, 1881–*

1967, edited by Charlotte J. Frisbie and David P. McAllester. Tucson: University of Arizona Press.

Mitchell, William E.
1963 Theoretical problems in the concept of kindred. *American Anthropologist* 65:343–54.

Mizuno, Koichi
1971 *The social system of Don Daeng*. Center for South East Asian Studies, Discussion Papers 12–22. Kyoto: Kyoto University.

Murdock, George Peter
1949 *Social structure*. New York: MacMillan.
1964 The kindred. *American Anthropologist* 66:129–32.

Murdock, George Peter (ed.)
1960 *Social structure in Southeast Asia*. Viking Fund Publications in Anthropology No. 29. Chicago: Wenner-Gren Foundation for Anthropological Research.

Myers, Cindy L., and Scott C. Russell
1983 A comparative investigation of artifact assemblages from Navajo sites in the N-41 right-of-way. In *The Navajo history and archaeology of east central Black Mesa, Arizona (CRMP-83-046)*, by Scott Russell, 201–19. Papers in Anthropology No. 21. Window Rock, AZ: Navajo Nation.

Navajo Times
1981a Chronology of events in the 1882 Executive Order area. *Navajo Times* (May 7) 23(19):15, 17.
1981b Report makes assessment on JUA condition. *Navajo Times* (May 21) 23(21):18, 19, 21.

Netting, Robert McC.
1982 Some home truths on household size and wealth. *American Behavioral Scientist* 25:641–62.

Netting, Robert McC., M. Priscilla Stone, and Glenn D. Stone
1989 Kofyar cash-cropping: Choice and change in indigenous agricultural development. *Human Ecology* 17(3):299–319.

Netting, Robert McM., Richard R. Wilk, and Eric J. Arnould (eds.)
1984 *Households: Comparative and historical studies of the domestic group*. Berkeley: University of California Press.

Nichols, Deborah L., and Erik T. Karlstrom
1983 The cultural resources of 1981 mitigation areas. In *Excavations on Black Mesa, 1981, a descriptive report*, edited by F. E. Smiley, Deborah L. Nichols, and Peter P. Andrews, 3–17. Research Paper No. 36. Carbondale: Center for Archaeological Investigations, Southern Illinois University.

Nichols, Deborah L., and Clifton W. Sink
1984 The 1982 field season. In *Excavations on Black Mesa, 1982, a descriptive*

report, edited by Deborah L. Nichols and F. E. Smiley, 3–30. Research Paper No. 39. Carbondale: Center for Archaeological Investigations, Southern Illinois University.

Nichols, Deborah L., and F. E. Smiley (eds.)
1984   *Excavations on Black Mesa, 1982, a descriptive report.* Research Paper No. 39. Center for Archaeological Investigations, Southern Illinois University at Carbondale.

Noisat, Bradley A.
1978   Navajo archaeology and settlement. In *The Bisti-Star Lake Project: A sample survey of cultural resources in northwestern New Mexico,* by Hannah Huse, Bradley A. Noisat, and Judith A. Halasi, 81–118. Albuquerque: Bureau of Land Management, Albuquerque District.

Ord, J. K.
1979   Time-series and spatial patterns in ecology. In *Spatial and temporal analysis in Ecology,* edited by R. M. Cormack and J. K. Ord, 1–94. Statistical Ecology Series Vol. 8. Fairland, MD: International Co-operative Publishing House.

Pehrson, Robert N.
1957   *The bilateral network of social relations in Konkama Lapp District.* Indiana University Publications, Slavic and Eastern European Series No. 5. Bloomington: Indiana University.

Peters, Emyrs
1960   The proliferation of segments in the lineage of the Bedouin in Cyrenaica. *Journal of the Royal Anthropological Institute of Great Britain and Ireland* 90(1):29–53.

Pinder, D., I. Shimada, and D. Gregory
1979   The nearest-neighbor statistic: Archaeological application and new developments. *American Antiquity* 44:430–45.

Rand, W. W.
1971   Objective criteria for evaluating cluster methods. *Journal of the American Statistical Association* 66:846–50.

Rappaport, Roy A.
1984   *Pigs for the ancestors: Ritual in the ecology of a New Guinea people,* 2d ed. New Haven: Yale University Press.

Reagan, Albert B.
1922   The 'flu' among the Navajos. *Transactions of the Kansas Academy of Science* 30(2):131–247.

Reeve, Frank D.
1957   Seventeenth century Navaho-Spanish relations. *New Mexico Historical Review* 32(1):36–52.

1960   Navaho-Spanish diplomacy, 1770–1790. *New Mexico Historical Review* 35(3):200–35.

Reichard, Gladys A.

1928   *Social life of the Navajo Indians.* Contributions to Anthropology 7. New York: Columbia University. (Reprinted, 1969, New York: AMS Press).

Reno, Philip

1982   *Mother Earth, Father Sky, and economic development.* Albuquerque: University of New Mexico Press.

Reynolds, Terry R., Louise Lamphere, and Cecil E. Cook, Jr.

1967   Time, resources, and authority in a Navajo community. *American Anthropologist* 69:188–99.

Roberts, Alexandra

1990   Ethno-history and archeology. In *The Wupatki archeological inventory survey project: Final report,* compiled by Bruce A. Anderson, 6.1–6.115. Professional Paper No. 35. Santa Fe: Southwest Cultural Resources Center, Division of Anthropology, National Park Service.

Rocek, Thomas R.

1984a   D:11:36. In *Excavations on Black Mesa, 1982, a descriptive report,* edited by Deborah L. Nichols and F. E. Smiley, 422–35. Research Paper No. 39. Carbondale: Center for Archaeological Investigations, Southern Illinois University.

1984b   Navajo cultural history. In *Excavations on Black Mesa, 1982, a descriptive report,* edited by Deborah L. Nichols and F. E. Smiley, 413–21. Research Paper No. 39. Carbondale: Center for Archaeological Investigations, Southern Illinois University.

1984c   Navajo sites investigated in the J-2 mining area. In *Excavations on Black Mesa, 1982, a descriptive report,* edited by Deborah L. Nichols and F. E. Smiley, 469–78. Research Paper No. 39. Carbondale: Center for Archaeological Investigations, Southern Illinois University.

1985   *Correlates of economic and demographic change: Navajo adaptations on northern Black Mesa, Arizona.* Ph.D. Dissertation, Department of Anthropology, University of Michigan. Ann Arbor: University Microfilms.

1988   The behavioral and material correlates of site seasonality: Lessons from Navajo ethnoarchaeology. *American Antiquity* 53(3):523–36.

1994   Recent Navajo settlement patterns: A spatial analysis. In *Coping with diversity,* edited by J. Dean and D. Oswald. Submitted to Smithsonian Institution Press.

Roessel, Ruth (ed.)

1974   *Navajo livestock reduction: A national disgrace.* Chinle, AZ: Navajo Community College Press.

Ross, William T.

1955   *Navaho kinship and social organization, with special reference to a transitional community.* Ph.D. Dissertation, Department of Anthropology, University of Chicago, Chicago.

Russell, Scott C.

1981a   The Navajo oral history and ethnohistory of northeastern Black Mesa: Eastern Lease Area. Ms. on file, Center for Archaeological Investigations, Southern Illinois University, Carbondale.

1981b   Navajo wood use behavior: Ethnographic and historical data. Ms. on file, Laboratory of Tree-Ring Research, Tucson.

1983a   Factors affecting agricultural production in a Western Navajo community. Ph.D. Dissertation, Arizona State University, Tempe.

1983b   *The Navajo history and archaeology of east central Black Mesa, Arizona (CRMP-83-046).* Papers in Anthropology No. 21. Window Rock, AZ: Navajo Nation.

n.d.   Unpublished field notes, on file, Center for Archaeological Investigations, Southern Illinois University, Carbondale.

Russell, Scott C., and Jeffrey S. Dean

1985   The sheep and goat corral: A key structure in Navajo site analysis. *The Kiva* 51:3–18.

Sahlins, Marshall D.

1968   *Tribesmen.* Englewood Cliffs, NJ: Prentice-Hall.

1972   *Stone age economics.* Chicago: Aldine Press.

Sasaki, Tom T.

1960   *Fruitland, New Mexico: A Navaho community in transition.* New York: Columbia University Press.

Sasaki, Tom T., and John Adair

1952   New land to farm: Agricultural practices among the Navaho Indians of New Mexico. In *Human problems in technological change,* edited by Edward H. Spicer, 97–111. New York: Russell Sage Foundation.

Saxe, Arthur A., and Patricia L. Gall

1977   Ecological determinants of mortuary practices: The Temuan of Malaysia. In *Cultural-ecological perspectives on Southeast Asia: A symposium,* edited by William Wood, 74–82. Southeast Asia Series No. 41, Athens, OH: Ohio University Center for International Studies.

Schroeder, Albert H.

1974   *A study of the Apache Indians.* New York: Garland Publishing.

Segalen, Martine

1984   Nuclear is not independent: Organization of the household in the Pays Sud in the nineteenth and twentieth centuries. In *Households, comparative and historical studies of the domestic group,* edited by Robert McC. Netting,

Richard R. Wilk, and Eric J. Arnould, 163–86. Berkeley: University of California Press.

1986   *Historical anthropology of the family.* Cambridge: Cambridge University Press.

Sessions, Steven E. (ed.)

1979   Spatial analysis of site type distributions in Block III. In *An archaeological survey report and mitigation plan for the Block III cultural resources—Navajo Indian Irrigation Project,* 77–84. Window Rock, AZ: Cultural Resource Management Program, Navajo Nation.

Shepardson, Mary

1963   *Navajo ways in government.* Menasha, WI: American Anthropological Association Memoir No. 96.

Shepardson, Mary, and Blodwen Hammond

1970   *The Navajo Mountain community: Social organization and kinship terminology.* Berkeley: University of California Press.

Spicer, Edward H.

1952   Sheepmen and technicians: A program of soil conservation on the Navajo Indian Reservation. In *Human problems in technological change,* edited by Edward H. Spicer, 185–207. New York: Russell Sage Foundation.

Spooner, Brian

1972   The status of nomadism as a cultural phenomenon in the Middle East. In *Perspectives on nomadism,* edited by William Irons and Neville Dyson-Hudson, 122–31. Leiden: E. J. Brill.

1973   *The cultural ecology of pastoral nomads.* Module in Anthropology No. 45. Reading, MA: Addison-Wesley.

Spores, Ronald

1980   New World ethnohistory and archaeology, 1970–1980. *Annual Review of Anthropology* 9:575–603.

Stokes, M. A., and T. L. Smiley

1964   Tree-ring dates from the Navajo land claim, II: The Western Sector. *Tree-Ring Bulletin* 26(1–4):13–27.

Stone, Glenn Davis

1991   Agricultural territories in a dispersed settlement system. *Current Anthropology* 32(3):343–53.

1992   Social distance, spatial relations, and agricultural production among the Kofyar of Namu District, Plateau State, Nigeria. *Journal of Anthropological Archaeology* 11(2):152–172.

Swidler, Nina

1972   The development of the Kalat Khanate. In *Perspectives on nomadism,* edited by William Irons and Neville Dyson-Hudson, 115–21. Leiden: E. J. Brill.

Swidler, W. W.

1972 Some demographic factors regulating the formation of flocks and camps among the Brahui of Baluchistan. In *Perspectives on nomadism,* edited by William Irons and Neville Dyson-Hudson, 69–75. Leiden: E. J. Brill.

Tapper, Richard L.

1979 The organization of nomadic communities in pastoral societies of the Middle East. In *Pastoral production and society,* edited by L'Equipe ecologie et anthropologie des sociétés pastorales, 43–65. Cambridge: Cambridge University Press.

Underhill, Ruth M.

1953 *Here come the Navaho: A history of the largest Indian tribe in the United States.* U.S. Bureau of Indian Affairs, Branch of Education, Washington, D.C. (Reprint, 1983, Tucson: Treasure Chest Publications).

1978 *The Navajos.* Norman: University of Oklahoma Press.

Underwood, Jackson

1985 Navajo sites investigated within Mining Area VIII. In *Excavations on Black Mesa, 1983, a descriptive report,* edited by A. L. Christenson and W. L. Parry, 353–69. Research Paper No. 46. Carbondale: Center for Archaeological Investigations, Southern Illinois University.

U.S. Bureau of the Census

1975 *Historical statistics of the United States, colonial times to 1970.* House Document No. 93-78. Washington D.C.: U.S. Government Printing Office.

U.S. Federal Trade Commission

1973 *The trading post system on the Navajo Reservation.* Staff report to the Federal Trade Commission. Washington, D.C.: U.S. Government Printing Office.

Utley, Robert M.

1961 The reservation trader in Navajo history. *El Palacio* 68(1):5–27.

VanStone, James W.

1974 *Athapaskan adaptations, hunters and fishermen of the subarctic forests.* Chicago: Aldine.

Van Valkenburgh, Richard F.

1941 *Diné Bikéyah.* Window Rock, AZ: United States Department of the Interior, Office of Indian Affairs, Navajo Service.

1956 Report of archaeological survey of the Navajo-Hopi contract area. Prepared for Indian Claims Commission, Navajo-Hopi Land Claim.

Vogt, Evon Z.

1961 Navajo. In *Perspectives in American culture change,* edited by Edward H. Spicer, 278–336. Chicago: University of Chicago Press.

1966   Geographical and Cultural Setting. In *The People of Rimrock,* edited by E. Z. Vogt and E. Albert, 34–45. Cambridge, MA: Harvard University Press.

Whallon, Robert

1973   Spatial analysis of occupation floors I: Application of dimensional analysis of variance. *American Antiquity* 38:266–78.

1974   Spatial analysis of occupation floors II: The application of nearest neighbor analysis. *American Antiquity* 39:16–34.

White, Leslie A.

1959   *The evolution of culture: The development of civilization to the fall of Rome.* New York: McGraw-Hill.

White, Richard

1983   *The roots of dependency.* Lincoln: University of Nebraska Press.

Wilk, Richard R., and Robert McM. Netting

1984   Households: Changing forms and functions. In *Households, comparative and historical studies of the domestic group,* edited by Robert McM. Netting, Richard R. Wilk, and Eric J. Arnould, 1–28. Berkeley: University of California Press.

Wilk, Richard R., and William L. Rathje (eds.)

1982   Archaeology of the household: Building a prehistory of domestic life. *American Behavioral Scientist* 25(6).

Williams, Aubrey W., Jr.

1970   *Navajo political process.* Contributions to Anthropology, Vol. 9. Washington, D.C.: Smithsonian Institution Press.

Witherspoon, Gary

1970   A new look at Navajo social organization. *American Anthropologist* 72: 55–65.

1975   *Navajo kinship and marriage.* Chicago: University of Chicago Press.

Wood, John J., Walter M. Vannette, and Michael J. Andrews

1982   *Sheep is life: An assessment of livestock reduction in the former Navajo-Hopi Joint Use Area.* Anthropological Papers 1. Flagstaff: Northern Arizona University.

Yengoyan, Aram A.

1971   The Philippines: The effects of cash cropping on Mandaya land tenure. In *Land tenure in the Pacific,* edited by Ron Crocombe, 362–74. London: Oxford University Press.

Young, Robert W.

1961   *The Navajo yearbook. Report No. VIII, 1951–1961. A decade of progress.* Window Rock, AZ: Navajo Agency.

1978   *A political history of the Navajo Tribe.* Tsaile, AZ: Navajo Community College Press.

Index

Abaa, 6

abandonment. *See* depopulation; site, abandonment

Aberle, David F., 6, 10, 28-30, 42, 45, 50, 54, 58, 61, 65, 67–69, 112, 141, 146, 149, 154, 205

acculturation, 9, 40–41

action group. *See* middle-level unit, action group

Adair, John, 30, 49, 63, 218

Adams, William Y., 20, 25, 35, 36, 40, 42, 44–45, 53, 59, 64, 65, 69, 75, 77, 149, 154, 162–63, 205

affinal relatives, 3, 6, 47, 48–50, 54–55, 57, 62, 64–66, 68, 143, 149, 151, 158–59. *See also* kinship

agriculture, 18–20, 23–27, 31–38, 40, 56, 59, 110, 112, 114, 125, 128–29, 137, 141, 154, 173; environmental constraints on, 15, 27, 35, 128; field data on, 112, 114, 114 (fig. 6.8); intensification of, 152–53, 164; joint labor for, 7–8, 11, 47–49, 53, 57, 62–64, 68

Ahlstrom, Richard V. N., 168, 170, 205

Amsden, Charles Avery, 24, 206

Anderson, Dana, 80, 131, 169, 170, 172, 174, 210, 211

Andrews, Michael J., 37, 160, 221

Andrews, Tracy J., 6, 10, 60–61, 66–67, 141, 214

Aneth, 16 (fig. 2.1), 24

Anglo-American, 18–19

animal units, defined, 30

annual round. *See* settlement, annual round

Apache, 16, 23

Appell, G. N., 3, 206

archaeological coding, 85–92, 167–85; accuracy and reproducibility of, 85–86, 133; association, 11, 89, 167–72, 174–78, 184–85; missing data in, 85, 109, 112, 120, 131, 133–34, 136, 138; seasonality determination, 86, 87, 97, 133, 136, 138, 173–74, 180, 198, 201. *See also* bias, in the archaeological sample; population, measured archaeologically; reliably dated site components, defined; site, defined; site, functional categories of; site, occupied

archaeological data: contrast with ethno-

About the Author

Thomas R. Rocek received his A.B. degree in anthropology from Princeton University in 1977, and his Ph.D. from the University of Michigan in 1985. He was awarded a Weatherhead Fellowship from the School of American Research in 1985. His research includes the study of recent social and economic change in Navajo society, as presented here, as well as the study of economic transformations in prehistoric agricultural village communities in New Mexico. His previously published works include journal articles on both topics, as well as a monograph, *The Henderson Site Burials: Glimpses of a Late Prehistoric Population in the Pecos Valley,* written with John Speth, published by the Museum of Anthropology at the University of Michigan in Ann Arbor (Technical Reports No. 18). He has taught at Oregon State University and is currently an assistant professor of anthropology at the University of Delaware.

DATE DUE